Organizational Rhetoric

Fortiter ac tenaciter repugnantibus

Organizational Rhetoric

Strategies of Resistance and Domination

Charles Conrad

polity

First published in 2011 by Polity Press

Polity Press
65 Bridge Street
Cambridge CB2 1UR, UK

Polity Press
350 Main Street
Malden, MA 02148, USA

ISBN-13: 978-0-7456-4716-6
ISBN-13: 978-0-7456-4717-3(pb)

A catalogue record for this book is available from the British Library.

Typeset in 11 on 13 pt Sabon
by Servis Filmsetting Ltd, Stockport, Cheshire
Printed and bound in Great Britain by MPG Books Group Limited, Bodmin, Cornwall

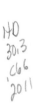

For further information on Polity, visit our website: www.politybooks.com

Table of Contents

Detailed Table of Contents

The author recommends that each chapter be read in two sittings. The asterisks below suggest appropriate points at which to pause and reflect on what you have read.

Detailed Table of Contents

Preface

In both everyday conversation and the twenty-first century's alternative to reasoned discourse, cable TV "news" shows, the term "rhetoric" gets very little respect. It is treated as meaningless adornment ("mere rhetoric") that masquerades as insight, a throw-back to the view that developed during the Middle Ages, when the church dictated what could and should be said, reducing rhetoric to the study of the optimal ways of expressing those pre-determined truths. Or it is treated as a synonym for lies. Rehabilitating rhetoric has been hampered by two paradoxes. First, style is an important part of the strategic use of symbols – it is what differentiates Martin Luther King's rhetoric from a bland memo on "diversity management." Second, lying is an unfortunately common rhetorical strategy, used by politicians, CEOs, and people involved in inter-personal relationships. But it does not have to be so. Underlying the flippant use of "rhetoric" as a label are some fundamental questions. For example, what is the relationship between language/symbol use, "truth," and "falsity?" How do members of different societies come to accept different assumptions as sacrosanct, as unquestioned and unquestionable statements about "reality?" What is the difference between "knowledge," accurate empirical statements, and "lies," big or everyday? How can those presumptions be challenged and revised when they no longer meet the needs of the societies that construct and sustain them?

Fortunately there are a number of alternative views of "rhetoric," ones that depict it as set of complex processes through which people construct distinctive views of reality, persuade others to share their beliefs and values, and create distinctive social, political, and economic structures that are legitimized through strategic discourse. During the last twenty years or so, this more fundamental view of "rhetoric" has been imported into organizational studies. This resulted in part from the simple observation that we now live in a world that is increasingly dominated by multinational corporations, which continually use rhetoric not only to sell their products and services, but to influence the political situations within which they operate. It also resulted from a shift in the ways in which scholars think about organizations and their relationships to society – a "discursive turn" that has led researcher–theorists to concentrate increasingly on the ways in which organizational actors use language and symbols to further their perceived interests. But, perhaps because the shift has been so recent, we are just beginning to integrate various perspectives on organizational rhetoric. However, the task is complicated by a number of paradoxes that are built into the relationships between rhetoric and society.

The most important paradox involves the *uses of rhetoric*. This paradox has been present since the ancient Greeks initiated the systematic study of rhetoric – it can be used to create open societies within which multiple voices are heard, multiple perspectives are articulated, and competing ideas are compared within democratic political structures. Or rhetoric can be used to silence dissent and perpetuate totalitarian rule. Moreover, it can be used to legitimize autocratic rule by corporate executives of corporations that operate within societies whose members say they are fully committed to democratic governance. In addition, democracy presumably involves open, public decision-making. But many political decisions in modern democracies are made in private, where organizations exercise their most significant influence. Indeed, organizational rhetors influence policymaking through two inter-related strategies: by strategically choosing the venues within which they will exercise political power, and by strategically crafting the arguments and appeals that best legitimize their actions with policymakers and the general public.

The tangible resources that organizations have available combine with their ability to maneuver through multiple venues to dominate the societies within which they operate. But, wherever there is power, there is a potential for resistance. These complicated, inter-twined dialectical relationships – between democracy and autocracy, between public decision-making and private influence, and between domination and resistance – provide the core issues discussed in this book.

A second paradox involves the *rhetoric of economics*. At least since the demise of the Soviet Union, the dominant ideology in the developed economies has been what financier George Soros has called *free-market fundamentalism* – a faith that the "invisible hand" of competition will miraculously lead to the creation of economic systems that maximize returns to individuals and societies as a whole, provided that government does not interfere in the process. Like all theologies, secular or scriptural, market fundamentalism is sustained by a complex rhetoric, one that obscures differences between "real" economies and the tenets of economic theory, and ignores the ways in which organizational rhetors use the ideology to legitimize having government intervene in ways *that aid them* – by making it more difficult for competitors (domestic or international) to enter the market, to restrict unionization, or to shift their costs of operation to individual taxpayers – while preventing government actions that might constrain their activities. Through rhetoric, corporate "persons" develop identities and images that legitimize their domination while undermining resistance.

A third paradox involves *organizations and the power relationships that exist within them*. Two ideological systems, the "organizational imperative" and "managerialism," both of which are supported by an extensive *myth of leadership*, link free-market fundamentalism to everyday organizational behavior. By casting positional leaders as "secular saviors" and by de-powering (and to some degree de-humanizing) followers, managerial dominance obtains legitimation. However, an alternative perspective, one that casts "leadership" as a set of skills and patterns of behavior rather than as attributes of the people who occupy positions at the top of organizational hierarchies, offers the possibility of ongoing resistance that both meets the needs of "followers" and improves the functioning of organizations.

My goal in this book is to examine each of these paradoxes, the guidelines and constraints that they impose on organizational rhetors, and, in turn, how they are managed through rhetoric. They will appear in each chapter, although in somewhat different forms, because the power of organizational rhetoric lies in their inter-relationships. Chapter 1 focuses on the paradox of democracy and examines the ways in which organizations have strategically used the courts and state–state competition to construct a political–economic structure that has been labeled the "American system": one composed of large, weakly regulated, and politically influential corporations. Chapters 2 and 3 examine the role that organizational rhetoric has played in the development of two sets of beliefs and assumptions that underlie the American system – free market fundamentalism (Chapter 2) and managerialism (Chapter 3) – and the ways in which organizations draw upon those assumptions to legitimize preferred policies and practices. Chapter 4 examines the role that rhetoric plays in public policymaking and the implications those processes hold for domination and resistance. Chapter 5 offers a similar analysis of the rhetorical processes through which organizational rhetors construct positive identities and images and draw upon those impressions in order to manage identity crises.

Each chapter includes a short-term research project, entitled "weekend fun," designed to allow readers to personalize the key issues being discussed in the chapter. They conclude with an extended case study, which applies the results of the "weekend fun" exercise to a concrete issue involving organizational rhetoric. Each chapter also includes a number of extended endnotes. I have included them for two reasons. The ideas that I will present are complex, and some of them are controversial. Some of the endnotes are designed to introduce readers to aspects of the issues that I was unable to present clearly in the text of the chapters. Others provide sources for readers to consult that present the "other side" of controversial issues. I hope that this book will encourage readers to keep thinking about the issues it raises. The

Preface

endnotes provide starting points for further research. I also recommend reading each chapter in two sittings. The Detailed Table of Contents includes a series of six asterisks, which indicate the point in each chapter at which I think readers should take a break and reflect on what they have read.

Finally, I would like to thank some people who were instrumental in my completing this effort. Every major project makes an author more difficult to live with than otherwise would have been the case, so every author should begin by thanking those people who have to live with him or her. So, thank you, Betty, Hannah, and Travis, for putting up with me. Second, I would like to thank three colleagues whose ideas, writing, and conversation influences almost everything I write these days: Jim Aune, Jim Barker, and George Cheney; and two whose works were invaluable to this book: Gail Fairhurst and Heather Zoller. Dennis Mumby, Kathleen Krone and Professor Cheney read an extended prospectus for the book and provided valuable advice; Professor Krone and Professor Fairhurst have read the completed manuscript and offered equally valuable suggestions for the final revisions. Third, I would like to thank the students in two sections of my COMM 446, "Communication, Organization, and Society" course, with a special thanks to Megan Dortch. They read early drafts of each chapter and "encouraged" me in many ways – to use shorter sentences, quit being so abstract, provide more examples, and so on. Their ability and willingness to discuss key concepts in depth even led me to make some substantive changes. Finally, I would like to thank my editors, Andrea Drugan and Lauren Mulholland, for their support, advice, and patience, and Manuela Tecusan for her careful copyediting.

Charles Conrad
College Station, TX, USA
January, 2011

1

What is Rhetoric? What is Organizational Rhetoric? Why Are They Important?

An emerging middle class is very helpful in the creation of democratic regimes. But it does not follow that economic prosperity necessarily leads to the evolution of democratic freedoms. [. . .] International banks and multinational corporations often feel more comfortable with a strong, if autocratic, regime. [. . .] Truth be told, the connection between capitalism and democracy is tenuous at best. Capitalism and democracy obey different principles. The stakes are different: In capitalism wealth is the object, in democracy it is political authority. The criteria by which the stakes are measured are different. [. . .] The interests that are supposed to be served are different: in capitalism it is private interests, in democracy it is the public interest.

George Soros (2000, 110–111)

[H]istory matters. [. . .] What comes first (even if it was in some sense "accidental") conditions what comes later. Individuals [policymakers] may "choose" these institutions, but they do not choose them under circumstances of their own making, and their choices in turn influence the rules within which their successors choose.

Carolyn Tuohy (1992, 8)

Core Concepts

- From its beginnings, rhetoric and its use have inherently involved issues of power and social control. Just as it can be used to foster the best forms of democracy, rhetoric can also be used to perpetuate the worst forms of totalitarianism.

- Rhetoric inevitably involves issues of truth and claims of superior knowledge.
- Rhetorical situations are composed of the beliefs, values, and taken-for-granted assumptions of an audience, and of the political and social structures within which rhetorical acts take place. Rhetoric also creates those beliefs, values, assumptions, and structures.
- The primary structure surrounding organizational rhetoric in the US has been called the "American system" – a unique combination of large corporations, minimal regulation, and high levels of political power.
- The American system developed incrementally over time, through a complicated combination of intentional actions and unintended consequences. It gives organizational rhetors a number of advantages, which, because of US economic power, influences rhetorical situations worldwide.

Why in the world would anyone choose to study "rhetoric?" Many, perhaps most, of the connotations that are attached to the term today are negative. It is viewed as a synonym for lies, a substitute for careful, objective analysis, and/or a group of meaningless adornments that are used to make bad ideas seem to be good (Foss, Foss and Trapp, 1991; Heath, 2009). This pejorative view is not new; its origins go back at least 2400 years, to the wealthy Athenian philosopher Plato. He viewed rhetoric as equivalent to "cookery," a technique of making food seem appealing even if it is not good for you, or to "flattery," which tricks people into feeling good about themselves and the institutions they have created instead of working to improve themselves or their societies. Of course, Plato had a much more positive view of his own rhetoric, which he believed would produce truth, not illusion.

It probably is not surprising that scholars who study rhetoric view it very differently. To them, rhetoric is a complex process through which people develop and refine their beliefs, values, and views of reality by communicating with others. In turn, they use rhetoric to persuade audiences to accept their ideas, their underlying values, and their modes of thinking. In the process people create stable societies, which fulfill the needs of at least some of their members, and change these societies when they no longer meet citizens' needs. Moreover, without public rhetoric, debate withers and democracy is impossible. This does not mean that all rhetoric is ethical and socially responsible. Lying, along with any number of other reprehensible practices, *is* a rhetorical strategy commonly used both by organizational and by political rhetors – and, if "reality-television" shows can be believed, by almost everyone involved in interpersonal relationships (Elliott and Schroth, 2002).

However, not even the worst abuses of the art of rhetoric warrant dismissing it out of hand. Just the opposite is the case. Societies function best when the widest possible range of interests is articulated, and the widest range of ideas is considered and tested. Through dialogue individuals and groups recognize that others have different views, prefer different policies and political systems, and have defensible reasons for their beliefs (Burke, 1969; Brummett, 1995; Heath, 2009). There are only three ways to correct abuses of rhetoric such as lies, character assassination, distortion, misinformation, and disinformation. Governments can attempt to dictate appropriate forms of communication, an approach that may inadvertently suppress legitimate communication and lead to totalitarianism in the guise of democratization. Or societies can encourage open debate, hoping that socially responsible rhetoric will offset or compensate for irresponsible discourse. Finally, societies can encourage their members to become critical consumers of discourse, not in the sense of being negative and cynical, but in the sense of learning to identify rhetorical techniques – good and bad – ask informed and analytical questions of rhetors, and understand how their own values, beliefs, and biases make them susceptible to some forms of rhetoric and resistant to others. In the best case, audiences will even understand that applying the label "true" (or "patriotic," or "God's will," or any number of other positively valued terms) to one's own claims

3

while dismissing opposing views as "mere rhetoric" is in itself a rhetorical act, one that is socially unproductive because it substitutes emotional labels for informed analysis. When Plato attached the label "rhetoric" to the discourse and practices of his rivals, he was engaging in "rhetoric" in the negative sense of the term, even though his use of the label was based on his genuine and deeply held belief that he was "right" and that his philosophical, educational, and economic rivals were wrong. The labels "truth" and "mere rhetoric" still are used today for precisely the same purpose – to encourage audiences to substitute labels for critical thinking and to short-circuit productive debate in an effort to get the rhetor what she or he wants.

It *is* socially important and scientifically interesting to ask why rhetors engage in deceptive or misleading rhetoric. It is *even more* important to ask why audiences respond as they do when this happens. Consider two examples. First, during the first years of this century, the Enron company declared bankruptcy. Among other things, the company's executives were condemned for freezing their employees' retirement plans during the weeks surrounding the company's declaration of bankruptcy. This step kept employees from selling their company stock and moving their funds to safer investments at precisely the time when the executives were dumping *their* Enron stock. But this criticism overlooks an important point: when the freeze was lifted and the company was officially bankrupt, Enron employees actually *bought* more Enron stock.[1] Why in the world would intelligent people do such a thing? What role did managerial rhetoric play in their decisions? (My answer to these questions can be found in Chapter 3.) Or, on a broader scale, during the "corporate bailout" era debate of 2008–2009, the vast majority of US citizens, as well as citizens of other countries who suffered because of shenanigans in the US financial industry, roundly condemned all of the participants – individual customers who took on excessive financial risk to buy houses they could not afford, workers in financial institutions who encouraged them to do so, corporate executives who garnered massive salaries and bonuses from actions that were at best misleading and at worst criminal, and the governments (pri-

4

marily in the US and UK) who chose to "socialize" private sector losses – that is, to bail out the companies and their executives and to require current and future (innocent) taxpayers to pay for those sins. But only a tiny proportion of the complaining citizens acted *on their own* to protect their remaining assets and punish the evil-doers. That is, almost no one withdrew his or her money from insolvent but bailed-out banks; almost no one moved her or his retirement funds to more responsible carriers; and almost no one did anything else to punish organizations whose employees had behaved irresponsibly or to reward the thousands of financial organizations that had been responsible stewards of the monies in their possession. This failure to act almost certainly did not result from a lack of information. The global media provided 24/7 coverage of the collapse and, even though the US government took extraordinary steps to disguise the identities and home addresses of the executives of bailed-out firms who subsequently received massive performance bonuses, almost everyone in the industrialized world eventually knew what had been going on. It also did not result from a lack of relevant expertise, since no one needs a degree in economics to decide that leaving one's savings in an organization that cannot survive without massive government aid might be foolish; neither does it require a PhD in ethics to decide to quit rewarding organizations whose powerholders enrich themselves beyond most citizens' wildest dreams by engaging in deceptive practices. But, instead of taking steps like these, which are completely under individual citizens' control and are precisely the kind of economically rational behavior on which capitalist economies depend, citizens have been much more likely to complain loudly about their government's irrationality and lack of integrity than to change their own behaviors. Why, and what role did organizational rhetoric play in their decisions about how to respond to these events? I will answer these questions at length in Chapters 2 and 4, but my current point is that understanding organizational rhetoric requires an analysis of the symbolic acts of rhetors, of the processes through which audiences interpret that rhetoric, and of the ways in which acts and interpretation mutually influence one another. Rhetoric is a complex interaction among social actors, cultural assumptions, and political structures. Understanding it requires us to begin at its beginnings.

Autocracy, Democracy, and the Functions of Rhetoric

Some time around 465 BCE, the citizens of Syracuse, a Greek colony on the island of Sicily, overthrew their tyrannical dictators and established a democracy. Suddenly the courts were filled with lawsuits regarding the rightful ownership of property. The people who had owned property before the tyrants took it away from them suddenly regained control of "their" property. But the people who had obtained titles to the property during the reign of the tyrants believed that it was rightfully theirs, especially if they had spent a great deal of their own money improving it. Were they not owed some compensation? Since Greek law required parties to speak for themselves in court and many of the would-be landowners were not skilled speakers, a group of entrepreneurs such as Corax initiated a new industry of training people in courtroom rhetoric. Worse yet, at least in the eyes of Plato and his followers, these teachers charged their students money. This made rhetorical training available to the growing middle class, whose members used it to win court cases against the wealthy elite. Soon Corax's student, Tisias, imported rhetorical training to mainland Greece, where it caught the attention of a group of itinerant philosopher–teachers called "sophists" (learned or wise people, *sophistai*).

Plato, Truth, Hegemony, and Social Stability through Rhetoric

Today democratic government, an educated middle class, and litigation are not especially shocking aspects of political and economic life. But, for the elites in Greek society, its very foundation (that is, control by the wealthy) was being destroyed. The elites did have a point. The "golden age" of Greek thought – which is so widely celebrated today – started around 600 BCE in trading colonies on the western coast of Turkey. Thanks to the development of a slave economy and the growth of international trade and finance – globalization, classic-style – the economic elite suddenly had the time and money needed to engage in research and systematic thought, and/or to sponsor others to do so. Most of the key ideas of Western philosophy and government originated in these investigations, just as the best of Western classical music was produced by composers in the employ of wealthy sponsors about two thousand years later. But the elites recognized that combining a democratic political system with educated non-elites would threaten their economic and political dominance.[2]

Plato was perplexed about rhetoric. On the one hand, he recognized how powerful it could be. The ancient Greeks believed that rhetoric had a divine power, and represented it in the form of the goddess Peitho.[3] When used by the "right" kind of people, rhetoric could create a stable and fulfilling society, which was designed and operated according to truth. But Plato's definition of "truth" was absolute and elitist, and his view of the "perfect" society was one of enlightened totalitarian rule by a philosopher–king aided by an equally elite group of guardians. For him, truth could be obtained only by members of this small group of individuals, who had been selectively trained in the process of dialectic. In Plato's perfect society, described at length in the *Republic,* people were divided into a strict caste system. Rhetoric did have a role in society, as the primary tool through which the philosopher–king taught different groups of citizens the role(s) they were ordained to play in society and persuaded them to play those roles happily. In Plato's utopia both the poor and powerless and the wealthy and powerful would accept the positions they occupied in society as right, just, and deserved. A broad consensus eventually would develop about how a society should operate, a *dominant ideology* that justified Plato's preferred social, political, and economic arrangements as "normal" (which means both "typical" and "morally correct") and "natural" (which means "inevitable").[4] By learning, accepting, and enacting the dominant assumptions of a society, its members demonstrate that they are qualified to participate in it, and thus can speak credibly about issues facing the society. Resistance would not only be futile, it would be virtually nonexistent.

7

This does not mean that achieving social control through rhetoric would be an easy task for the philosopher–king. Audiences are composed of active, thinking people, who sometimes interpret messages in ways that differ from the rhetor's intent. Consequently the philosopher–king must constantly be on guard against unapproved interpretations of the truth and must actively intervene to correct these "false" doctrines. For Plato, almost any technique would have been acceptable as long as it was being used in the pursuit of truth and social stability. From the tactics described so powerfully by George Orwell in *1984* and *Animal Farm* to withholding information about a government's activities in the guise of "national security," to allowing a corporation's management to keep its finances secret from its stockholders and regulatory agencies as "proprietary information," to allowing governments to seize private property for the use of private developers, or to imprisoning or executing critics, any mode of social control would be acceptable. Dissenting voices should be silenced, and forms of rhetoric that invite varied misinterpretations – theater and music – should be banned. In Plato's *Republic*, society would be closed to foreign ideas and foreign influences, and to the socially destructive activities of public debate and democratic impulse. As philosopher Karl Popper and others have pointed out, throughout Western history Plato's views of the ideal society have repeatedly been used to justify totalitarianism and xenophobia – physical, economic, and symbolic force used in the name of ultimate truth – and have repeatedly been used by dictators since his time to legitimize their actions (Popper, 1944; Soros, 1998).[5] In short, Plato advocated using rhetoric as a mechanism for suppressing dissent and for maintaining a stable society in which the many were dominated by the few, rather than as a process of testing competing ideas in a democratic intellectual marketplace.

The Sophists, Democracy, and Contingent Truths

Another view of "rhetoric," the one that Plato condemned so loudly, was intimately tied to social change. It was grounded in a fundamentally different perspective on the nature of truth, knowledge, and human nature. The ancient Greeks had long debated the possibility of knowing absolute, constant truth. They wanted to believe that the universe made sense, that there was some principle, or force, or process that was present in every part of the universe that made the physical and the social world stable and predictable. But this quest is paradoxical. By definition, this "truth" (the Greek term was *alethes*) had to be abstract and unchanging. However, the world that humans experience is tangible and ever-changing – an idea captured in the statement, attributed to the Presocratic philosopher Heraclitus, that "we cannot step into the same river twice." The "river" of life is different from one moment to another, and stepping in it adds another element of change. Furthermore, as long as we are trapped in our physical bodies, we must experience the universe through our senses. While they are adequate for understanding the concrete, physical world, they can never allow us to know abstract truths completely. Plato responded to this paradox by arguing that *some* people could obtain an *approximation* of truth through dialectic. Admittedly, the knowledge obtained by these gifted few would be imperfect – like trying to know what someone is like by viewing his or her shadow on a wall – but it would be much closer to the truth than the kind of knowledge available to people who had not been trained in dialectic.

Plato's intellectual and economic rivals, the sophists, offered a very different response to the paradox. To them, absolute truth might not even exist. If it does, we humans can not gain an accurate knowledge of it; and, even if we could, we could not communicate it to one another because language is a human creation – powerful but inherently imperfect. So the best we can do is to focus our efforts on understanding the "here and now" and to learn to choose the best course of action in the everyday situations we face. Language and rhetoric may not be perfect, but they are good enough to allow us to create that kind of everyday knowledge.

Although different sophists adopted different versions of this idea, all of them focused on rhetoric as the key to creating a good society and successfully participating in it. Protagoras focused on debate, because he believed that there are multiple "sides" to every issue; Gorgias believed that the power of language was grounded in its poetic dimensions, which could be taught through training in impromptu speaking; and Isocrates, who lacked the skills and confidence to speak in public, focused on teaching his students to use rhetoric for political maneuvering – a form of knowledge that the sophists called *apate* (deceit or beguilement) or *metis* (cunning) (Heidelbaugh, 2001, 2007). In the process, they accepted – perhaps even celebrated – the "messiness" of democratic decision-making and the advantages of having multiple, diverse points of view introduced into debates – and they rejected the purported certainty and stability promised by Plato's *Republic*. The sophists were not so radical as to advocate changing Athenian democracy to the kind of "one person, one vote" system that twenty-first-century democrats often have in mind. Like the authors of the US Constitution, they accepted a view of democracy that limited political rights to propertied Greek males. But their ideas and practices allowed a much wider range of political participation than would ever have been tolerated in Plato's *Republic*.

Aristotle: Western Society's Great Systematizer

Aristotle was Plato's student, but his ideas differed from his mentor's in important ways. He was a keen observer of the world around him and spent his life trying to make sense out of it, primarily through categorizing its every aspect. Like Plato, he recognized the power of rhetoric and was very much concerned that it could be used to bring out the worst elements of human nature. Also like Plato, he observed that some teachers of rhetoric taught techniques for swaying the emotions of judges and legislators instead of teaching their students how to help an audience arrive at the best decisions for itself and for the broader society. But rhetoric could also be used to bring out the best in human beings and to help them construct the best possible societies. Proper training could allow rhetoric to become the "ethical branch of politics" (Aristotle, 1962).

How, then, could a rhetor persuade an audience to make good decisions, to create good societies? Aristotle offered three answers to that question. His first answer applied to all human beings, to what today's philosophers call "human ontology." All of us share certain features. We are thinking beings, so we can be persuaded by what we believe to be "rational" arguments (*logoi* in Aristotle's Greek). Persuasion is most likely if rational arguments are made by people who seem to embody what we value most highly (*ethos*, character), and are presented in ways that appeal to our deepest desires or passions (*pathe*).[6] But human beings are also products of their environments, which means that different audiences are "prepared" (or "conditioned") by their experiences to respond positively to different kinds of rhetoric. This difference underlies Aristotle's second answer to the question of how people can be persuaded.

During his travels Aristotle noticed that there were a number of different political systems in the ancient world, each of which celebrated and magnified some aspects of human nature while de-emphasizing others. Each society had distinctive laws and economic systems, and its citizens had characteristic modes of thinking, forms of education, rituals, religious beliefs, and types of rhetoric. Members of each society had also come to accept a particular set of *ideas*, which told them what to think, how to make sense out of events and experiences, how to act, and what kind of social, political, and economic structures to construct. These core ideas coalesced to form *ideologies* within which each idea supports and strengthens the other ideas. Citizens learn to evaluate their actions and the actions of others in terms of that ideology. By acting, thinking, and speaking "rightly," one demonstrated that one belonged in a particular society and should be taken seriously by others. In other words, one developed "ethos." Similarly, different societies developed different views of what constituted "logical" reasoning and different conceptions of the passions. For example, human beings seemed to share a deeply held, passionate commitment to social justice. But different societies developed different beliefs about what states of affairs constitute "justice" and "injustice." When rhetors base their arguments and appeals on the dominant ideology of a society – that is, when they conform to accepted definitions of logic, enact dominant values, and describe a circumstance or event in ways that activate the passions of members of that society – they increase the likelihood that their rhetoric will be successful. In the process, they demonstrate that the core ideas of the society actually can be used to address the challenges that its members face in their everyday lives, thereby strengthening that ideology.[7]

Aristotle's third form of persuasion was narrower still. The observation that societies develop dominant ideologies does not mean that they are homogeneous. Within every society some people develop views of reality that deviate from socially accepted norms, and they legitimize their views through communication with like-minded others. Sometimes these differences are related to social class – today's wealthy suburbanites take for granted different beliefs and values than long-term unemployed residents of "urban jungles" do. Sometimes the differences are linked to an auditor's profession, training, or daily experiences – engineers think differently from lawyers or artists. Sometimes they are related to the audience members' age (and thus to their past experiences). Whatever the source of a particular audience's views, differences among its members create a significant challenge for rhetors: the challenge of adapting their appeals to the specific audience they face, while also acting in ways that are consistent with broader social assumptions and values. Fortunately, as the sophists realized, the dominant ideologies of societies are full of tensions, incongruities, and contradictions. Most of the time citizens are not conscious of those incongruities; in fact ideologies make our lives stable and predictable partly because we are able to ignore the inconsistencies. As a result, rhetors have a wide range of socially acceptable *topoi* to draw upon. Rhetors can take fundamentally different positions on key issues *and* legitimize those positions in terms of socially accepted assumptions that define a society. In the process, they both affirm and reinforce the ideas they draw upon and, by raising contradictions to a conscious level, they facilitate social change.[8]

Unfortunately, over the centuries, Aristotle's systematic,

complex view of rhetoric was misinterpreted as a simplistic "cookbook" of techniques (Kennedy in Aristotle, 1991). What we do know is that Aristotle viewed rhetoric as a practical *art*. It had no subject matter of its own but could be used to help people make decisions on a wide variety of topics.[9] It could be used for good or for ill; but, no matter how it was used, it would have an important impact on society.

Summary: Issues and Lessons from the Classics, or Why Ancient Greeks Matter

Two important implications emerged from the debates over rhetoric that took place during the classical era. The first implication is that *rhetoric and its use inherently involve issues of power and social control*. For Plato in the *Republic*, rhetoric was a tool to be used by philosopher–kings to inculcate a particular set of beliefs, values, and frames of reference in the citizens of the *Republic*. It was to be used to facilitate "right thinking" and "right action" and to silence incorrect views and political dissent. Virtually any rhetorical tactic was acceptable as long as it was used for the "good," as defined by the philosopher–king. Like most of today's social theorists, Plato recognized that, even in the most tyrannical states and institutions, resistance is always possible and rhetoric is the primary means of achieving both social stability and social change. A stable society based on the "truth" was possible only if the power of rhetoric could be harnessed by philosopher–kings, that is, if their "voice" dominated the marketplace of ideas.

The second implication of the debates of the classical era is that *rhetoric inherently involves issues of truth and claims to knowledge*. The debate between the sophists and Plato and his followers was grounded in different views about the nature of truth, the processes through which it is discovered, who is capable of discovering it, and how it is to be applied in concrete decision-making situations. Rhetoric is made of claims about what counts as "knowledge," as opposed to "myth" or "mere rhetoric." "Facts" are contrasted with "opinion," "divine revelation" with "heresy," "science" with "mythology," and so on. The essence of rhetoric

13

is to create and manage these truth claims; the power of rhetoric lies in the capacity to attach these claims to particular positions on social, political, and organizational issues. More than his mentor, Plato, Aristotle understood that there are many different kinds of societies and political systems that can meet their members' needs. Even in the most totalitarian societies or institutions (for example in prisons or psychiatric institutions), there would always be differences, tensions, contradictions, and resistance. The role of rhetoric is to manage those tensions, paradoxically to sustain stability while facilitating change. This contrast, between the use of rhetoric to ensure domination by an elite and the use of rhetoric to articulate multiple voices reflecting the interests of multiple stakeholders in a democratic process, will be the central issue examined throughout the remainder of this book, just as it has been the central issue in the history of Western civilization.

Essential Issues in the Study of Organizational Rhetoric

Why study *organizational* rhetoric? The simple answer to that question appears in a phrase from the 1960s – that's where the action is. In short, "organizations have replaced individuals as key figures in society" (Heath, 2009, 18; see also Cutlip, 1994). As I will explain in the remainder of this chapter and in Chapter 4, organizational rhetoric influences public policies, both directly and indirectly. Equally important, organizational rhetoric also influences popular attitudes and beliefs, even to the extent of molding the core taken-for-granted assumptions that guide and constrain our actions and interpretations of reality (Greider, 1992, 1997; Soros, 1998, 2000; Phillips, 2002). Organizations have long influenced public policy, particularly in the US. But, with the advent of globalization, US organizations today have now significant effects on the lives of people who live halfway around the world.[10] The size and power of the US economy means that any comprehensive analysis of organizational rhetoric should begin with an assessment of the "American system." Aristotle's

14

observations on different societies provide a model for such an assessment. Societies are defined by a dominant ideology – a set of assumptions that, while not universally accepted, are treated as normal and natural by most of the people most of the time; they justify a particular social, political, and economic structure. Those structures guide and constrain the experiences of members of the society in ways that provide evidence which seems to support the dominant ideology. The two – ideologies and structures – are so tightly woven together that they should be separated only briefly, and only in order to explain them more clearly. In the remainder of this chapter I will explain the processes through which the structure of the American system developed, and I will discuss ideology only when necessary. In Chapters 2 and 3 I will examine the ideological basis of that system and explain how our taken-for-granted assumptions legitimize its structure. In the process I will argue that the structure provides organizational rhetors with a wide range of *strategic* options regarding the times and places in which they act, and the taken-for-granted assumptions provide them with the *topoi* that they can draw upon when they do so.

Characteristics of the "American System" today

In many ways the US economy is different from that of the other industrialized democracies. The "American system" has four key characteristics: (1) a preference for large organizations, which (2) are allowed, even encouraged, to be politically active; (3) face little government regulation; and (4) are not expected to be governed in a democratic fashion (Perrow, 1991, 2002; Roy, 1997; Prechel, 2000). Some countries have one or more of these characteristics, but not all four. For example Japan, South Korea, and some European countries tolerate or encourage the development of large limited-liability corporations, but they compensate for the resulting concentration of economic power by regulating them closely. Although executives in US firms and their political allies complain loudly and repeatedly about the regulatory burdens imposed on them, when compared to other industrialized countries US organizations are weakly regulated. It is true that the US regulatory system is exceptionally complex because of the country's "federal" political structure. A company operating in more than one state may simultaneously be subject to regulations from dozens of federal agencies, a number of similar agencies in each state, and local governments, all of which impose different and sometimes contradictory rules. This makes it difficult and expensive to comply with all of the regulations that corporations face, but the overall rigor of the regulations faced by US firms is light in comparison to that of other industrialized nations (Dempsey, 1989; Vietor, 1994). I will discuss regulation and regulators more extensively in Chapter 4.

Some of the limits to regulatory power are statutory. For example, in the US, worker safety is primarily regulated by the individual states, which means that the protections vary widely. Some states have extensive protections, while others, such as Arizona and Texas, do not even require employers to give water breaks to employees working in the sun in temperatures above 100 degrees F (38 degrees C). Similarly, statutes governing the Food and Drug Administration (FDA) do not allow it to force a company to remove foods infected with salmonella from the market, or to require pharmaceutical firms to recall a previously approved drug when dangerous side-effects are detected. The regulator can only request voluntary withdrawals and ban advertisements that have been found to be false and/or misleading.

Other limits to regulatory power are economic. For example, if an employee is killed at work because of a company's failure to meet federal Occupational Safety and Health Act (OSHA) requirements, the maximum fine that can be imposed is $7,000 *per death*. If you need a bit of context for this number, in August, 2009, ExxonMobil agreed to pay $600,000 in fines and penalties for negligently allowing 85 migratory birds to become trapped in uncovered storage tanks ($7,058 *per bird*); and in June, 2009 a federal judge fined Jammie Thomas-Rasset $80,000 *per song* for illegally downloading music for her own use.[11] In other cases fines may *seem* to be large, but pale in comparison to the profits made through illegal activity. For example, in 2006, Pfizer, Inc. was slapped with a $2.3 billion fine for illegally marketing four of its prescription drugs, the largest such fine in US history. But that "total stands small compared to the $44.2 billion in pharmaceutical sales the world's largest drugmaker made last year." Indeed, one of the drugs, Lyrica, "registered $2.6 billion in sales" (Murphy, 2009).[12] In 2010 two of the financial institutions most responsible for the 2008 collapse of the global financial industry and resulting "Great Recession" received similarly trivial fines. Citigroup's $75 million settlement with the Securities and Exchange Commission (SEC) for "materially misstating" its exposure to risky "subprime" mortgages equaled *one third* of *one percent* of its revenues for the *second quarter* of 2010. When Judge Ellen Huvelle of the Federal District Court for the District of Columbia accepted the settlement, she observed that the fines were not large enough to "deter anyone [in corporate America] from doing anything" (quoted in Wyatt, 2010; see also Gordon, 2010). Similarly, Goldman Sachs and Co., whose former (and future) employees occupy key positions in the agencies that are charged with regulating the industry, paid $550 million to settle fraud charges, the largest fine levied against a Wall Street firm in the history of the SEC. The amount

was less than 5 percent of Goldman's 2009 net income, about fifteen days of the firm's profits (Creswell, 2010; Gordon, 2010). In theory, the economic discipline provided by regulation is supplemented by lawsuits filed by aggrieved workers and consumers. However, during the past twenty years or so "tort reform" has limited or eliminated this option in many states, and entire industries are exempt from lawsuits in federal courts (Vibbert and Bostdorff, 1993). So, while US organizations are subject to a patchwork quilt of regulations, the actual impact of those regulations is much less than in other industrialized countries (Banting and Corbett, 2002).

Corporations also receive preferential treatment in tax policies. In the late 1950s, when President Dwight Eisenhower warned against the growing power of a military–industrial complex, about half of the US government's income came from corporate income tax. The percentage declined to an historical low of 4 percent in 2009, less than the Treasury collected from excise taxes on tobacco, alcohol, and other products, and only one-sixth as much as it collected in either individual income taxes (26 percent) or social security, Medicare, and other retirement taxes (25 percent). In fact few large companies pay any federal income tax, and many have a negative tax rate because they receive more money in government subsidies than they pay in taxes. A 2004 report by the Government Accounting Office indicated that 61 percent of US corporations paid no income taxes from 1996 to 2000, a period of rapid economic growth and very strong corporate profits; 94 percent had an effective tax rate of 5 percent or less (the statutory tax rate for corporations during this period was 35 percent). Between 2000 and 2003 almost a third of the 275 most profitable Fortune 500 companies (which had combined profits of more than $1.1 trillion) paid no income taxes or had a negative tax rate. The companies that were most successful in avoiding federal income taxes were Prudential Financial (profit of $437 million; effective tax rate of −262.3 percent), Boeing ($1,069 million; −159 percent), and Entergy (a Texas-based utility company, $562 million profit, −135 percent tax rate).[13] Corporate rhetors argue that tax breaks and subsidies allow organizations to grow and add more jobs, but there is no statistically significant relationship between effective tax rate and these outcomes (Soros, 1998; Prechel, 2000). Yet, opinion polls make it quite clear that US citizens *believe* that US organizations are excessively regulated and taxed, a tribute to the effectiveness of organizational rhetoric.

Finally, and perhaps most importantly, US firms have much more political power than organizations in other industrialized countries do. This has resulted from a number of unique historical events, which can be understood only through a brief examination of US economic and political history.

Weekend Fun 1

At the end of each chapter I will provide a case study that can be personalized to the lives and experiences of each reader. For the system to work, you probably will have to do some background research, which will be more difficult in some cases than in others. Early in each chapter I will describe the research that you need to do in anticipation of the case study. Hopefully this will give you adequate time to collect the data before you get to the case study itself. For the first case, you need to choose a legal prescription drug. This exercise works best if (1) the drug is a non-generic drug (unless you are a resident of Canada, where generics, too, will work for the exercise), and (2) it is near and dear to your heart, that is, it is taken regularly by you or someone who is emotionally and/or financially close to you. Find out how much the drug costs US residents who do not have health insurance. Find out how much it costs US residents who are eligible for Medicare, or who get their drugs through the Department of Defense Office of Veterans' Affairs (a hint: a good starting point is the website of Families USA), and how much each prescription costs US taxpayers. (If you really want to get your adrenaline flowing, also find out how much it costs a US Congressperson.)

This will not be easy. As I explain in Chapter 2, a crucial strategy used by organizational rhetors is to keep secret the information that customers need in order to make rational purchasing decisions.

For example, Congress (with presidential support) has forbidden the FDA from making comparative cost–benefit information on prescription drugs available to consumers. With only a couple of exceptions, states have followed suit. For example, in August, 2005, New York's (Republican) governor George Pataki signed a law requiring the state to create an easily used website that allowed consumers to compare prescription drug prices across the state. The pharmaceutical industry tried to block the bill, but failed – the bill passed both houses of the New York legislature unanimously. Five months later, Pataki inserted a provision that would repeal the law "deep in one of the budget bills" that he proposed. When the reversal became public, the governor's office quickly backed off, but the outcome is still in doubt and the website still does not exist (Cooper, 2006). The governor of Oregon, John Kitzhaber, successfully fought *for* the creation of a website with comparative information, and, at the time I wrote this chapter, that website was still functioning. So getting price information will be more difficult than you might imagine that it would be, or feel that it *should* be. But keep trying; eventually you will find it. Once you succeed, find out how much the drug would cost in a country other than the US. Another hint: it is easiest to compare your costs to Canadians', because that's what recent political rhetoric in the US has done. For example, the staff of former Democratic Representative and Presidential Chief of Staff Rahm Emanuel compared the prices of ten oft-prescribed drugs at Costco stores in Chicago and Toronto, and found a $1,500 USD difference in a one-month's supply (CBC News, 2007). Of the ten drugs, only one (Viagra) could be purchased less expensively in the US. Overall, Canadians spend between 50 and 70 percent less than US residents for identical prescriptions, depending on the drug and the province where it is purchased.[14] When Congressman Emanuel and North Dakota Senator Byron Dorgan introduced the Pharmaceutical Market Access and Drug Safety Act on January 10, 2007, they estimated the potential savings to US consumers at $50 billion USD over the next decade. But, since Canada has the *second-highest* prescription drug costs in the developed world – almost double those paid in European countries – it will be much more fun to choose a different non-US country. Save your results.

20

What is Rhetoric? What is Organizational Rhetoric?

Creating the Structure of the American System

One of the best summaries of the development of the American system is provided by Yale sociologist Charles Perrow in his 2002 book *Organizing America* (see also Sklar, 1988 and Perrow, 1991). Societies, and their economies, can be organized as communities, markets, or hierarchies (bureaucracies), Perrow notes. In "communities" economic units tend to be small and family-owned, and economic exchanges often do not involve money. Social roles are fixed, based on traditional patriarchal family relationships, and playing them requires low levels of skill. Communities are governed by elders, whose control is grounded in religious beliefs and/or custom. In "markets" the economic units are small, but they are more specialized than in "communities," which means that the goods and services that are exchanged are more varied and entrepreneurial activity is valued and rewarded. Social roles are governed by short-term contracts and relationships depend on economic motivations and rational calculations. People move from one occupation and one set of contracts to another rather easily, although some tasks require high levels of skill and training. There is little government role in the economy, although government does enforce contracts, while trade and professional organizations provide some informal controls. In "hierarchies" economic units are large, benefiting from the "economies of scale," which come from size, and from the power that comes from being a monopolist or oligopolist. Hierarchies rely on mass production and the daily routines that accompany it, and are highly bureaucratic – tasks are segmented and require *specialized* skills, each supervisor is directly responsible to his or her immediate supervisor and for her or his subordinates, and decision-making is *centralized* at the top of the organization. Typically these companies hire from within or through interpersonal relationships for jobs that vary widely in the level of skills and training required. The economy is governed by large corporations, government, trade and professional associations, and unions – in that order of power. A heated debate over which form should characterize the United States was present from its beginning.

On the one hand, there was a perspective typically attributed to Thomas Jefferson. Fearful of concentrated power, either in government or in large organizations, Jefferson glorified societies whose economies were dominated by agriculture and small producers and shopkeepers, "communities" in Perrow's model. Government should occur through some form of direct democracy, such as the stereotypical New England town meeting. As in the democratic city states of ancient Greece, whose history, philosophy, and politics Jefferson knew very well, citizenship should be limited to propertied free (white) males. Social stability would come from connections among people who actively participated in politics and were economically interdependent.

A contrasting model, usually attributed to Alexander Hamilton, focused on a fear of economic stagnation. Even in 1800, industrialized economies seemed to be prone to repeated boom-and-bust cycles and economic depressions that often led to social unrest, as evidenced by the French Revolution and Reign of Terror. Still, Hamiltonians glorified industrialization as the only long-term means of ensuring economic growth in the new nation, which they assumed would provide social and political stability. They also believed that sustained economic growth requires technological progress, which requires in turn capital investments that go beyond what is possible to get from neighbors supporting neighbors. Further, large capital investments require centralized authority – an active and influential federal government, courts that are sensitive to the economic effects of laws, and a national bank – in short, what Perrow would call a "market" mode of organizing. Unlike the Jeffersonian model, in which government's proper role is to represent the interests of the people, government's role in a market system is to aid organizations directly, which would in turn provide the economic growth necessary to provide jobs, goods and services needed by the people, and a stable society. The distinction may seem to be a small one from the perspective of the twenty-first century, but policymakers at the time realized that it involved a fundamental choice, one that would influence the kind of society future generations were to live within.

In 1800 the community model was dominant. By 1850 the

economy had moved toward a market system, although fear of concentrated power had limited the development of large bureaucratic organizations. In market systems, relations between organizations and between them and their customers are oriented toward long-term cooperative interactions based on mutual trust. Perrow notes that "trading partners share information, resources, and even personnel at times; accommodate each other's needs; rely upon trust and unwritten agreements; and share risks through reciprocity" (2002, 25). But the Civil War accelerated the shift to an hierarchical system: the war "helped pave the road that eventually led to large-scale industrial corporations; it created a national currency and banking system. It stimulated the first truly large-scale securities [stock] market in the United States" (Roy, 1997, 129).[15] War is expensive and disruptive of social institutions. While small, local banks had been able to block the formation of a national bank for decades; desperate times led to desperate measures, including the National Bank Act of 1863. The improved transportation systems that were created in order to facilitate the movement of troops and equipment allowed organizations to expand their operations over long distances and across state lines. This combination set the stage for a progressive shift to large, hierarchical organizations with highly concentrated economic, and eventually political, power.

Completing the Structure of the American System I: The Rise of Limited-Liability Corporations

The shift to a bureaucratic/hierarchical economic system created an opportunity for organizations to dominate the US political–economic system. But it did not provide the legal structure that was necessary. US citizens had long been skeptical of the idea of a corporation. Its core concept, "limited liability," means that owners (and, later on, professional managers) would be financially responsible for the operations of a company only to the extent of their investment in it. This doctrine inevitably shifted the risks involved in creating and operating a company from its owners and operators to its creditors and stockholders. Since creditors only exercised indirect control over the operations of corporations, this shift was very controversial. Owners and managers would be making bets with other people's money, creating what came to be called a "moral hazard."[16] Although this phrase developed in the financial industry (insurance, to be specific), it refers to any situation in which one party makes decisions about how much and what kinds of risks to take, and will profit handsomely if it makes the correct decision, but someone else will bear the cost if the decision is a bad one (Krugman, 2009; Posner, 2010). As a result, state governments were careful to grant organizations the right to incorporate *only* if their owners and managers could demonstrate that doing so would meet *public* needs that could not be met efficiently in other ways, for instance building a canal or railroad or turnpike. As a result, every decision to allow incorporation was a political battle, one that had to be justified rhetorically.[17] Ironically, some of these justifications were grounded in Jeffersonian ideas: corporations "would offset the centralized state and prevent the concentration of wealth in the hands of the few who would have the economic and political clout to secure charters" (Perrow, 2002, 38, 39). Others were the outgrowth of the Whig Party's belief that the superior wisdom of educated judges should take precedence over the emotions of the unschooled masses. Others were clearly Hamiltonian – entrepreneurs must take risks, and it is in the public's interest to limit those risks. Indeed governments would be wise to form partnerships with entrepreneurs in order to encourage, assist, and protect them. Incorporation seemed to offer a means of addressing public needs that is, inherently, economically more efficient than government ever can be (Perrow, 2002, esp. 35–45, 112–128).

In the midst of this debate, the US Supreme Court made a series of what seemed to be at the time rather innocuous decisions. But, when combined with other political decisions, these decisions changed the political–economic structure of the US forever. In 1819 the *Dartmouth College* v. *Woodward* decision declared that corporations were "persons" and thus had all of the constitutional rights and obligations afforded individual citizens (save the right to vote) – a principle that was broadened and re-affirmed in its 1886

Santa Clara v. *Southern Pacific Railroad* decision. Representing Dartmouth College, Daniel Webster explicitly argued that private corporations must be *protected from* democracy, from "the rise and fall of popular parties and the fluctuations of political opinion." This view was not unprecedented. Thomas Cronin, former White House Fellow and award-winning political scientist, reminds us

> that "most of our framers [*sc.* Founding Fathers] were skeptical [. . .] and even hostile to notions of popular democracy. They had fought their war of independence in large part to get away from monarchy [. . .] Yet democracy was regarded as a dangerous and unworkable doctrine. The very term *democracy* appears neither in the Declaration of Independence nor in the US Constitution. (Cronin, 1987, 35)[18]

Chief Justice Marshall favored Webster's position and delayed hearings on the case until the court had both a clear pro-corporation majority and a series of favorable lower court decisions that it could use as precedents. Perrow concludes: "The Dartmouth decision [. . .] was not a mistake, an inadvertence, a happenstance in history, but a well-designed plan devised by particular interests" (Perrow, 2002, 41). Ironically, corporations obtained the constitutional rights of "persons" fifty years before Black Americans and more than a century before women. As a result of these decisions and of the economic growth and technological advancement that followed the Civil War, the large inter-state corporations of the "robber baron" era became possible. By the end of the century some corporations had budgets many times the size of the federal government's.[19]

Over time, the size and power of the federal government did increase; but so did the constitutional rights of corporate persons. In 1889 (*Minneapolis & St. Louis Railroad Co.* v. *Beckwith*) and in 1893 (*Noble* v. *Union River Logging Railroad*) the due process and equal protection provisions listed in the Fifth and Fourteenth Amendments to the US Constitution were applied to corporations. In 1906 (*Hale* v. *Henkel*, 201 US 43) they were protected against search and seizure; in 1908 they received the right to a jury trial in criminal cases (*Armour Packing Company* v. *US*, 209 US 56), a right that was expanded to civil cases in 1970 (*Ross et al. Trustees* v. *Bernhard et al.*, 396 US 531). The First Amendment right to free speech – was expanded in 1976 to cover *commercial* speech in addition to political discourse (for example product advertising: *Virginia Pharmacy Board* v. *Virginia Consumer Council*) and in 1978 to cover the expenditure of money (*National Bank of Boston* v. *Bellotti*). A second series of court decisions, starting with the *Minneapolis and St. Louis Railroad* case, gave corporations the right to challenge state statutes (Ritz, 2001, 2007). Hundreds of cases followed which struck down states' rights to regulate corporate activity: a Minnesota statute banning the sale of milk in plastic, nonreturnable, nonrefillable containers (in order to reduce the amount of non-biodegradable trash in landfills); a Vermont statute requiring milk producers to label milk that was produced by using the controversial bovine growth hormone BST (the First Amendment protects a corporation's right both to speak and not to speak); state laws banning the use of taxpayer money to buy products from objectionable states such as South Africa during its apartheid era; ordinances banning the construction of cell phone towers in residential areas – and so on. For corporations, the courts became a primary site for making and resisting public policy, one that is much less expensive than lobbying every state and municipality.

In addition, the decisions created a curious kind of "personhood" for corporations. In theory, legal rights are accompanied by legal responsibilities – the right to private property, for example, means that an individual must respect other people's ownership rights. Individuals who fail to fulfill those responsibilities are dealt with through the legal system. But the US legal system is designed to deal with *individuals* who commit crimes for *individual* motives. Corporations are collections of individuals, but it is difficult to prosecute individual employees for following illegal orders when refusing to do so could cost them their jobs.[20] On the other hand punishing an entire corporation for the actions of a few seems unfair and unwise, because doing so will hurt many innocent parties, including citizens who are supposed to be protected by the legal system. Moreover, bureaucratic structures serve to protect employees, at all levels, from being held responsible for actions they take as members of corporations. This is especially true for those employees at the top of corporate hierarchies (Jackall, 1983, 2009). When combined, these two factors make it exceptionally difficult to ensure that corporate persons meet the *responsibilities* of citizenship that accompany the *rights* of personhood.

In sum, it is almost impossible to overestimate the importance of these largely forgotten court decisions. They meant that corporations could challenge any state or federal laws that regulated or otherwise constrained their activities. More importantly, they shifted policymaking about corporate power and practices from elected legislatures to appellate judges. In the process, the government's role in the economy shifted from protecting the rights of *individual* workers, customers, and citizens to protecting the rights of *corporate* persons (Cheney, 1992; Cheney and Carroll, 1997). In fact the doctrine of corporate personhood has had such profound effects on the balance of political power in the US that other countries have consciously sought to avoid going down the same path. For example, when Canadians drafted their Charter of Rights and Freedoms in 1984, they made an explicit distinction between the extensive rights of "human" persons and the more limited rights of organizations.

The power of large, bureaucratic/hierarchical, limited-liability corporations became clear during the late 1800s. Instead of restricting or strictly regulating them, as had been the case for decades, some states decided that encouraging their development would be economically advantageous. The first state to make incorporation easier was New Jersey, and corporations rushed to move their headquarters to the Garden State. By 1901, 71 percent of large US firms (defined as those valued at more than $25 million USD) and two-thirds of those worth $10 million USD were incorporated in New Jersey. Tax revenues generated by these firms were so large that the state was able to avoid creating a state income tax, unlike most other eastern states. Other states followed New Jersey's lead, notably Delaware and Connecticut, creating an unofficial competition to establish the most pro-corporation state laws. However, like the court decisions, all of this went "virtually unnoticed in the financial press or national newspapers" (Roy, 1997, 152; see also Horwitz, 1992).

A wave of incorporations and corporate mergers started during the Depression of 1898 and was over by 1902. In only four years the aggregate value of stocks and bonds of large corporations had increased eight times. Suddenly, warnings about the concentration of power that would result from what was called "easy incorporation" were proving accurate. The small, public-oriented corporations of the eighteenth and early nineteenth centuries had been replaced by behemoths that had seemingly unlimited finances and economic power. They also seemed suddenly to have unlimited political influence.

Completing the Structure of the American System II: Economic Giants Go Political

In 1900 Congress banned corporations from contributing directly to political candidates. Soon afterwards President Theodore Roosevelt embarked on his campaign to "bust" the largest corporations. But the US Supreme Court re-entered the picture with a series of decisions declaring that organizational size alone was not illegal or unconstitutional, and Roosevelt, along with the Jeffersonian ideal of a society of small organizations and direct democracy, rode off into history. Both economists and the general public rationalized the change by lauding the economic efficiencies that large corporations offered to consumers. Additional court decisions gave large corporations even more legal legitimacy; and the rapid economic growth of the 1920s broadened popular support. The 1929 stock market crash and the social and economic dislocations of the Great Depression revived public debate about the advantages and limitations of the American system. The public lost confidence in the ability of private enterprise to manage the economy on its own, the size and regulatory role of the federal government increased significantly, and new power blocs – unions, farmers, and so on – formed and grew in power. When the economy improved after World War II and the fear of "socialist" institutions such as unions and farmer cooperatives re-emerged during Red Scare of the late 1940s and 1950s, the pressure on corporations waned. Although there were multiple corporate scandals during this era, criticism of the American system virtually disappeared (Wells, 2002).

Beginning with the 1976 *Buckley v. Valeo* decision, in which the US Supreme Court ruled that campaign donations were "speech" and thus protected by the First Amendment, opportunities for corporations to influence political decision-making grew rapidly. *Buckley* solidified and accelerated a cycle that had already developed – Congress engages in substantial rhetoric about "campaign finance reform" and enacts some restrictions, which encourages corporate attorneys and accountants to develop creative ways of getting around the rules and mount court challenges designed to invalidate them. Limitations on corporate political influence become less effective, leading to actual or perceived campaign finance scandals, which culminate in a new round of relatively weak restrictions, and the cycle starts over again.

US citizens understand these processes, and have become quite cynical about them. They also largely reject the claims made by defenders of the system that campaign contributions do not "buy votes" but only provide contributors with access to policymakers. They realize that access is important in itself – if only one interest group is allowed to discuss an issue with policymakers, especially if those discussions occur in private, policies favoring that interest group are likely. A recent, methodologically sophisticated study concludes that business contributions, although not those from labor unions, significantly influenced votes in the US House of Representatives.[21] Of course, the US campaign finance system allows any individual citizen, regardless of his or her wealth or income, to contribute to political campaigns up to $2,400 per candidate per election (including primaries) or up to $30,400 per year to political parties. But the superior resources and greater political sophistication of corporate interest groups give them more influence over the political process. I will examine in depth corporate influence on public policymaking in Chapter 4, but the overall process is simple. Corporations "work, quite deliberately and often rather covertly, as political actors, and often have direct access to those at the highest levels of formal political and administrative power with considerable success" (Sklair, 1998, 284).[22] The structure of the American system was complete.

The American System Goes Global

To this point I have discussed the development of the American system as if it were important only within the borders of the US. This may never have been true, and certainly it is not true today. With the economic globalization that accelerated after the collapse of the Soviet Union in 1990, both the structures and the ideas that comprise the American system have permeated the entire world. Central to this expansion were two structures: non-governmental organizations created at the Bretton Woods Conference after the end of World War II – the International Bank for Reconstruction and Development (usually called the World Bank); and the International Monetary Fund (IMF). Not only did World War II leave the economies of Japan and Europe in ruins, it virtually stopped international trade and finance. The World Bank was designed to make up for the lack of direct investments that would normally come from private sources and governments. The IMF is a *public* institution, funded by taxpayers around the world, and is "based on a recognition that markets often did not work well – that they could result in massive unemployment and might fail to make needed funds available to countries to help them restore their economies" (Stiglitz, 2002, 17; see also Greider, 1997; Soros, 1998; Stiglitz, 2010). From their inception, these organizations were dominated by the United States. The latter has always been able to appoint directors of the World Bank and has a bloc vote large enough to veto any IMF policy it opposes. Eventually the missions of the two organizations became closely entwined and their operations shifted away from their original goals. Nobel prize winner George Stiglitz explains:

30

Founded on the belief that markets often worked badly, it [the IMF] now champions market supremacy with ideological fervor. Founded on the belief that there is a need for international pressure on countries to have more expansionary economic policies – such as increasing expenditures, reducing taxes, or lowering interest rates to stimulate the economy – today the IMF typically provides funds only if counties engage in policies like cutting deficits, raising taxes, or raising interest rates. (Stiglitz, 2002, 12–13; see also Moore, 1995; Mohammadi, 1997; Soros, 1998, 2000; Narkunas, 2005)

Unfortunately, the strategies have had mixed success. The IMF admits that half of its interventions have failed, and the World Bank's failure rate may reach 80 percent in its African projects, sometimes because the recipient countries lacked the structures necessary to make free markets work, and sometimes because the World Bank left local monopolies in place or encouraged the development of new ones. Efforts to expand the reach of the American system also have generated a great deal of resistance, in part because of resulting increases in poverty and unemployment, in part because they have often allowed developed countries to retain policies that protect the latter's industries while requiring developing countries to dismantle theirs, and in part because they have been anti-democratic. Consequently the twenty-first century has seen both developing countries, especially in Latin America, and developed countries revise or reject the US model.[23]

Implications

At this point you may be feeling a bit overwhelmed. Since I have covered much of the history of Western society from 600 BCE to the present in one single chapter, it is probably time to take a breath and assess where we have been. There are three important ideas to take away from this chapter. *First, studying organizational rhetoric involves analyzing fundamental issues about the nature of society and of the systems that comprise it.* Western society has from its beginning been about a tension between democracy and autocracy. Rhetoric is central to both of these conceptions of what

31

constitutes a "good" society, and such tension is reflected most clearly in discourse about the role that corporations – decidedly undemocratic and autocratic institutions – play in modern capitalist democracies. Dictatorial modes of operation that we say (and may even believe) we would never tolerate in our political system are allowed – indeed, they are celebrated – in our corporations. Ironically, we willingly grant those undemocratic institutions the right to exert significant influence over democratic decision-making, while rarely suggesting that corporations should grant their employees, stockowners, or customers a significant voice in corporate decision-making.

This inconsistency is partly the result of our ambivalence about democracy itself. It is a very messy process – democratic decision-making takes a great deal of time and energy and is emotionally involving, which means that it makes people feel vulnerable. While the structure of democracy seems to give everyone a chance to make his or her voice heard, it does nothing to ensure that having a voice or a vote means having influence over decisions. People who are more articulate, have access to more or better information, and are more familiar with rules and political processes tend to dominate democratic decision-making (Mansbridge, 1973; Habermas, 1984). But our ambivalence about democracy also results from an ideology and a rhetoric, present for centuries but dominant since the early 1980s, that financier George Soros (1998) has called "free-market fundamentalism" (which I will examine at length in Chapter 2). Because of that ideology, people throughout Western democracies have come to take for granted the assumption that organizations should be evaluated in terms of efficiency and profitability, not of democracy or social responsibility. Why and how this has happened, and the role that organizational rhetoric has played in the development and continuation of such an ideology, is the primary focus of this book.

Second, social/economic/political systems are complex creations which, once established and legitimized, guide and constrain future rhetoric. As a result, they are very difficult to change. Rhetorical situations have two dimensions – social/economic/ political structures, and taken-for-granted assumptions. This chapter has focused on the structural dimension. Chapters 2 and 3 will focus on the assumptions. Rhetoric is central to both structures and assumptions; it is guided and constrained by them, but it also creates, reproduces, and sometimes transforms them.

Finally, rhetoric and its effects are ambiguous and unpredictable. Rhetors, organizational and otherwise, often succeed in creating and legitimizing the structures and assumptions that make up rhetorical situations. But the unintended, long-term consequences of their efforts may be very different from what they had anticipated. The *Dartmouth* decision was about a very specific issue – the state of New Hampshire's right to place a trustee or two on the college's board of trustees in exchange for the provision of taxpayer support. But over time the precedent created by the U.S. Supreme Court's *Dartmouth* decision combined with other specific actions to change fundamentally the nature of the US political and economic system. The effects of seemingly minor events can be magnified over time in ways that no one anticipates, just as the impact of what initially seems to be a momentous change sometimes dissipates over time. Furthermore, the structures that are created may outlast the rhetoric used to justify them, or the rhetoric may become a permanent fixture of political and organizational life long after the structures change. Rhetoric is about maneuvering within the constraints that make up rhetorical situations and about drawing upon the taken-for-granted assumptions of a society to legitimize one's preferred course of action. Its effects are complicated and unpredictable, but this is what makes it interesting.

I will return to these ideas repeatedly in the chapters to come, so hopefully they will become increasingly clear over time. In Chapter 2 I examine the ideas that accompany, support, and are supported by the structure of the American system, focusing on the ideology of free-market fundamentalism. Chapter 3 examines the development of a dominant mythology about leaders/leadership and workers/followership. Chapter 4 traces the processes through which organizational rhetors influence public policymaking, and Chapter 5 explores the role that rhetoric plays in the construction and defense of organizational identities and images.

Case Study: Dealing (Legal) Drugs

Prescription drugs cost more in the US than anywhere else in the developed world. US spending for prescription drugs in 2004 was more than $188 billion USD, more that 4.5 times the $40.3 USD billion spent in 1990, which makes it the fastest-growing component of health care spending (Gubonski et al., 2010; Gardner, 2007). The rapid increase from 1990 until 2003 was driven by increases in the number of prescriptions written (up 71 percent), increases in drug prices (which more than tripled the average annual inflation rate), and a shift toward expensive "new" drugs and away from older name-brand drugs and generics. Price inflation moderated a bit between 2003 and 2005 because of a reversal of the last two trends, but escalated again after 2006.

Drug companies typically rely on PhRMa, the industry's lobbying group, to offer public justifications of drug prices. PhRMa's rhetoric is quite predictable: it claims that the industry produces miracle drug after miracle drug, which have lengthened the lives of millions of patients, improved the quality of life of millions more, and reduced or controlled overall health care costs by providing alternatives to surgery or hospitalization.[24] Because of government "price controls" in countries other than the United States, maintaining high profits from sales in the US is necessary for research to continue. Since Americans use more prescription drugs than any other country, its citizens benefit most from that research. Drug development is expensive, time-consuming, and very risky – it takes twelve to fifteen years for a research idea to reach market, only one drug in fifty survives clinical trials with animals, only one in five out of those that reach the human-trial stage will make it to market, and only one in three drugs introduced to the market will reach a break-even point. When drugs are designed for a specialized market, for example AIDs patients in advanced stages of the disease or septic shock patients, prices must be exceptionally high to warrant their being developed, and it is the profits firms make on other drugs that allow them to embark on the research that leads to such drugs. Pharmaceutical firms recognize that risks are inherent in a capitalist market, but they are willing to incur those risks because of the potential payoffs, which are possible only in a capitalist system unfettered by government intervention (Aune, 2001).

Critics generally admit that drug firms must make *reasonable* profits in order to sustain risky research and development, but they argue that the industry's assertions wildly overstate the case and ignore a wealth of conflicting empirical evidence. First, the industry is incredibly profitable, maintaining annual profits in the 18–25 percent range per year for the past two decades. This profit margin is more than four times the profit margin of the oil and gas industry, and six times that of Fortune 500 companies as a whole. Second, very few of the "new" drugs that reach market actually have new active ingredients; most are "copycat" drugs, which differ from their competitors only in terms of inert ingredients or, in some cases, of packaging, which require trivial R&D (research and development) expenditures. Of the twenty drugs approved by the US FDA in 2005, only seven actually had new active ingredients, and *all* of those were developed by European firms, where drug costs (and pharmaceutical profits) are less than half of the cost in the US; in 2004 the figures were thirty-six approvals, ten involving new compounds, eight of which were developed in Europe. Indeed, allowing companies to make massive profits on copycat drugs actually reduces the likelihood of their creating new compounds, because it encourages them to spend R&D funds on low-risk products: "the more we spend on the latest overpriced, oversold, me-too drug, the more we encourage industry to concentrate resources on producing and plugging more of the same" (Agovino, 2006).

Third, industry research and development spending is wildly exaggerated. Industry figures extrapolate the most expensive form of drug research – new chemical compounds developed entirely in-house – to all drugs, including "me too" (that is, duplicate) compounds. Their estimates of development costs are also exaggerated through creative accounting. Instead of reporting actual overall costs, drug PhRMa estimates development costs by multiplying the expenses involved in creating the tiny number of drugs that do reach market by the massively larger number of chemical compounds that start the process but are rejected before incurring significant expenses (Collier, 2009). Industry data also fail to subtract the tax breaks given by the federal government for R&D, or the value of the federal grants that fund between 25 percent and 40 percent of total R&D spending. However, even with all of this manipulation of the data, the industry's reported research costs average only about 15 percent of spending, less than profits, administrative overhead, or advertising. In addition, the industry spends millions on campaign contributions and lobbying, more than any other industry. In 2002, drug companies spent $91 million USD at the federal level and at least $48 million more in the forty-two states that require detailed reporting (Angell, 2004).[25]

Discussion Questions

1 Scholars interested in rhetoric long have recognized that every rhetorical act is in a way autobiographical, that there is an implied author whose beliefs, values, and ways of thinking are constructed by the text. In an important 1970 article, Edwin Black argued that there also is an implied auditor, a listener/reader whose beliefs, values, and ways of thinking would make the rhetoric especially persuasive (Black, 1970). What are the key characteristics of the "perfect" auditor constructed in the drug industry's rhetoric (said another way, what would a person have to believe, what hierarchy of values would they have to hold dear, and what modes of thinking would they have to use for PhRMa's rhetoric to be especially persuasive)? Why? Conversely, what are the key characteristics of the "perfect" audience for the industry's critics? Why?

2 Recall the results of your "weekend fun" search. Given what you've found, and what you've just read, explain the price differences across countries. Explain your reactions to your findings.

2

Creating Topoi for Organizational Rhetoric

Getting the most out of capitalism requires public intervention of various kinds, and a lot of it: taxes, public spending, regulation in many different areas of business activity. It also requires corporate executives to be accountable – but to the right people and in the right way.

Clive Crook (2005, 1)

Markets are useful things, but they should not have been turned into a religion. Politics is, ultimately, the search for the optimum balance of exit and voice in a polity. It is no accident that the quality of public argument has declined so dramatically since the ascendency of the market.

James Arnt Aune (2001, 166; see also Hawken,
Lovins, and Lovins, 1999, 261)

The [current] depression is a failure of capitalism, or more precisely of a certain kind of capitalism ("laissez-faire" in a loose sense, "American" versus "European" in a popular sense) and of capitalism's biggest boosters.

Richard Posner (2009, 260; see also Posner, 2010)

Core Concepts

- All societies are defined by a characteristic set of taken-for-granted assumptions, which provide citizens with a sensible, stable, and predictable perceptual world, but also function as a powerful form of social control.

• Core assumptions are articulated through a variety of symbolic forms, including rhetoric, myths, and ritual. When people enact them, their power is reinforced.

• An important assumption in Western capitalist democracies, especially in the US, is the "organizational imperative," which claims that all good things come to people via formal organizations, and thus are threatened by any actions that restrict organizations.

• The organizational imperative culminates in "corporate colonization of the lifeworld," a pattern of dependency relationships that encompass the tangible requirements of modern life and a sense of individual identity.

• Another important assumption has been labeled "free-market fundamentalism," a group of ideas that hold true in only a few sectors of capitalist economies but are treated as being universally applicable. Its rhetorical power stems from its simplicity and reliance on bi-polar contrasts.

• When combined, the organizational imperative and free-market fundamentalism provide a powerful set of rhetorical *topoi* that can be strategically manipulated by organizational rhetors.

In Chapter 1 I explained that rhetoric always takes place in particular situations, and that those situations have two primary components. The structural component embraces everyday practices that have been accepted as normal and natural, as well as the social, political, and economic institutions that have developed and been legitimized in a society. Rhetorical situations also have an ideological component: the set of beliefs, values, and frameworks for making sense out of reality, which have come to be accepted by a society in general and by the specific audiences that rhetors face within it. The debate between Plato and the sophists focused on the first dimension. Plato wanted to create a political structure within which the only voice that was heard belonged to the philosopher–king, and the only rhetoric that was allowed was designed to persuade citizens to accept his view of truth without

38

question and to act in accord with it. The sophists believed that many different definitions of truth were possible and that democratic societies depend on structures that encourage citizens to use rhetoric in order to pursue their self-interests. Aristotle accepted the legitimacy of a wide variety of social/political/economic structures, each of which has its own institutions and rhetorical practices.

The final sections of Chapter 1 focused on the structural component of rhetorical situations, using the development of the "American system" as an extended case study. In the present chapter and the one that follows, I will focus on the ideological component of rhetorical situations and on the *topoi* that are available to organizational rhetors. Here I will examine three cultural myths that underlie contemporary organizational rhetoric in the US: the myth of upward mobility, the "organizational imperative," and "free-market fundamentalism." I will conclude with an extensive case study that re-links ideas and structure, an analysis of organizational rhetoric and the "baby-selling" industry. Chapter 3 will focus on the development of taken-for-granted assumptions about managers and workers and will conclude with an analysis of the role that cultural myths and social structures play in issues regarding executive compensation.

Rhetoric and Societal Myths

The dominant values of a society are articulated in social myths. These myths may or may not be true in an empirical sense, but they are *believed* to be true by members of a society. The details of key myths may or may not be internally consistent, and they may or may not be congruent with other widely accepted myths. For example, although US society is highly individualistic, it still includes values of connectedness and community, especially to family or people of the same religion/race/ethnicity/geographic location/economic level. Still, social scientists have long observed a fundamental tension between individuality and broader notions of community. Alexis de Tocqueville noticed this tension when he toured the United States soon after it became a nation. Almost 200 years later, sociologist Robert Bellah and his associates found that the obsession with individualism and resulting feelings of isolation from "different" people had expanded and deepened since the end of World War II. These changes have made us long even more strongly for connection and community, and have rendered even more influential a rhetoric of nostalgia that celebrates a lost era of individuality and unity (Reynolds and Norman, 1988; Bennis, Parikh, and Lessem, 1994; Bellah et al., 1995).[1] However, as Chapter 1 has pointed out, the presence of tensions and contradictions does not mean that the dominant ideologies and institutions of a society are fragile. Ironically, contradictions can provide stability – rhetors can "pick and choose" preferred ideas and ignore or de-emphasize the rest without having to abandon the overall system of beliefs and values (Abercrombie, Hill, and Turner, 1980; Orren, 1995).[2]

Myths of Opportunity and Mobility

Perhaps the most important myth in Anglo-US society involves economic opportunity and upward mobility. According to the myth, the United States is the land of opportunity, which, unlike Europe, has no fixed class structure. Capable individuals who work hard and "play by the rules" will succeed beyond their wildest dreams; those who do not will not. Like almost all social myths, this one is both partly true (empirically verifiable) and partly an illusion. First of all, inter-generational mobility in the United States (the likelihood that a child's adult income be higher than her or his parents') has varied historically with a number of factors, the most important of which is access to education, especially higher education. Researchers interested in mobility typically begin their data analysis by dividing a population into five groups (quintiles) that are arrayed around the statistical median (the value at which half of the data points are higher and half are lower). If one organizes US family income in this way, the years immediately after World War II were especially good times.

Among men whose fathers' incomes placed their families in the bottom quintile of the population, 23 percent made it all the way to the top quintile. For them, the mobility myth was an empirical reality. The years between 1968 and 1971 and between 1974 and 1976 were good times too, although not to the same extent as the post-World War II years. While 60 percent of US citizens stayed in the same income quintile, almost all of the remaining 40 percent moved up. Economic growth during the Vietnam War years and between the oil embargoes of the 1970s combined with low tuition rates and high federal support for education to provide high levels of opportunity.

But, after 1976, the percentage of those who either stayed in the same quintile or fell into a lower one (no mobility or negative mobility) started to increase. These figures reached 67 percent in 1990 and approached 90 percent at the beginning of the 2008 Great Recession – roughly the same level as during the "robber baron" era of the 1890s. Between 2000 and 2008 median family income (adjusted for inflation) actually fell, for the first time since the figures were first compiled during the 1960s. The number of poor people in the US grew by 5.2 million (to 40 million) – a 15.4 percent increase, more than double the overall rate of population increase. More than half of this increase took place among people who lived in the suburbs, traditionally the locale of greatest economic stability and growth. More than 30 percent of the US population (92 million people) fell below 200 percent of the federal poverty level, $22,000 for a family of four. As a result, by 2008 the United States had fallen to tenth place in upward mobility among the twelve members of the Organization of Economic Cooperation and Development (the developed countries, abbreviated OECD), with only Italy and the UK having less upward mobility. In Denmark, Australia, Norway, Finland, and Canada, upward mobility was more than twice the US level (Corak, 2006; Vogel, 2006; d'Addio, 2007). The downward trends accelerated after the start of the Great Recession in 2008 (Krugman, 2003; Herbert, 2010).[3] The trends have been so significant for so long that many Americans are beginning to doubt the viability of the mobility myth – a majority believe that their

41

children will have a lower standard of living than they themselves have, and a few have recommended that their children emigrate to economies where their prospects are brighter (Uchitelle, 2010).

These trends were primarily related to a decline in the number of well-paying manufacturing jobs and to declining access to higher education. The US economy added virtually no private sector jobs between 2000 and 2009. No previous decade since the Great Depression had a job creation rate of less than 20 percent. Jobs *were* created in the service sector – health care (2.4 percent per year), law (0.7 percent), finance (0.9 percent), and management and technical consulting (5 percent) – but these gains were too small to compensate for losses in auto manufacturing, computer and electronics assembly, construction, and even retail, except in stores that cater to lower-income customers (e.g. Walmart; see Norris, 2009b). The "solution" to this shift, according to politicians and media pundits, is for people to retrain for the "new economy." But those jobs typically have lower salaries and benefits, and retraining for them has become quite expensive. In 1972 federal Pell Grants, which are awarded to low-income students, covered 72 percent of the average cost of a state four-year institution; in 2003 they covered 38 percent. Even education benefits for veterans declined substantially in real value (that is, adjusted for inflation), although the "Post 9/11 G. I. Bill," which became operational in August, 2009, seems to be reversing this trend somewhat (Wise, 2009; Foderaro, 2010). Largely because of increased costs relative to income, today only 18 percent of students who enter high school earn a college degree within ten years. This completion rate places the US in tenth place among the twelve developed countries. Although this shortage should make it even more valuable to have a college degree for those who do obtain it, changes in the structure of the US economy have meant that today's graduates are experiencing far less return on their (or someone's) investment than was the case in the past (National Commission on the Cost of Higher Education, 1998; Uchitelle, 2005; Dionne, 2009; Scott, 2009). As the new decade began, some steps were taken to stop this trend. Ivy League universities (and

a number of "near-Ivys") announced that they would shift financial aid packages from loans to grants for students whose family
income was "middle class" or lower (the median household income
in the United States is approximately $50,000 USD per year), and
changes in the federal student loan program allowed a significant
increase in the size and number of Pell Grants to be awarded.
However, the Great Recession has already led some universities to reverse themselves, and the Congress elected in 2010 has
passed a budget including a massive reduction in funding for Pell
Grants.

At the same time real incomes have fallen and both income and
wealth have become more unequally distributed (especially if total
tax burden is taken into account). Since 2000, the average real
income of the bottom 90 percent of households fell by 7 percent,
while the income of the top 1 percent rose by 148 percent. The
average income of the top 0.1 percent rose by 343 percent, and the
income of the top 0.01 percent rose by 599 percent. Interestingly,
during times of increasing inequality, the amount of rhetoric
supporting the mobility myth seems to increase. For example,
the recessions and declining mobility of the 1890s spawned the
"Horatio Alger" stories, named after the writer of a series of short
books in which the key character, always someone from a highly
disadvantaged background, faced a series of challenges. Thanks to
personal grit, talent, determination, and the unbounded opportunity provided by the US free-market economy (and often with the
direct assistance of a "Daddy Warbucks" character), he (all of the
Horatio Alger heroes were male) eventually overcame these challenges, to become an economic and social success. The 2000s gave
us updated versions of these stories, for example the movies *Maid
in Manhattan* and *The pursuit of happiness*, or any biography of
Oprah Winfrey. The revival of this rhetoric during difficult times
is not surprising. The mobility myth is a central part of US cultural
identity, and rhetoric supporting it is an important cultural ritual.
When economic times are at their darkest, cultural myths are most
comforting, and the rhetoric that supports them is most important
(Cawelti, 1974; Cloud, 1996).

43

Weekend Fun 2

One of the fastest growing industries in the US involves reproductive technologies. For a variety of reasons, many women and couples are unable to reproduce "the old-fashioned way." Entrepreneurs have adapted technologies originally developed in agriculture to meet this need – for a price, of course. Some of these technologies involve purchasing human eggs or sperm (or both) from producers. Some societies ban or limit this trade, but the United States, which is the largest market, does not. You can easily obtain more detailed information on the processes, costs, locations, and corporations that ply this trade on the internet; but a short drive near your campus will turn up a number of organizations that will be happy to pay you to participate in this industry.

Like any other commodity, human eggs and sperm vary in perceived value. While some customers have unique preferences – some potential mothers prefer to purchase eggs harvested from someone who looks like them or who is from the same ethnic background, for example – the overall value of an egg (or "donation" of sperm) corresponds to the dominant ideology of a culture. In the United States this means that sperm and eggs that are likely to produce tall, athletic, blonde (natural, not chemical), highly intelligent children are more valuable (expensive) than ones that are likely to produce children with other characteristics. Your assignment for the weekend is to:

1 find out what your eggs or sperm are worth on the open market;
2 find out how their value compares to others'; and
3 explain the differences you have observed.

As a starting point, you can peruse the on-line campus newspapers of Ivy League universities (if you want to be a little less elitist, throw in Stanford, Northwestern, and Duke). For the purposes of this exercise, you need not find exact figures. Realistic estimates are adequate for our purposes, which is a good thing – because prices vary frequently and sometimes in unexpected ways. For example, in 2005 fears regarding the spread of "mad cow" disease led the US to

44

ban the importation of "sperm" (very few modern cattle breeds can reproduce on their own; the industry depends almost wholly on in vitro fertilization). Unfortunately, some of the laws were written so broadly that they interfered with the international trade in *human* sperm as well as with the importation of *livestock* sperm. Since US corporations specializing in human reproduction had become dependent on sperm from Scandinavian countries (which have an abundant supply of the Aryan-looking men whose sperm is preferred by US customers), the ban created shortages, and the value of domestic sperm skyrocketed. Once the laws were revised to exclude human sperm, the value of Aryan sperm stabilized (Canadian Press, 2007b; Rabin, 2007). Keep your results. We will return to the topic at the end of this chapter.

P.S. If you're especially adventuresome, compare the likely income associated with a career as an egg/sperm donor with that associated with your college major. You may have found a new career option, although it is important to recognize that, like professional athletes, egg/sperm donors have relatively short careers (consumers prefer eggs and sperm from young adults – people like you).

The Myth of the Organizational Imperative and Dependency Relationships

Near the end of the social upheaval of the 1960s and 1970s, two organizational sociologists, William Scott and Donald Hart (1979), published an influential and thought-provoking analysis of the role that formal organizations had come to play in US society. They started with the observation that, historically, US culture was unique in two ways: through its citizens' optimism about the future and through their faith in individual "know how." Our optimism stemmed from the incredible natural abundance that European settlers found in the New World and from three hundred years during which each generation had a higher standard of living than the previous one – the historical basis of the mobility myth.

Faith in the individual resulted from two hundred years of

rhetoric celebrating the frontier experience – the lone rancher, farmer, miner, or captain of industry conquering the wilderness and transforming a vast wilderness into the world's greatest economic engine (Turner, 2008). But "the times, they were a changin'," to paraphrase Bob Dylan. The Vietnam War and oil crises of the 1970s had led many to believe that the post-World War II era of US global dominance was coming to an end; and the social stability of the 1950s had given way to social movements focused on creating a more equitable and just society. By 1980 these economic, social, and political trends had become so pronounced that they triggered a conservative counter-movement (Scott and Hart, 1979). During times of social stress and change, formal profit-making organizations seemed to be the most stable institutions and provided the greatest hope for resurrecting the economy. Faith in the lone individual and in democratic government was being replaced with faith in and dependency on the large bureaucratic organizations of the "American system."

The Organizational Imperative

In its pure form, the organizational imperative is simple: all good things come via formal organizations, and all policies, attitudes, and behaviors should be designed to strengthen them. But the imperative is paradoxical. On the one hand it demands that democratically elected governments subsidize or otherwise assist corporations; on the other hand it obscures the fact that large bureaucratic organizations are decidedly un-democratic institutions with little or no accountability to the general public. On the one hand it demands that society accommodate itself to a particular mode of decision-making, one that focuses on expedient, short-term considerations; on the other hand it is justified through the long-term gains that autocratic organizations promise to members of a democratic society.

This reverence for formal organizations coincided with an increasing dependency on them, both for tangible needs and for individual identities. There was a time when people relied on organizations for income, but the rest of life's needs were met by interpersonal relationships and/or informal organizations. Child care was provided by extended families, or churches, or cooperative exchanges among neighbors. Health care was provided by professionals with whom people had personal relationships – a neighborhood, or a small-town doctor, or a midwife. Emotional support was provided by friends, family, or ministers, and no money changed hands when it was provided. Everyday life, especially outside of "work," was spontaneous and un-organized – children might get together at a neighbor's house or in a vacant lot to play baseball. Individuals knew what was best for them on the basis of beliefs and values communicated to them across generations by their families and neighbors. Leisure time was an opportunity to strengthen one's interpersonal relationships or to participate in communal activities that were *individually* meaningful.

But, increasingly after World War II, "home life" became more and more *organized* and *commodified*. Child care was provided by relative strangers working for (low) pay, in daycare centers licensed by the state and organized like any other bureaucracy. In the "best" cases it was provided by "family-friendly" corporations in on-site daycare centers. Health care was funded through insurance plans designed and selected by one's employer, who also decided which physicians are acceptable and what medical procedures should be covered. Health insurance became a "fringe benefit," provided in lieu of increased wages and salaries and subsidized by government (that is, by taxpayers) through generous tax credits and deductions (today these reduce federal income tax receipts by more than any other part of the tax code). Neighborhood baseball games were replaced by bureaucratic and expensive "youth sports" conglomerates, which are allowed – in fact encouraged – to monopolize public spaces. And all of these things were given a price: in other words they could be bought and sold like any other commodity.

Leisure too was transformed into a fringe benefit, offered by corporations (often grudgingly), so that employees could re-charge and re-energize in order to improve their productivity *at work* (Habermas, 1984, 1987; Deetz, 1992a). Spontaneous informal interactions between neighbors were replaced by block parties, organized by bureaucratic Homeowners' Associations or as "nights out" scheduled in the nation's capital. Even the highly personal process of finding one's mate or partner was transformed from an informal process involving one's friends and family to a commodity purchased from a quintessential impersonal bureaucracy: eHarmony and its on-line clones. The process itself has been bureaucratized and corporatized. For example, Jess McCann's popular 2008 book, *You lost him at hello: A saleswoman's secrets to closing the deal with any guy you want* advises modern women that "dating and relationship building is exactly like making a sale. [. . .] There's strategy to making it work" (Casey, 2008; McCann, 2008). As a result of these changes, almost all of modern life depends on one's relationships with bureaucratic organizations, a condition that social theorist Jurgen Habermas has labeled the corporate colonization of the lifeworld (see Deetz, 1992a).

In addition to these functional dependencies, people's individual identities have become increasingly tied to their work organizations. Of course, a link between who one is and what one does pre-dates the industrial revolution – barrel-makers adopted the surname Cooper, and slaves took the surnames of their masters, for example. But during the 1950s people started proudly to proclaim "I am an IBMer" (or a minion of some other employer). Conversations among strangers, which once started with a discussion of one's family of origin, now started with questions about where the two parties work. By the 1980s, management "how to" books and organizational research advised organizations to encourage employees to "identify" with their organizations (see Chapters 3 and 5). "Identity" was transformed, from something that an individual develops over a lifetime through communication with a number of "significant others," into a mechanism for motivating (which is a euphemism for controlling) employees without having to rely on expensive reward systems.[4] By the early 1990s organizational communication scholar Stan Deetz could accurately observe:

Corporations have frequently, wittingly and unwittingly, replaced religious, familial, educational, and community institutions in the production of meaning, personal identity, values, knowledge, and reasoning. [. . .] With such institutional domination in place, every other institution subsidizes or pays its dues. (Deetz, 1992a, 17)

As a result, leaving an organization today means not only losing the tangible connections that make everyday life possible – day care, health care, friendships – but also possibly losing one's sense of self.

An Entire Generation (or Two) of Resisters?

In Chapter 1 I explained that, while societies can be characterized by their dominant ideologies, those collections of beliefs, values, and perceptual sets are filled with contradictions – tensions that create opportunities for resistance, and sometimes even for social change. The economic trends described in the first section of this chapter have supplied empirical evidence that has led some Americans to doubt the tenets of the organizational imperative. This resistance seems to be most pronounced in the two youngest cohort groups: "Generation Xers" (who matured between the mid-1980s and the mid-1990s) and the "Millineals," whose adolescence took place around the turn of the century.[5]

First consider Xers. They matured during a time of increasingly unstable core relationships. By the mid-1970s, two-career families had become the norm and divorce rates were increasing rapidly. Between 1985 and 1995 two-thirds of white-collar employees experienced downsizing or major organizational restructuring, and millions of blue-collar (manufacturing) jobs disappeared forever. By the early 1990s the fastest growing sector of the labor market was that of temp/employment agencies, and college students had come to "expect corporate disloyalty. A [typical] 24- or 25-year old says 'I am responsible for my own life. No one's going to take care of me, [I know,] because they threw my dad out of work'" (Carnegie–Mellon University Professor Richard Florida, cited in Walker and Moses, 1996, n.p.; see also Jackson, 1999).

Under these circumstances it had become rational to keep one's résumé polished and one's network connections active, to plan one's own career, and to develop the skills necessary for seizing new opportunities. All of these steps reduced one's dependence on a particular employer. The actions legitimized by the organizational imperative – being subservient to bosses, accepting multiple cross-country moves, putting in long hours without overtime pay, or accepting regular overnight travel – no longer made sense. Developing lasting interpersonal relationships at work is a waste of time if one expects to move on at a moment's notice.

Millineals may also be engaging in resistance, albeit in a somewhat different form. Like the Xers, the only thing they trust are themselves and their established interpersonal relationships (families and long-term friendships). Electronic technologies permit them to maintain these trustworthy relationships, even over long distances, which also allows them to avoid the risks involved in establishing new relationships. Some observers say this orientation breeds cynicism and disconnection from one's community, while others note that it breeds a high level of social activism. This combination makes sense if Millineals are rejecting the organizational imperative – they feel connections to others, but they are alienated from formal organizations. They do volunteer work, but *decidedly do not do so* in order to get National Honor Society points. They may devote a great deal of time and energy to meeting the needs of less fortunate people, but they are more likely to do so through informal groups or grassroots organizations than through established organizations such as the United Way or Sierra Club (Alsop, 2008; Cappelli, 1999; Connelly, 2003; Howe and Strauss, 2003; Kamenetz, 2005; Green, 2007). They do seem to be more optimistic than the Xers, because they are more confident in their *individual* ability to plan their own lives and they adapt strategically to the situations they face. They are optimistic, but they are so disposed on the grounds of self-reliance, somewhat like settlers on the frontier of the nineteenth century – *not* on the strength of their faith in organizations or institutions. If they participate in the political process, they do so because they are excited about an individual candidate or cause, not because of party identification or of a broad sense of patriotism or political responsibility. They are constantly involved in negotiations over everything – terms of employment, vacation days, task assignments, and so on – because they are immersed in a society in which everything is unstable and contingent.

However, the Great Recession has given them a massive dose of realism. In 2008 seventeen percent of college-educated Millineals were either unemployed (5.5 percent) or no longer looking for work (11.5 percent). Both figures were record highs, and both were increasing. The percentage of graduates who were living with their parents in 2010 was higher than in any year since 1940, the end of the Great Depression. The figures were much worse for Millineals without college degrees, and the trends continued as the recession deepened. By mid-2010, 37 percent of 18–29-year-olds were unemployed or underemployed, and their official unemployment rate was more than 15 percent, compared to an overall rate of 9.5 percent. Unfortunately, recent research shows that entering the job market during a recession has adverse long-term effects – for example, the salaries of students who graduated from college during the less severe recession of the early 1980s are 8–10 percent lower than the salaries of those who graduated during the better economic times of the 1990s (Uchitelle, 2010). It is too early to assess the long-term impact that these economic realities will have on the Millineals' optimism, self-confidence, and expectations. It is clear that they had little trust in organizations before the recession and that they have even less now. They *seem* to be adopting more traditional behaviors – negotiating less, becoming more compliant to organizational demands, and being more patient about their pace of advancement. But, if you dig beneath the surface, former Deloitte consultant Stan Smith notes, "their underlying values are still there. [. . .] They want flexibility. They want work-life balance. But for now, they are just not as vocal about how they want it served up" (cited in Krischner-Goodman, 2010, B6; see also Smith, 2008 and Uchitelle, 2010). Which set of beliefs will win out? Time and the economic condition will tell.

The Mythology of Free-Market Fundamentalism

A third core mythology that is available to organizational rhetors is a doctrine that financier George Soros (1998) has labeled "free-market fundamentalism."[6] Historically, and increasingly since 1980, US citizens have been told that the optimal economic system is laissez-faire capitalism, one that focuses on maintaining private property and on minimizing government intervention in the economic realm. It is not a new concept, and acceptance of it has waxed and waned throughout US history. There have been times in which it worked quite well. In "communities," when small, family-owned organizations bought and sold goods and services to friends and neighbors involved in long-term personal relationships with their members and when the economy was organized in a "market" structure characterized by trading partners who had cooperative, long-term, mutually adjusting relationships, informal social controls ensured that no economic entity would victimize others. In parts of the US these circumstances still exist. But in a bureaucratic/hierarchical economy with wide variations in economic power, a laissez-faire system is an invitation to manipulation and abuse. Free-market fundamentalists have creatively, often brilliantly, legitimized their theoretical framework in part by blurring the distinction between community/market systems and bureaucratic/hierarchical ones, and in part by focusing attention on some of the "taken-for-granted" assumptions that define US society while de-emphasizing others (Kuttner, 1996; Cheney et al., 2007; Baker et al., 2009). The overall effect of their rhetoric has been to legitimize government actions only when they assist large, bureaucratic corporations, and to de-legitimize them when they restrict corporate activities in some way. In the process, the proverbial "playing field" gets tilted, so that the interests of some organizations and stakeholders, especially large, politically influential ones, are privileged, while the interests of other organizations and stakeholders are sacrificed. In the remainder of this chapter I will describe the underlying assumptions and rhetoric of this perspective and briefly outline the key arguments and appeals of its critics.

Outline of the Faith

Free-market theory is based on the assumption that a laissez-faire economic system has sufficient checks and balances in place to ensure that the legitimate interests of all members of a society will be met. Individuals compete with other individuals and organizations compete with other organizations in pursuit of their own self-interests, and an invisible hand ensures that over the long term the most productive, efficient, and/or innovative individuals and organizations will triumph and the weaker ones will disappear. If organizations are making larger profits in one sector of the economy than in others, investors will shift their funds to the most profitable firms in the most profitable sectors. New firms will increase the pressure on existing ones, either by using more efficiently the same technologies that the latter possess or by developing more innovative techniques; the increased competition will increase the supply of whatever goods or services are being produced in that sector of the economy; prices will fall; and consumers will benefit. Existing firms will be forced to become even more efficient, to move to sectors in which they can compete more successfully, or to go out of business – a process that economist Joseph Schumpeter labeled "creative destruction." In the long run, which is an economic abstraction rather than a specific time period, every sector will approach an equilibrium point at which demand almost perfectly matches supply and does so at the lowest possible price. Since an equilibrium is by definition the most efficient way for an economy to allocate resources, everyone will benefit because individuals, organizations, and capital will have moved to the sector of the economy in which they are best able to compete.

When considered at a global scale, free-market competition maximizes "comparative advantage." That is, some areas of the world have natural advantages that should attract certain industries and repel others. For example, as long as there are no artificial (that is, political and/or cultural) barriers to trade, banana production will concentrate in tropical climates, not in Sweden or Canada. The invisible hand will ensure that every other product or service will also move to the parts of the world that have a corresponding comparative advantage. But, for the global economy to reach *its* equilibrium, *everything* must move freely from country to country – capital, labor, *and* technology. Unfortunately, at least according to market fundamentalists, a number of artificial barriers to freedom of movement can exist. These barriers usually are imposed by governments who are more interested in maintaining their local industries than in adapting to the economic realities of a global economy. As a result of globalization, today there are fewer barriers to the capital markets than to labor and technology. It is very difficult for governments to limit the flow of capital, especially in the age of electronic funds transfer. The ease and speed of capital movement was illustrated with a vengeance during the financial market meltdown of 2008 and 2009. For example, free flows of capital had allowed Icelandic financial institutions to invest heavily in UK banks, which had been free to invest heavily in undercapitalized US financial organizations, which had been free to write millions of high-risk, "subprime" mortgage loans in Nevada, California, and Florida. Once the bottom fell out of the Las Vegas housing market, Iceland's bankruptcy was virtually inevitable, short of a bailout by its trading partners. But that is the whole point of "creative destruction," globalization-style. Capital flows are tightly interconnected, in ways that eventually punish actors who take on excessive risks and reward those who do not, unless governments intervene by providing subsidies, tax breaks, or other forms of artificial support.[7]

Globalization has also increased the flow of technology as patent and copyright laws – which, free-market fundamentalists argue, impose artificial, efficiency-reducing barriers – have been relaxed. Barriers to the movement of labor have been more resilient. For example, during the 1970s and 1980s almost all of the textile corporations in the US moved their production facilities to China or Latin American countries that had a "comparative advantage" in wages (often paying less than a dollar an hour), weakly enforced or nonexistent labor laws, and/or lax environmental standards. When Latin American and Chinese wages started to rise, these same textile firms moved their operations to

Vietnam, Cambodia, or Bangladesh, where a well-paid worker earns about $64 a month, compared to $117 to $147 a month in China – just as the theory of comparative advantage would have predicted (Bajaj, 2010). In theory, textile workers in the US would have moved along with their jobs, unless their skills and abilities equipped them to move to other domestic industries, with wages and benefits that exceeded those they could receive in Latin America or Southeast Asia. But none did, because of artificial social barriers (wanting to stay near family, for example) or artificial political barriers (laws limiting migration). Conversely, the easy immigration of workers from low-wage economies into the developed countries during the 1990s and early 2000s has been limited by domestic political considerations, especially during recessions, just as had been the case during the 1890s and early 1900s (Mann, 1973; Higham, 2002; Skerry, 2009).

Of course, all of these trends have been controversial. During the past thirty years many of the developed countries of North America and Western Europe have allowed the entire manufacturing sectors of their economies – not just textiles – to move offshore, and/or they have relied more and more heavily on immigrant labor to staff the industries they have retained. As a result, less than 30 percent of workers in the developed economies today work in manufacturing. Even Germany, which traditionally has been the most manufacturing-intense economy in Western Europe, saw manufacturing's share of its Gross Domestic Product (GDP) fall from 32 percent in 1990 to only 22 percent in 2009. In the US the figure dropped below 10 percent during the 2008–20011 recession, which is lower even than in France. At least 30 million full-time US employees lost manufacturing jobs during these decades, and either became unemployed or moved into the service sector, which has lower pay and weaker benefits. Economist Louis Uchitelle observed that, "rather than try to outstrip foreign competitors in innovation, a costly and risky process, we [US] gave up in product after product" (Uchitelle, 2009, n.p.; Hoffman, 1997; Uchitelle, 2007; Dougherty, 2009; Irwin, 2010). This shift is important because manufacturing has long been viewed as an essential pillar of a powerful economy. It generates millions of well-paid jobs for those with only a high-school education, which represents a huge segment of the population. No other sector contributes more to a nation's overall productivity. As manufacturing declines, the country becomes ever more dependent on imports of merchandise, computers, machinery, and the like – running up a trade deficit that, in time, could undermine the value of its currency and its capacity to import what it needs.

Critics of free-market fundamentalism argue that decisions to abandon manufacturing were unwise. In exchange for increased profits that primarily benefited the very wealthy, the living standards of the vast majority of Americans (or Europeans) have declined precipitously. Somewhat ironically, since the economies of the developed countries are largely driven by consumption (about 70 percent of the US GDP is a function of consumer spending), reduced living standards also undermine economic growth. In response, free marketeers claim that the movement was not really a function of choices, but was an inevitable aspect of globalization – the invisible hand working invisibly. In fact the concept of inevitability is central to free-market rhetoric because it implies that resistance is futile, and inefficient as well. Moreover, through the process of creative destruction, the *global* economy has been strengthened. For example, thanks to the shift of textile manufacturing, workers in Southeast Asia now have jobs and incomes that some day may allow them to purchase goods and services produced in the developed countries. Production costs have plummeted, and residents of the developed world can now go to their local Walmart and purchase Chinese-made hoodies for less than $10 USD, just as the theory of comparative advantage predicted.

The Proper Role for Government in Free-Market Economies

It should be clear by now that free-market fundamentalism allows only a very limited economic role for governments. They may need sometimes to ensure that economic markets remain competitive (through anti-monopoly laws, for example), that property rights are protected, and that contracts are enforced. For example, even market fundamentalists seem to agree that it is probably not wise to allow people to practice neurosurgery without a government-regulated license, even though such laws interfere with market mechanisms. Licensing requirements clearly restrict freedom of entry into the health care market, reduce competition, and drive up costs. However, many fundamentalists do complain that licensing laws and other seemingly innocuous laws create a "slippery slope" that encourages governments to interfere with market processes when it is not necessary for them to do so. For example, in addition to restricting who can be a neurosurgeon, some states also forbid dental hygienists – or midwives, or psychiatric social workers, or family therapists, or nurse practitioners, or any number of other professions – to practice on their own, without being employed by dentists, psychiatrists, and physicians. These decisions are based primarily on political rather than economic considerations, and there is little question that they drive up health care costs, thereby reducing access to health care. There is little reliable evidence that such restrictions create any benefits for consumers, in spite of what the rhetoric of dentists, psychiatrists, and physicians claims. As I will explain in greater detail in Chapter 4, in the United States government regulations and regulatory agencies are created far more often in order to protect existing corporations or professionals from competition than in order to protect stakeholders from corporations. When governmental decisions about the economy are driven by political pressures supported by rhetorical appeals, market processes are short-circuited and stakeholders are harmed.

For example, when Southwest Airlines first requested permission to fly out of Dallas' Love Field, the major carriers at the newly opened Dallas Fort Worth (DFW) International Airport persuaded Speaker of the House Jim Wright (D–TX) to try to block the move. The public rhetoric of the "legacy carriers" (the companies that were in operation when the industry was de-regulated in 1979) and their political allies claimed that restricting competition in this way would protect taxpayers who had invested millions of dollars in the new DFW airport. However, the action was such a blatant attempt to undermine competition and to drive up the prices paid by customers who fly through Dallas that Congress balked. The bill was amended to allow Southwest to fly from Love Field, but only to airports in states that border Texas. It is a tribute to Southwest's management that they were able to succeed in spite of this government interference in an industry that it had supposedly de-regulated.[8] It is a tribute to the political power of American and Delta Airlines that it took Southwest almost thirty years of effort to persuade Congress to overturn the Wright amendment.

Thus, market fundamentalists argue, government is best when it does the least. This view of government's role in the economy is grounded in three assertions. A *futility thesis* states that governments simply cannot effectively direct a society or economy. The presumed "miracle" of the free market is that its processes work "invisibly" and thus do not have to be managed, or even fully understood.[9] The presumed lesson of the demise of the Soviet Union is that centralized economic planning by government is doomed to fail. When governments do act, they do so on the basis of an incomplete understanding of social and economic processes and often base their decisions on considerations other than market values (that is, considerations of what one person is willing to pay another in a free economic exchange). In very rare instances governments may accidentally do what the market needs to have done at a particular moment, but it is much more likely that government intervention will worsen the condition that the action is designed to solve (*a perversity thesis*). Even more importantly, government activities inevitably produce additional serious, unintended, and unanticipated consequences. For example, "zero-tolerance" drug possession laws may be well-intentioned, but they have massively increased the size of prison populations, driven up incarceration costs paid by taxpayers, weakened families in communities in which maintaining stable family units is especially difficult, and, thereby perpetuated the cycle of welfare dependency. Similarly, free marketeers argue, minimum wage laws encourage organizations to replace workers with technology, thereby reducing the job options available to unskilled or semi-skilled workers. Finally, government intervention in the market is likely to jeopardize the virtues of a society or the economic gains that have been achieved through the free market (*a jeopardy thesis*; Hirschman, 1991; see also Viner, 1960; Kuttner, 1996).[10]

Rhetoric and the Critique of Free-Market Theory

Free-market *theory* has been criticized on a number of grounds, from its unrealistic assumptions to its ethical implications. There is a broad consensus in support of free marketeers' claim that capitalism does a better job of producing wealth than any other economic system. The debate is over how a society can obtain this advantage without allowing individuals to pursue wealth in ways that undermine society. On the one hand, many free marketeers now reject the extreme version of market fundamentalism. Economic crisis after economic crisis – the insider stock trading scandal of the mid-1980s, the savings and loan crisis of the late 1980s and early 1990s, the "corporate meltdown" and bankruptcies of the early years of the new century (Enron, WorldCom, Adelphia, and so on), and the financial industry meltdown and Great Recession of today provided very clear evidence that market discipline alone is not sufficient. Moreover, it also is clear that the market fundamentalists who occupied important regulatory roles during these two decades were repeatedly blinded by their ideology and missed very clear signs that crises were coming. As a result, some of the most important free-market theorists now are explicitly rejecting extreme versions of market fundamentalism and calling for a more realistic and less ideological perspective (see for example the quotation by Judge Richard Posner at the start of this chapter). However, a second critique goes further: it argues that even moderate (that is, non-fundamentalist) free-market theory fails to recognize that there are many cases in which the assumptions underlying free-market theory are simply not fulfilled in real-world economies.

Market Automatons and Real People

One unrealistic assumption involves the people who make up "markets." In theory, the invisible hand can work properly because people are economically rational decision-makers. They are able to obtain the information they need to make the best decisions (the economics expression is "to maximize utility"), they are able to process that information, and they are sufficiently mobile to make optimal purchases. The moderate critique is that, especially given the complexity and specialization that characterize contemporary societies, this is often not true. For example, even with the information available on the internet, few people can make economically rational choices among medical treatment options, insurance plans, cell phone contracts, auto repair strategies, or plumbing fixes. In addition, the internet may actually have reduced the "rationality" of consumer decision-making, because it does little to screen out inaccurate or irrelevant information. Customers quickly experience information overload, which leads to decisions that are as nonrational as those made with too little information. Systems like Microsoft bing.com have been created solely to help customers deal with this problem.

In addition, organizations often work very hard to ensure that consumers or potential employees do not have access to accurate information. Like most professional associations, medical associations in most states make it difficult to obtain the success/failure rates of surgeons, or even the records of physicians convicted of criminal offenses. Recent legal changes have made information about hospital death rates more readily available and the results have been shocking. *Houston Chronicle* business columnist Loren Steffy explains and provides an example:

> Earlier this week a Houston Chronicle and Hearst Newspapers series exposed the staggering number of people [in the US] – an estimated 98,000 – that die annually from preventable medical errors. Another estimated 99,000 fall victim to infections they contract while in the hospital. Most of these deaths occur behind a veil of secrecy that prevents consumers from knowing the full scope of the problem. Attempts to shine a light into this shadowy corner of the medical world has [*sic*] been met with staunch resistance. [. . .] As it stands now, our mythical "free market" for health care – which really is a web of government-and-employer-subsidized care – is predicated on the notion of consumer choice. [. . .]. Yet for all the talk about patient choice, most patients lack the basic information they need to make informed decisions about their care. [. . .] Instead, patients across the health care system are left to founder in the darkness of carefully

constructed ignorance. We don't know the mortality rates of our local hospitals. We don't know how many people may have died or suffered unnecessarily because their insurer denied a treatment their doctors deemed necessary. (Steffy, 2009d, 1D)[11]

In addition, the purpose of advertising is often to encourage people to make decisions that are not economically rational (as illustrated in B. F. Skinner's 1976 fictional utopian society, in which only unadorned information could be provided to consumers), although advertising executives rarely describe the activities of their firms in quite these terms.

However, even if consumers did possess the requisite information and expertise, they often may not be able to process it. Humans tend to overestimate the likelihood of "good" outcomes and to underestimate the probability of "bad" ones. For example, no matter how much information students are given about past patterns of grading in a course and about their own academic records, they invariably seem to overestimate their chances of receiving As and Bs and to underestimate their chances of getting Cs, Ds, or Fs. Similarly, people may not learn much from experience. We tend to focus on experiences that are easiest to recall, not on ones that are most relevant to the decision we are trying to make. Or we rely on information that is readily available rather than painstakingly search for higher-quality information, which is more difficult or expensive to obtain (this is called the *availability bias*). If a decision must be made in a very short time frame, it may not be possible to gather or fully process the relevant information. If decisions are highly complex or inherently ambiguous, decision-makers may not even know what kinds of information they need, much less when they have enough of it. In short, because human rationality is constrained, people rarely act like the "utility-maximers" depicted in free-market theory.[12]

Finally, the rationality assumption included in free-market theory overlooks the fact that markets are made of human beings who are connected to one another in complex networks. Their choices are strongly influenced by their interpersonal relationships and by their feelings, especially trust. While computer models of "market behavior" (a rather strange rhetorical construction, since markets can neither make choices nor act – only humans can) can predict collective action, real networks depend on the trust that exists among the members of a network. This is the primary reason why complex computer models of investment risk failed to predict the 2008 collapse of the world financial markets:

> "they were too simple-minded. They focused mainly on figures like the expected returns and the default risk of financial instruments. What they didn't sufficiently take into account was human behavior, specifically the potential for widespread panic. When lots of investors got too scared to buy or sell, markets seized up and the models failed" [. . .] [concluded] Stephen Figlewski, a professor of finance at the Leonard N. Stern School of Business at New York University [. . .] "[W]hen trust in counterparties is lost, and markets freeze up so there are no prices [being negotiated], it shows how different the real world was from our models." (Lohr, 2009, n.p.)[13]

Of course, free-market purists argue that all of these limiting factors involve weaknesses in the people who operate within an economy, not in the theory itself. Consequently, it is people who need to be "fixed," not the model.

Limits to Competition and the Strength of the Invisible Hand

The moderate critique of free-market theory also questions its assumption that rational choices made by groups of individuals will combine in ways that benefit societies as a whole. Three arguments make up this criticism. The first is that, while individual "utility maximization" (which may just be a fancy phrase for greed) is a powerful motivator, if left unchecked it can be socially destructive. The patron saint of free-market theory, Adam Smith, was well aware of this problem. Fifteen years before publishing his treatise on the free market, *The wealth of nations*, Smith examined the moral aspects of economics in a companion book that is almost completely ignored by free-market economists (Farrell, 2002). In *The theory of moral sentiments*, Smith struggled with the need to constrain greed without undermining the economic advantages of the free market. In early editions of the book he argued that informal constraints would be adequate. As people mature within a community, they come to accept its definitions of right and wrong and develop a commitment to the welfare of the other members of the community. Some people learn these lessons completely and become saints (Smith noted that this is "a select, though, I am afraid, a small party"). "Normal" people also learn the Protestant values of prudence and self-control, and usually act in accord with their own consciences. But they will be inevitably tempted by material gain, so they will need the additional encouragement of public opinion and informal social pressure. The potential shame that would come from being viewed as excessively greedy or from being caught engaging in unfair economic behavior would be enough to constrain the vast majority of citizens. It is for this reason that Smith advocated having factory owners live in the same town in which their factories operated – doing so creates interpersonal relationships, which fosters feelings of shared responsibility, which encourage all parties to act in ways that respect one another.

There are some people, Smith despaired, who have neither conscience nor a capacity to feel disgrace. If allowed to roam free in an economy, they will engage in vicious economic behavior that is destructive to their society, and in the long run to themselves – one cannot have a full and meaningful life without a connection to one's community (the lesson that Ebenezer Scrooge learned one cold winter night). This potential for excessive greed, Smith observed, is greatest among people working in the capital markets – banking, international finance, and trade – in part because it is easier to cover up one's indiscretions when working with money than when making tangible, visible products, and in part because the vast sums of money floating around in these industries attract moral reprobates.[14] Regrettably, Smith concluded, excessive greed sometimes has to be constrained through the power of the state.

During Smith's lifetime England became more and more industrialized and more and more urban. Smith realized that these trends brought increased geographical mobility, decreased surveillance exercised by members of a person's community, and a reduced chance that "normal" people would internalize the values of prudence and self-control. Without effective informal controls, a greater number of "normal" people will fall prey to excessive greed, so a more activist government would be necessary. Smith clearly preferred a limited government presence in markets, but he also recognized that some interference is necessary in order to help the invisible hand perform its functions.

Although today's free-market theorists ignore *The theory of moral sentiments* almost completely, this treatise articulates the most important ethical issue facing societies with capitalist economies – how can a free society simultaneously obtain the economic advantages of the "invisible hand" and avoid the socially destructive excesses of human greed?[15]

A second limitation to the power of the invisible hand involves the relationship between individuals' motivation and the needs of the broader community. Financier George Soros notes that there is no automatic link between the two:

> the common interest does not find expression in market behavior. Corporations do not aim at creating employment; they employ people (as few and as cheaply as possible) to make profits. Health care companies are not in business to save lives; they provide health care to make profits. Oil companies do not seek to protect the environment except to meet regulations or protect their public image. Full employment, affordable medicine, and a healthy environment may, under certain circumstances, be [unintended] by-products of market processes, but such welcome social outcomes cannot be guaranteed by the profit principle alone. (Soros, 1998, 205; see also Soros, 2000; Aune, 2007; Cheney, Roper, and May, 2007; McMillan, 2007)

Indeed, Nobel prize winner Milton Friedman, the primary spokesperson for free-market theory during the late twentieth century, extended the observation that managers *are not* concerned about broader social issues to argue that they *should not* be (1970). Corporate executives, Friedman argued, have only one responsibility: to "make as much money as possible, while conforming to the basic rules of society." It is only through the pursuit of profit that managers fulfill their responsibilities to owners and investors.

Using an organization's resources to pursue other goals, no matter how noble they might be, imposes a tax on shareholders without their permission. Furthermore, managers have no particular expertise in social issues, and capitalism has no means of holding them accountable for their efforts to be socially responsible. Those are political issues, and thus should be managed by elected officials. In short, values and issues regarding "community" are not excluded from free-market theory by accident – excluding them is necessary and desirable.

This distinction is especially important, because individuals pursuing their economic interests often act, both consciously and by accident, in ways that undermine their communities. One example involves the "tragedy of the commons." The phrase harkens back to the Middle Ages, when communities held an area in common where every citizen could graze his or her livestock. The "tragedy" is that these incentives lead citizens to use the commons as much as possible in order to save their own pastureland. Individually rational action eventually will lead to the commons being over-grazed, which will make them useless to everyone. A more modern example involves what is called the "paradox of thrift." Capitalist economies rely on both consumption and savings (thrift). Consumption is the enactment of demand and is necessary in order for capitalist economies to function. But thrift is also important because the money that consumers save becomes the capital that entrepreneurs borrow to start innovative businesses and that established firms borrow in order to expand and grow. Thrift is paradoxical because actions that are rational for individuals may be just the opposite of what the economy needs. During recessions some people lose their jobs. Their consumption falls, and their savings rate usually drops to zero. People who keep their jobs tend save more than they otherwise would, because they are worried about losing their jobs. Without their consumption, the economic downturn worsens, making it more likely that they will lose their jobs, which makes them spend even less, and so on in a downward spiral. Increased savings mean that more money is available for investment, but, faced with declining demand, the rational decision for entrepreneurs and managers is to cut back, not to expand. In extreme cases, "saving" becomes "hoarding" and prices begin to fall, which discourages consumption further, since it is individually "rational" to wait until prices bottom out before buying. A deflationary cycle is set in motion.

Conversely, when the economy is booming, consumers are more confident and spend more, creating inflation, which in turn encourages people to spend more in order to "beat" the coming price increases, which makes prices rise even further and faster. Increased demand increases inflation, and so on, unless governments interfere to slow the economy. For example, in 2005 and 2006 the US had a negative savings rate of around 0.1 percent, the lowest figure since the depths of the Great Depression in 1934. By mid-2009, during the worst recession since the 1930s, the savings rate had risen to 6.9 percent, the highest level since World War II. Individually rational consumers were doing just the opposite of what the overall economy needed them to do. The paradox of thrift exaggerates economic cycles, not because individuals are behaving irrationally, but because they *are* being as rational as they can be given the information they have available. But individual rationality can lead to negative outcomes for the economy and for society as a whole.

A third difficulty with the concept of the "invisible hand" involves "externalities," the costs of economic activities that are not included in transactions themselves. *Positive externalities* are benefits afforded economic actors but paid for by people who do not directly participate in or gain from the transactions. For example, public education or transportation systems are paid for by taxpayers, many of whom do not benefit directly from corporations' uses of their investments. So, for the corporations which use the taxpayer-funded infrastructure and their customers, the "externality" is a positive one. *Negative externalities* are costs that are imposed on people who do not participate in an economic transaction or benefit directly from it (for example the people who breathe polluted air or drink polluted water, or the taxpayers who pay for cleaning up toxic waste). Sometimes externalities are accidental, but much more often externalizing some or all of the costs of doing business is a conscious organizational strategy. Pressure to maximize short-term profits creates powerful incentives for managers to shift costs to outsiders, and the nature of bureaucratic structures (see Chapters 3 and 5), combines with the international scope of large organizations' operations, to make it easy to do so (Hawken, 1993; Mitchell, 2001). Once a corporation's management chooses to externalize costs, the managers of competing firms face intense pressure to do the same. Governments can adopt policies that minimize externalities, either directly, by requiring corporations to pay for externalities, or indirectly, by taxing corporations and/or consumers and using the monies gained to build (or rebuild) infrastructures. But these are political decisions. Markets themselves neither require costs to be internalized nor compensate external stakeholders for the costs that are imposed on them (Lindblom, 1997, 2001).

In each of these cases – commons problems, the paradox of thrift, and the effects of externalities – the only viable alternative is for government to interfere with the operations of the free market with policies that stimulate the economy during recessions or slow it down during rapid growth, regulate an industry at least to a limited degree, and/or "socialize" the costs of building and maintaining infrastructures. Of course, all of these steps violate the tenets of free-market theory and can be criticized as government meddling in the economy, which free marketeers claim is always futile, perverse, and/or jeopardizes positive elements of society.

What's so Good about Competition Anyway?

Critics of free-market fundamentalism also argue that, ironically, its advocates often ignore its underlying assumptions. Capitalism works because of competition – it drives innovation and efficiency, and in the long term leads markets toward equilibria that benefit everyone. But in the short term (the one we actually live in) it gives capitalists an absolute incentive to try to avoid or undermine the discipline of competition. Creative destruction may be a wonderful thing in theory, and may even be a good thing when applied at a market or global level, but it is much less attractive to the owners, managers, or employees of the corporations that are being creatively destroyed. In free-market theory, organizations that continue to innovate and/or increase their efficiency will continue to prosper, and thus have nothing to fear from market discipline. But following this strategy is risky. For example, most new companies that are founded by an innovative entrepreneur may fail over the mid-term because they cannot continue to innovate fast enough or because they are absorbed into larger, less innovative bureaucracies. Consequently it is much less risky, and thus economically more rational, to find ways of undermining competition than it is to actively participate in a highly competitive market.

Ironically, the primary strategy used by capitalists to avoid competition is to enlist government as an ally. As early as the late 1800s, conservative economists had largely abandoned the free-market notion that governments should not interfere in markets, especially those that involve significant economic risks (for example oil exploration) or significant capital investments (for example building railroads). No one would opt to invest in these industries, these economists formerly known as free marketeers argued, unless one could be guaranteed substantial profits. But the only way to guarantee profits of sufficient size is to insulate these organizations from open competition (you may recall PhRMa's use of this argument from the case study at the end of Chapter 1). Since capital-intensive industries are necessary for long-term economic growth, deviating from free-market principles seemed to be warranted. Armed with this new academic wisdom, owners and managers of corporations in capital-intensive industries pushed for laws that would allow them to form monopolies or oligopolies, even though doing so undermines the discipline provided by competition. Quickly, the trend toward monopolization expanded. Rhetors in every industry, regardless of its capital requirements, attempted to persuade policymakers that *they too* should be granted preferential treatment because *they too* face excessive competition and overwhelming risks.

However, existing corporations can also avoid competition on their own, without government help. They simply use their market power to destroy potential competitors, primarily through what is called "predatory pricing." For example, in the US more than

80 new airlines have come and gone since the industry was de-regulated in 1979 – only Southwest Airlines, (to a lesser extent) Jet Blue, and handful of intra-state airlines, have prospered. Most failed because the legacy carriers cut their fares below their new competitors' costs on routes served by start-up airlines, absorbing the loss through profits made on other routes. Predatory pricing is illegal, but laws are difficult to enforce, and administrations that favor de-regulation (every one that the US has had since 1979) have little incentive to enforce the laws. Alternatively, if the start-up airline does manage to become a threat, existing firms can simply buy the company. Now that Southwest has come to occupy a monopoly/oligopoly position in many markets, it seems to be adopting this tried-and-true strategy. In 2009, it tried to purchase bankrupt Frontier Airlines (ironically, one of the legacy airlines whose lobbying helped create the Wright Amendment). *Houston Chronicle* business columnist Loren Steffy asked: "why would Southwest want to buy a marginal player at a time when revenue across the industry is getting hammered by the recession? The answer is to keep anyone else from buying it" (Steffy, 2009c, D1–2; see also Bush, 2008; Free, 2009; and Steffy, 2009b).

Finally, corporations can avoid competition by obtaining direct financial support from government through preferential taxa-tion, direct subsidies, or socializing losses. Subsidy programs exist in all of the major economies. In the US they grew steadily in importance during the twentieth century, reaching $92 billion per year by 2006 (Perelman, 2006; Perrow, 2002). They have been especially controversial when applied to food production. They invariably are justified as necessary to save family farms, ranches, wineries, and so on, but they are typically administered in ways that favor multinational agribusiness corporations and millionaires whose income primarily comes from activities other than agriculture. Because subsidies reduce the costs of doing busi-ness for large corporations, they actually hurt more efficient and innovative small producers. For example, in spite of restrictions included in the 2002 farm subsidy bill, from 2003 to 2006 almost 3,000 multi-millionaires (defined as those with incomes of more than $2.5 million USD), including residents of Saudi Arabia and

Hong Kong, received $49 million USD in farm subsidy payments. As a result, subsidies have been criticized both by the political left and by the political right, which eventually owed them the pejorative nickname "corporate welfare" (Margasak, 2008).[16]

Although tax breaks for large corporations are not often discussed in the media, they have the same effects as direct subsidies (recall the net-tax data presented in Chapter 1). As with farm subsidies, the large corporations that receive tax breaks incur lower costs of doing business than the smaller firms with which they compete, so the policies encourage additional monopolization and further reduce the incentive for large firms to innovate. Of course, they are justified in a number of ways, from the omnipresent assertion that business taxes are inherently evil to claims that they spur innovation and create jobs – assertions that are rarely supported by the available empirical evidence. Since most jobs are created by young, rapidly growing firms and since most innovation comes from middle-sized firms, these claims are ironic at best (Kuttner, 1996). They are persuasive only because they are grounded in pervasive cultural myths.

The final pro-corporate intervention occurs when government shifts the losses that result from bad management decisions to investors and taxpayers – that is, when private losses are "socialized." The positive rationale for many such programs is that they protect innocent bystanders. For example, the Federal Deposit Insurance Corporation (FDIC) and the Federal Savings and Loan Insurance Corporation (FSLIC) in the United States protect depositors if their banks and savings and loans go bankrupt. The rationale is that, since depositors almost never have any influence over the decisions that lead to bankruptcy and since, unlike the banks' owners and managers, they are not protected by "limited liability" laws, they should not be punished. Protecting small depositors also makes sense from an economic perspective because, if depositors believe that it is risky to put their money in a financial institution, there will be much less capital available for investors, and thus less economic growth. However, if the protections are administered in a way that rewards the people who *are* responsible for the bank's failure, they defeat their economic purpose. Furthermore they violate the social rationale by encouraging excessively risky decisions and policies in the future by creating moral hazards (recall Chapter 1). It is precisely this problem that has led many people to decry the financial industry "bailouts" carried out by the US and UK governments during 2009 and 2010 (Johnson, 2009, 2010c; Kindleberger, Aliber, and Solow, 2005).

Of course, a free-market fundamentalist rhetor *should* reject all forms of government interference in the economy – excessive regulation as well as various forms of unwarranted aid – because they all undermine competition. But economic realities *sometimes* warrant violating the theory, and political considerations often override theoretical purity. The resulting ambiguity opens up a space for organizational rhetors, even allowing them to claim that it is necessary to violate free-market theory in order to protect free markets.

Adjusting Free-Market Theory to Fit Economic Realities

Economist Robert Kuttner (1996) has persuasively argued that, when all of the complicating factors described in the previous sections are taken into account, the either/or distinction between "free markets" and "(government)-controlled economies" that characterizes fundamentalist rhetoric is both unrealistic and misleading. Of course, there are cases in which the assumptions underlying free-market theory are met in "real-world" situations – economic actors are able to make rational (utility maximizing) decisions and do act with prudence and self-control. Competition is sufficient to reward efficient and innovative actors while punishing those who are not. At the same time, the economy will be able to avoid massive boom-and-bust economic cycles that are socially and economically destructive, and so on. But, if any of these "heroic" (Kuttner's term) assumptions are not met, the invisible hand alone will not be sufficient to make markets work properly. "Market failures" will occur and when they do, government should intervene in order to *supplement* market forces. The distinction between "first best" (pure markets) and "second best" (markets plus necessary government involvement) is crucial, Kuttner argues, in part because "second-best" markets make up between one half and two-thirds of capitalist economies.[17] More importantly, trying to force "second-best" markets to behave more like free markets, through de-regulation or some other strategy, will reduce economic efficiency and create openings for opportunism (excessive greed). Of course, to be helpful, government actions must increase rationality and competition, not protect the power and profits of existing firms or serve other political ends.

In the relatively rare cases in which *none* of the heroic assumptions are met, government will have to own and operate those industries. If government exerts excessive control, or owns and operates sectors of the economy that would function better as second-best or free markets, the economy and society suffer. The challenge for policymakers is to figure out which sectors are of which type and to resist the temptation of lumping all parts of the economy into the same basket. Instead of arbitrarily and simple-mindedly assuming that government interference in markets always is bad, they should ask:

- To what extent do economic actors have the information, expertise, incentives, and options necessary to be rational actors?
- What can and what should government do to enhance their rationality?
- To what extent does a particular sector of the economy have the amount and type of competition needed for the market to operate properly?
- What can and what should government do to enhance competition, so that it will provide adequate discipline and sustain innovations that will have long-term value?
- To what extent will rational actions by individuals lead to positive outcomes for the society as a whole?
- What can and what should government do to increase the link between individual rationality and positive outcomes for society?

In summary, the moderate critique suggests that free-market

theorists are correct when they claim that the incentive systems of capitalism are exceptionally powerful motivators. However, their analysis does not take those incentives seriously enough – the rational approach for organizational actors to take is to avoid competition, not to embrace it. Conversely, the moderate critique argues that markets are stronger and more resourceful than free marketeers admit, and operate quite well even with a significant degree of government involvement. This capacity explains why the most "socialistic" of the capitalist democracies (e.g. the Scandinavian countries) are among the most innovative and efficient, year after year. Government "interference" is necessary in order to make markets work as they are supposed to, steps that go far beyond licensing professionals and enforcing contracts.

The Power of Free-Market Rhetoric

Given all of the complications and limitations outlined in the previous section, one might reasonably ask: Why did free-market fundamentalism become dominant? It will not come as a surprise that my answer to this question involves structures *and* ideas – both of which are created and sustained through rhetoric.

The Structure of the Free-Market Ideology Industry

Private, not-for-profit "think tanks" whose avowed goal is to advise policymakers on important social issues have had a long history in the US. Many are officially non-partisan, and are viewed that way by policymakers and members of other think tanks. Their primary function is to provide decision-makers with un-biased data and advice (for example, the Rand Foundation, which is the largest think tank, and the Hoover Institute, which focuses on international affairs). Other think tanks see themselves as "fair and balanced" sources of information and perspective, but are viewed by partisan policymakers as biased sources of propaganda (examples include the Brookings Institution, which conservatives tend to view as "liberal," although historically it has opposed the key domestic policies of a series of Democratic presidents, and the American Enterprise Institute, which now is viewed by leftists as a far-right group). Still others are avowedly political, and some of the most influential of these think tanks advocate free-market fundamentalism. In the US, the most important ones are the libertarian Cato Institute, founded in 1977, and the larger Heritage Foundation, founded in 1973 by a grant from Colorado brewer Joseph Coors. Although Cato is concerned with removing government constraints on the individual freedoms of adults regarding a variety of issues – for example it supports legal equality for gay people, opposes restrictions on pornography (if the latter does not involve minors), and favors the legalization of marijuana (again, for adults) – its greatest impact has been on economic issues (Altheide and Johnson, 1980; Tuohy, 1999). Edwin Feulner, founder of the Heritage Foundation, explains that organization's goals:

> The Heritage Foundation takes an aggressive, entrepreneurial approach to its mission. This is reflected not only in our emphasis on marketing [including its "pioneering" use of talk radio] and our pioneering use of shorter policy papers for busy policymakers, but also [in] our approach to management. Everyone at Heritage works from a common policy perspective. We have no prima donnas thinking their own deep thoughts in shuttered cloisters. [. . .] Instead we seek out and equip those conservative thinkers who are highly motivated to wage, and win, battles in the never-ending war of ideas. (Quoted in McGann and Weaver, 2000, 73; see also Crawford, 1980; Smith, 1991; Abelson and Carberry, 1998; Abelson, 2002)

In short, the goal of organizations such as Heritage is to create, legitimize, and encourage citizens to internalize a particular set of "taken-for-granted" assumptions about economic issues, and to apply those assumptions persuasively to a variety of public issues. To achieve their goals, advocacy organizations employ two primary rhetorical strategies: that of providing what seems to be objective "evidence" on policy issues and that of producing "realist" rhetoric.

The Ideas and Rhetoric of Free-Market Fundamentalism

Perhaps most importantly, free-market think tanks provide a structure through which research papers on issues of economic policy can be created and publicized, advocacy programs in universities can be funded (more than $100 million a year during the mid- to late 1990s), and writing by like-minded university faculty can be supported. The resulting documents are focused, direct, and simple enough to be easily understood by the general public. When there is a dearth of relevant information on an issue, or so much information that it is daunting (or impossible) to sort through it all, this form of rhetoric is especially powerful. As rhetorical critic James Arnt Aune points out, free-market economic analysis is spectacularly simple:

> It reduces social complexity to a few simple principles: the inexorable law of supply and demand, the perfidiousness of government intervention, the glorious and open future promised by the elimination of government intervention. It also [. . .] relies on irony as a mode of explanation: human actions may have perverse effects, especially in cases of social engineering. [. . .] This makes the economist appear to have both worldly wisdom *and* a sense of humor. (Aune, 2001, 31)

Of course, critics argue that the ideological research produced by free-market think tanks distorts complex issues and employs questionable research methods; but it is very difficult to argue persuasively those positions with audiences who do not have expertise in the intricacies of social science research. This is especially true when the simple conclusions of free marketeers are supported by what *seems* to be highly complex research. Rhetorical acts that begin with phrases such as "that depends on what your definition of *x* is" usually fail (and did so long before President Clinton made the caveat infamous), *even if* an issue is so complex that making rational policy choices actually does depend on precise definition.

But the persuasiveness of free-market rhetoric goes beyond simply maneuvering around gaps in data. Aune attributes its success to its "realist style." First of all, free-market rhetoric maintains an image of scientific objectivity. By establishing "boundary conditions" for their research, free-market rhetors make it virtually impossible to disconfirm their underlying assumptions and predictions. Aune notes that, by starting with the caveat "everything else being equal" ("the economist's equivalent of the magician's 'abracadabra'"), one can explain any unpredicted result of economic research (2001, 22; see also McCloskey, 1985, 1994; Perelman, 2006). When de-regulating an industry fails to achieve its goals, economists can always argue that the sector has not been "deregulated enough." Kuttner (1996) shows how this argument has been used to explain the mixed results of de-regulating the airline industry. All of the loose ends are tied up, and no empirical evidence can disconfirm the claims made in the rhetoric.

Second, social values that cannot be neatly included in models of economic exchange are excluded from analysis for the sake of clarity, precision, and predictability. Soros concludes that "[free-market fundamentalism] is a belief in perfection, a belief in absolutes, a belief that every problem must have a solution. It posits an authority that is endowed with perfect knowledge even if that knowledge is not readily accessible to ordinary mortals" – one whose persuasive power is that of magic: awe and belief without understanding (1998, 227).

Third, like Plato, free-market rhetors cast all policy debates as bi-modal, either/or comparisons, and depict any opposition to the dominant ideology as "mere rhetoric" or dangerous heresy. Proposals to increase "corporate social responsibility" or to "increase equality" are depicted as impinging on the individual rights of someone – an especially powerful argument in individualistic societies such as the US. Even if government does succeed in "leveling the playing field," something that is *assumed* to be true of free markets, these inevitably give aid and comfort to "free-riders," people who unfairly exploit otherwise defensible programs. Special interests have learned to dominate political decision-making, so government policies and programs inevitably favor their interests over those of "normal," hard-working, middle-class citizens. The messiness of democracy is contrasted with the clarity of the market and defined as a social evil, not as a necessary compromise.

Conclusion

The mobility myth, the "organizational imperative," and "free-market fundamentalism" provide valuable *topoi* for organizational rhetors. When combined, they form a powerful rationale which can be used to legitimize almost any action that an organization's management might want to take and to blunt almost any suggestion that organizational operations should be constrained. Any policy proposal can be depicted as a threat to some benefit on which people have come to depend. Any action by government or by any stakeholder group (labor, environmental advocates, and so on) can be cast as a threat by "special interests" to corporate profits and/or economic stability and growth. Similarly, government subsidies, tax-breaks, and anti-competitive regulations have existed for so long that they have come to be viewed as "normal" and "natural" parts of economic–political relationships. Ironically, moves to reduce this preferential treatment can be cast as unwise government *interference* in normal ways of doing business. Regardless of their actual impact, regulations and regulatory agencies become handy scapegoats for organizational failures and/or excuses for negative organizational activities (see also Chapters 4 and 5).

Finally, the combination of bureaucratic structures and doctrines of the "invisible hand" allows executives to deny responsibility for any decisions they make that harm external stakeholders ("these job cuts are outside of my control, they are forced on the organization by the irresistible power of globalization," or by "self-serving actions taken by government, labor, environmental advocates, or other 'special interests'" – and so on). At the same time, rhetoric that depicts managers as "corporate saviors" (which will be the focus of Chapter 3) allows them to claim credit for the organization's successes regardless of the impact that their actions actually had.

Case Study: Markets and Community Values – Buying Babies[18]

In 1978 Richard Posner, currently a judge on the US Court of Appeals for the Seventh Circuit and a faculty member at the University of Chicago School of Law, co-authored an article that was widely interpreted as advocating the creation of a "free market" in babies. You have encountered his name a couple of times in this chapter, but only in passing. Before I summarize the "baby-selling" proposal, it is important for you to get a better of idea of his stature. Now that Milton Friedman has passed away, there is no more important advocate of free-market theory in the US. Kuttner (1996, 335) describes him as a free-market extremist who believes that taxation, income transfer from the rich to the poor, and government spending are forms of legalized theft; James Aune's *Selling the free market* (2001) devotes more space to him than to anyone else. Posner's writings, both judicial decisions and books – he publishes books faster than most people read them – have provided crucial intellectual support for free-market theory and the related "law and economics" movement. He was twice considered by President George W. Bush for a position on the US Supreme Court.[19]

Landes and Posner (1978) started with a simple observation. The number of US couples who would like to adopt a healthy white infant (HWI) vastly exceeds the supply – exact data are difficult to produce, but most estimates suggest an imbalance of 25:1 or more between couples who have completed applications and extensive "home studies" designed to ensure that they would be good parents on the one hand, and the number of available HWIs on the other. Since the application process is complicated and expensive, and the odds of obtaining a HWI are so low, many more couples decide not to complete it. Consequently the overall demand–supply ratio may be as high as 200:1. The ratio of "special needs children" (that is, those who, because of race, age, disability, and other attributes are not HWIs) to couples interested in adopting them is roughly the opposite, about 25 children to each interested couple.

The insufficient supply of HWIs, Landes and Posner argue, results largely from improper government interference in the adoption market. Laws typically do allow prospective adoptive parents to pay a birth mother's medical expenses and living expenses during the later stages of her pregnancy, but they ban direct payment for her baby. As a result, far fewer women in crisis pregnancies complete their pregnancies and make their children available for adoption than would otherwise be the case. The resulting supply–demand imbalance for HWIs has three effects:

1 it drives up the cost of adoption (Landes and Posner cite costs ranging from $9k to $40k; they are much higher today), pricing tens of thousands of potentially excellent parents out of the market;

2 it allows middle-persons (adoption agencies and attorneys who specialize in adoptions) to impose "demanding (and sometimes arbitrary) criteria of age, income, race, and religion to limit demand to supply" (1978, 1); and

3 it has created a black market in HWIs, as always happens when demand vastly exceeds supply.

In short, adoption of HWIs is a paradigm case of what happens when government interferes in a market and distorts normal processes of matching supply and demand.

So, Landes and Posner propose, why not allow qualified adoptive parents to pay birth parents for their offspring? Supply would increase, prices would fall, the black market would disappear or be reduced significantly, and abortion should become less common because women in crisis pregnancies would have an economic incentive to carry a fetus to term. Of course, the protections currently in place that screen potential adoptive parents should be retained or strengthened if necessary, because babies are a very special commodity. The organizations who profit so handsomely from the current arrangement would strongly oppose the proposal – monopolists never want to give up their monopoly power – probably with cries of "the immorality of baby selling" – all the while pretending that we do not currently sell babies. The truth is that we do sell babies, but we do so through a system that makes no economic sense and creates a number of social problems. Landes and Posner also recognized that their proposal could affect adversely the supply–demand imbalance for "special needs" children, but they offered a number of proposals for offsetting those effects.

Discussion Questions

1 How would a free-market purist (someone who believes that government intervention in the free market is inherently evil) respond to Landes and Posner's proposal? Why? How would someone who believes that it is proper for government to tell individuals how to live their lives, as long as some larger societal good results from the "intervention" respond to the proposal? Why? What values and hierarchy of values are embedded in each of the responses you've described?

2 What is *your* response to the proposal? Should "everything (including HWIs) be for sale," to paraphrase the title of Kuttner's book? If not, are you willing to allow government to dictate who can and cannot become parents, and who will receive the tens of thousands of dollars that exchange hands during baby-selling transactions? What values and value hierarchy are embedded in your response? Are you comfortable with that hierarchy? Why – or why not?

3 Now, find your answers to the "Weekend Fun" exercise at the beginning of this chapter, and apply the value hierarchy you developed in response to question 2 to the market in human sperm and eggs.[20] Should your country have a free market in the components of babies, but not in babies themselves? What about embryos, which currently are not regulated in the United States? What about women "renting" their wombs (surrogate motherhood)? What about other practices made possible with today's medical advances – selecting the sex of children using a couple's own eggs and sperm, using in vitro fertilization techniques to produce babies of a desired height, IQ, etc.? Who should make these decisions? The "invisible hand?" Government agencies? Employers, who make decisions about which procedures are covered under their employees' health insurance (Levine and Agence France-Presse, 2006; CBC News, 2006, 2007; Goodman, 2008; Grady, 2007)? What about other medical issues – the supply of organs, for

80

example?[21] What would your answers suggest about other cases of government interference in markets? Should private insurance companies (usually in negotiation with employers) be able to decide which of these procedures should be funded? (Note: if insurance companies do not cover a given procedure, it will still be available to wealthy couples.) Why, and what does your answer say about the ability of market processes to deal with broader social values? What does it say about your values and the extent to which you accept the tenets of free-market theory?

3

Constructing the Leadership Mythos

At the heart of any public company [corporation] is an implicit bargain: the managers promise to run the company in the owners' interest, and the stockholders agree to hand day-to-day control over to the managers. Unfortunately, there is no easy way to ensure that the managers don't slack off or divert some of the stockholders' money into their own pockets. Adam Smith was among the first to identify this problem: "The directors of such companies [. . .] being managers of other people's money than of their own, it cannot well be expected that they should watch over it with the same anxious vigilance [. . .] Negligence and profusion, therefore, must always prevail, more or less, in the management of the affairs of such a company." [*The wealth of nations* (1776)]

Cassidy (2002, 64)

As a counter to Athenian democracy as it existed, Plato promoted the transcendental abilities of the philosopher–king, who is possessed of magical skills and of superhuman wisdom. In short, modern leadership theory, even the theory of democratic leadership, is still attempting to make a case for Plato's philosopher–king.

Barker (2001, 483)

Core Concepts

• Workers in organizations in the United States and Canada support a much heavier managerial burden, both in terms of

82

numbers and compensation, than workers in other industrialized countries do. This difference is grounded in a complex set of cultural assumptions labeled "managerialism," which are sustained through an equally complex rhetoric.

- Although thousands of studies of leadership have been conducted and many thousands of pages have been written on the topic, there is no agreed-upon definition of the term or unambiguous links between the concept and other ideas. This ambiguity allows organizational rhetors to base their rhetoric on whatever conceptual scheme best legitimizes their claims in particular rhetorical situations.

- Leadership rhetoric largely ignores followers and followership. When they are mentioned, followers are depicted as objects – human "resources," like steel orders or photocopy machines – or as flawed leaders, some of whom can be repaired through the actions of skilled leaders.

- The simplest and most common definition of "leader" equates leadership with occupying a position at the top of an organizational hierarchy. This definition is sustained by a combination of rhetoric and organizational structures, which are used in combination to dismiss evidence of leader incompetence and protect positional leaders from being accountable for their actions.

- Other definitions of "leadership" focus on leader traits and behaviors. Thousands of studies have failed to identify traits or behaviors that predict leadership effectiveness or organizational success, although research has delineated the traits and behaviors that people *believe* to constitute leader effectiveness.

- Resistance is a complicated phenomenon because it is motivated by a web of individual and collective motivations, including improving organizations and their operations. Consequently, it has multiple, incongruent effects. Resistance by individuals is transformed into collective resistance through strategic rhetoric, often by using the strategies labeled "leadership."

As the quotations at the beginning of this chapter suggest, one of the most important taken-for-granted assumption in modern capitalist democracies is the notion that it is legitimate – "natural" and "normal" – for professional managers to dominate organizations. "As a result of deeply ingrained cultural assumptions," organizational behavior scholars Gary Gemmill and Judith Oakley note, "approaches to the study of leadership usually start with the idea that leaders are unquestionably necessary for the functioning of an organization." Like the commonly held belief in the naturalness of hierarchy, the presumed need for leaders "takes its power chiefly from the fact that it is an undiscussable aspect of reality [. . .] outside of conscious awareness" (Gemmill and Oakley, 1992, 113; see also Anthony, 1977; Campbell, 1977). Questions like "what problems or issues in our organization make it necessary to anoint someone as our official 'leader'?" are simply not asked. Dominant cultural assumptions also declare that the people who occupy leadership positions effectively represent the interests of all of the stakeholders whose lives are affected by the organization's actions. Managers are, after all, hired by the owners of corporations to represent their interests in the everyday operations of the firm; they are constantly watched and evaluated by a supposedly independent Board of Directors; and they are motivated by what they believe to be best for the long-term success of the organization and its many stakeholders. They are assumed to have expertise that other members of their firms lack (or, like the scarecrow at the end of *The wizard of Oz*, to at least have a diploma that *symbolizes* their superior expertise). Only *they* know the optimal strategies for maximizing the efficiency of the firm's everyday operations, and only *they* know how to strategically adapt their organizations to meet the ever-changing demands of a global, competitive free market. When managers succeed, they are handsomely rewarded, because everyone benefits from their success; when managers fail, everyone suffers, but managers are especially penalized. Managerial power, influence, and rewards are assumed to be both earned and richly deserved. They are "secular saviors" – to use the phrase of Harvard Business School professor Rakesh Kuhrana (2002) – whose visible hands make the miraculous "invisible hand" of capitalism work (see also Rost, 1991; Alvesson and Sveningsson, 2003c; Collinson, 2005). The interests of all other stakeholders – stockholders, workers, and the communities within which organizations exist – are secondary, because in the end "what's good for management is good for everyone."

In this chapter I will examine each of these assumptions as both the product of strategic rhetoric and the basis of managerial dominance. I will also note that there is little empirical evidence to support any of them. Chapter 2 explained that cultural assumptions about the functions of capitalist economies and the proper roles for various actors, including governments, to play in them are legitimized by the rhetoric of free-market theory. In this chapter I develop a parallel argument about cultural assumptions regarding "leadership" and "followership." Like the rhetoric of free-market economics, rhetoric about leadership permeates everyday discourse and influences the processes through which we all make sense out of organizational life. Our shared frames of reference in turn influence the content and the taken-for-granted assumptions of leadership research and theory. In a complex cycle, cultural myths about leadership influence research, which generates rhetoric that reproduces cultural assumptions.

The Presumptions, Practices, and Rhetoric of "Managerialism"

Managers are especially revered throughout the developed world, but especially so in the United States and Canada. This reverence is evidenced by their sheer numbers and the size of their compensation. Using data from the US Bureau of Labor Statistics, David Gordon compared the ratio of managerial and administrative employees to non-managerial employees in the organizations of nine developed countries. In the United States the figure was 13 percent. The second highest figure was in Canada (12.9 percent) – which is not surprising, given the influence that the US economy has on that of its largest trading partner. But the next highest percentage was *half* that level (Norway, at 6.8 percent). In Japanese and German firms it was less than one-third the US/Canadian level (4.2 percent and 3.9 percent respectively). After viewing these data, David Gordon concluded: "because managers do not contribute directly to the products made by or services provided by a firm, US organizations became progressively less competitive and non-management employees had to be increasingly productive in order to compensate for the increasing bureaucratic burden" (1996, 27).

The advent of computer technology and the "downsizing" campaigns of the 1980s and 1990s were touted as means of streamlining US firms in order to make them more competitive in the global economy. A key part of this strategy was to flatten organizational hierarchies and to empower lower-level employees to make everyday decisions, thereby increasing organizational efficiency and effectiveness by reducing the bureaucratic burden. However, the strategies were implemented in ways that achieved the opposite result, actually *increasing* the managerial burden from 12.6 percent in 1989 to 13.6 percent in 1995, a trend that continued during the economic boom of the 1990s. Fully 25 percent of the jobs created during the Clinton Administration (1993–2000) were managerial/supervisory, double the percentage among the jobs being created at the beginning of the period.[1] As a result, non-management workers in US and Canadian corporations entered the new century supporting a much larger managerial burden than workers in corporations headquartered in the rest of the developed world and that gap continues to grow.

The cost of the managerial burden is exacerbated by compensation systems. The ratio of average executive compensation to average worker pay increased in the US from roughly 40:1 in 1979 to 140:1 in 1992, then to 530:1 in 2002, when it exceeded 1000:1 in Fortune 100 firms. Over the course of a single decade, the 1990s, chief executive officer (CEO) pay jumped by 535 percent – five times the increase in corporate profits and seventeen times the increase in average worker pay. Had the average pay for US factory workers increased at the same rate as CEO compensation, it would have been $114,035 at the end of the period (instead of $23,753); had the federal minimum wage increased at the same rate, it would have been $24.13 instead of $5.15. These trends actually *accelerated* in the US during the first decade of the new century, while the ratio of management-to-worker pay remained stable in many developed countries (Sweden, Norway, Denmark, and Germany, for example) and increased only modestly in others (the UK, Canada, and Italy). Those countries whose economies were closely tied to the US experienced much greater inflation of executive compensation than the countries less closely connected economically (Galbraith, 1998; Parker, 2005; Phillips, 2002).[2] Even greater discrepancies exist in the amount that executives are paid for failing. For example, Tony Hayward, the BP CEO who lost his position as a result of his mishandling of the Deepwater Horizon explosion and oil spill, received a "golden parachute" of $1.6 million USD (one year's salary) plus the pension benefits he had acquired (an additional $17.5 million USD). But that figure represents less than a tenth of the what Robert Nardelli got for "running Home Depot into the ground" – a company that is

> far smaller, easier to manage and less prone to catastrophic disaster. [...] Then there's the Wall Street crowd, led by Merrill Lynch's Stan O'Neal, who laid waste to the firm and walked away with $161.5 million, and Ken Lewis, who bought Merrill after O'Neal was done with it, misled shareholders about its losses, and still got $125 million for leaving. Charles Prince oversaw huge write-downs at Citgroup related to subprime mortgages and was given $42 million in defeat. (Steffy, 2010c, D1–2)

Weekend Fun 3

Choose an organization with which you have an economic link – one that you work for or have invested in, or one that gave you a scholarship or employs one of your parents, your significant other, and so on. Find out how much its CEO has made during the past decade. Find out what has happened to the number of people employed by the firm, both in your home country and in other countries. If possible, include jobs that have been "outsourced" to other companies and/or other countries. Then find out what has happened to the income of stockholders (who are the legal owners of public firms) through dividends paid and increases (or decreases) in the value of the company's stock. Finally, find out what has happened to the overall value of the stocks of companies in the same sector of the economy. One way to do this is to locate a mutual fund that specializes in that sector (e.g. health care, energy, and so on). Save your results.

Both dimensions of the managerial burden – the numbers of managerial employees and their pay – are supported by, and in turn support, an ideology that organizational communication scholars have labeled "managerialism." Just as the organizational imperative said that organizations are the only thing that really counts in modern society, managerialism claims that the only thing that really counts in organizations are managers (especially upper management), and their distinctive expertise: values, actions, and ways of thinking and communicating. While the various assumptions underlying managerialism are widely accepted, especially in the US, it is important to recognize that none of them is "true" in an empirical sense. The primary assumption, that there is no difference between owning a corporation and managing it (because managers are hired by owners to do what is best for them and for the corporation), is simply not true. Managers in modern firms are rarely owners/entrepreneurs – they have almost never invested their lives in building the organizations they work for. Neither do managers plan to invest their future in a particular organization or have any concern for passing on to their heirs a stable and profitable organization. They are "hired guns," who move from organization to organization in an effort to build their own careers. They often know very little about a particular organization's history, values, culture, or even about the tasks that are performed within it. Their expertise is in subjects that are easily transferable from firm to firm – finance or operations management, for example – even in very specialized industries. This does not mean that they are sociopaths (the excessively greedy people Adam Smith worried so much about). It does mean that they are trained to focus on their own careers, not on the organization that currently employs them. In fact, today's Master of Business

88

Administration (MBA) programs provide would-be managers with extensive advice about how to develop their own market value, so that they can easily move from company to company (Pfeffer, 1998; DiTomaso, Parks-Yancy, and Post, 2003; Kuhrana, 2010). The success of the organizations they run is a means to their career development, not an end in itself. Organizational reward systems encourage these same attitudes and behaviors, giving executives little reason to be primarily concerned with the long-term condition of the organizations they leave behind.[3]

As a result, it is not surprising that there is little evidence that executive performance is a valid or reliable predictor of organizational success, regardless of how it is defined. Changing leaders does not produce improved organizational performance over the long term, although it often generates short-term increases in stock values because investors *believe* that any change will be an improvement (Staw, 1975; Calder, 1977, 2002). This does not mean that executives never are corporate saviors – there are many cases in which their actions stem organizational declines or stimulate organizational growth (Child, 1972; Bass, 1985; Kotter, 1988, 1990; Tedlow, 2002). But there also are many cases in which executives weaken or destroy organizations, or sacrifice the interests of other stakeholders to their own short-term financial gain. Executives' actions are only one in a myriad factors that influence organizational success, and the impact of their actions is often dwarfed by factors that have a much stronger relationship to firm performance: the structure and degree of competitiveness of the industry in which a firm is located, the culture and/or "intelligence" that was in place in the firm when the executive was hired, the legacy of past innovation and/or investment decisions, and so on (Pfeffer and Salancik, 1978; Hambrick and Finkelstein, 1987; Hannan and Freeman, 1989; Carroll and Hannan, 2000; Alvesson, 2002).[4] So the correlation between what executives are paid and how well their organizations perform is statistically nonsignificant (no greater than chance). Harvard Business School's Rakesh Kuhrana concluded that the available data show "just how little connection exists, in practice, between the financial rewards showered on CEOs and the interests of corporations and their shareholders" (2002, 190–191; also see Pfeffer, 1998). In short, the mythology that supports managerial dominance is just that – a set of assumptions that have been cultivated through strategic rhetoric and sustained through the operation of social/ economic/organizational structures created to maintain that dominance (Deetz, 1992a, 222). As I explained in Chapters 1 and 2, social myths do not have to be empirically verified, or even verifiable, in order to be powerful – they succeed because people *want* them to be true, *believe* them to be true, and *interpret* empirical evidence through the frames of reference that they provide.

Of course, no cultural mythology is universally accepted, even if it is generally believed. An ideology can still be dominant even if there are many doubters. In addition, cross-cultural comparisons make it clear that the degree to which managerialism is accepted uncritically varies widely (Scott, 1990; Collinson, 1992; Murphy, 1998; Kassing and Avtgis, 1999; Kassing, 2001; Sewell and Fleming, 2002; Ganesh, Zoller, and Cheney, 2005). Even in societies such as the US, where it is widely accepted, the number of doubters has increased substantially as a result of recurring managerial scandals at the beginning of the new century – at Enron, WorldCom, Adelphia, and other firms in the United States and at Guinness, Maxwell, and Shell Oil in the United Kingdom – and the financial industry crisis and government bailout at the end of its first decade. The doubts have been exacerbated through the contrast between managerial corruption and greed and the economic suffering experienced by workers, the vast majority of whom have acted in ethical ways and have made significant contributions to their organizations, even in the most difficult circumstances. But the mythology supporting managerial dominance is amazingly stable, being sustained by a complex and omnipresent rhetoric, which constructs particular views of leaders and leadership, followers and followership.

Organizations, Rhetoric, and the Cult of Leadership

Ambiguity is an unavoidable and inescapable aspect of human experience. This may be even more true of our conception of leadership than of any other construct. At one level, everyone knows what leadership is. Although we may not be able to define it, we know it when we see it. We *should* know what it is, since it may be the most studied concept in the social sciences and humanities. For example, the most recent edition of Bernard Bass's oft-cited *Handbook of leadership* (Bass and Bass, 2008) is more than 1,500 pages long, even though it is only a partial *summary* of existing research. Joseph Rost's (1991) survey of 587 works on leadership found that 63 percent (366) of them did not even define the term. When it was defined, the definitions were inconsistent with one another, even within the same work. K. B. Lowe (2006) found thirteen different definitions *in the same book*, and in 2005 David Collinson and Keith Grint introduced the new journal *Leadership* with the observation that "there is little consensus on what counts as leadership, whether it can be taught, or even how effective it might be" (cited in Barker, 1997, 346). Of course, not having a clear understanding of what "leadership" is makes it impossible to differentiate "good" leadership from "bad," "toxic" from "transformative," "counterfeit" from "real/authentic," or "effective" from "failed" – to rehearse just a handful of commonly used adjectives. It also means that a very important and complicated concept is often reduced to simplistic slogans such as "leaders are people who do the right things (Bennis and Naus, 1985)". This definitional problem, communication researcher Steve Banks concludes, is endemic – "the words used to define leadership are contradictory, the models [developed to analyze it] are discrepant, and the content of leadership is confused with the nature of leadership" (Banks, 2008, 11).

For scholars and practitioners who believe (or wish) that leadership studies were "scientific," this state of affairs is frustrating at best. But, for people interested in the rhetoric of organizations, the existence of tensions, contradictions, and ambiguity merely suggests that there is sufficient conceptual space for rhetoric about leadership to be important. When multiple inconsistent definitions exist *and* seem to be legitimate, organizational rhetors can draw upon the definition(s) that best serve their purposes in a particular rhetorical situation. When the situation changes, they merely shift to another seemingly legitimate definition. Thus the key question, for scholars of organizational rhetoric and for practitioners alike, is not "what is leadership?" – but how do interested parties (1) use rhetoric to construct preferred depictions of leaders, leadership, followers, and followership; and (2) use those definitions to legitimize their actions, power, and rewards.

Constructing "Followers" and "Followership"

One of the few terms that are included in every definition of "leadership" is "follower"; one of the few conclusions that are included in almost all leadership theories is about the relative unimportance of "followership." In general, "leaders" are defined as people whom someone follows, and "leadership" is the process of persuading followers to pursue the organization's and the leader's goals, even if doing so involves sacrificing their own goals and well-being. Leaders are successful when they have motivated followers to actively, even happily conform to the demands made of them. "Good leaders" are defined by their ability to induce a kind of "massive learned helplessness," which prompts workers to become "cheerful robots" (Goffee and Jones, 2001, 148). So, in mainstream leadership research and theory, a primary function of leadership is managing dissent, either by preventing it altogether or by channeling it in directions that will aid organizations through "improved decision-making" (Gemmill and Oakley, 1992; Barker, 2001; Wicks, 2002). At its best, leadership involves the ability to get workers to pressure *one another* into conforming, being motivated to work harder than their tangible rewards warrant, and suppressing dissent – a process that organizational communication scholars have labeled "concertive control" (Banks, 2008, 13; see also Barker, 1993; Barker, Melville, and Pacanowsky, 1993; and Sunstein, 2003).

But what are the attributes of a "good" follower? Somewhat

92

ironically, mainstream leadership rhetoric rarely discusses followers explicitly. This is probably not all that surprising – whether you peruse an airport bookstore or a university library, you will find many works on leadership, but it is unlikely that you will find a single book or magazine article on followers or followership.[5] Almost every college and university in the Western world offers undergraduate and graduate work in "leadership"; almost none offers even a single course in followership, even though almost every student will spend the vast majority of his or her life as someone's subordinate. In those rare cases in which followers or followership are mentioned, it is only in passing – as "unproblematic and predictable cogs in the [leadership] machine [. . .] empty vessels waiting to be led, or even transformed, by the leader" (Banks, 2008, 11; see also Goffee and Jones, 2001). Mainstream leadership rhetoric does little to explain what constitutes effective followership because there is so little to explain. When followers are described at length, they are depicted as either flawed leaders or as objects to be molded and/or tools to be used.

There is hope for some followers, those who are "leaders-light," wannabes who aspire to become leaders but do not yet have the necessary experience, expertise, or maturity to be elevated to the position of leader. Their key virtue is that they are especially responsive to leadership. Thus they are capable of being "fixed" by leaders who know how to do it. This definition was most blatant during the late nineteenth century. One perspective, popularized by Herbert Spencer, was called "Social Darwinism." Its proponents claimed that leaders, indeed all members of social and economic elites, held their positions because they were better adapted to the social and economic climate of the time. Consequently it was natural, normal, and proper for the strong to thrive at the expense of the weak; indeed it was morally correct for leaders to dominate the subordinates. Workers were workers because they were genetically inferior beings. Harsh discipline, coercion, and threats of (or use of) violence – all were appropriate ways for naturally superior leaders to obtain compliance from naturally inferior, but potentially useful, followers.

A second perspective, labeled "industrial betterment" or

"welfare capitalism," also started from the assumption that workers were inferior, but it was more optimistic about the possibility of improving them through education and/or placement in appropriate environments (this was a kind of "Eliza Doolittle goes to work" perspective). Rapid industrialization had led US firms to rely increasingly on immigrant labor, and many of them brought foreign and dangerous ideas – socialist notions of worker rights – which led to frequent and sometimes violent confrontations between owners and labor. Superior people had a moral, religious, and societal responsibility to reform these workers and to instill in them a Protestant sense of duty and middle-class, "American" habits and character – frugality, industriousness, temperance, neatness of dress, and "circumspection of manners." Not only would these efforts improve society, they would reduce hostility between labor and owners and promote increased profits, which could be shared. As the treasurer of a pioneer in industrial betterment, the Waltham Watch factory, noted: "anything that tends to lighten the strain of labor upon the mind, or serves to provide cheerfulness and contentment, is an economic advantage" (Gilman, 1899: 117; see also Buder, 1967; Korman, 1967; Barley and Kunda, 1992). These efforts began in the railroad industry, when Cornelius Vanderbilt established Young Men's Christian Associations (YMCAs) along trunk lines, to minister to the railroaders' physical and spiritual needs, stem drunkenness, and foster a more reliable workforce. By the 1880s and 1890s advocates of industrial betterment were building libraries, providing organized recreational activities, improving the sanitation and aesthetics of factories, and even building entire communities in which their employees could be isolated from the social ills being imported from Europe.

Although the industrial betterment movement met a precipitous decline when the economic depressions of the late 1890s led to escalating labor–management tension and violence, the underlying assumption that workers were inherently deficient continued. The assumption may not have been as explicit, yet the leadership models developed during the twentieth century advocated "employee development" in one form or another. As the century progressed, a new academic discipline – industrial or organizational psychology – developed to support the core beliefs of managerialism. Psychological health, at least at work, meant "fitting in," becoming integrated into one's organizational role without feeling conflicts between membership in the organization and one's values or self-interest (Scott, 1985; Driskell and Beckett, 1989; Deetz, 1992b). For example, Paul Hersey and Kenneth Blanchard's still popular "situational leadership" model calls for leaders to adapt their strategies to the level of "maturity" and "willingness" of each subordinate. A *mature* follower is one who has sufficient training and skill to take on and accomplish an assigned task in the manner desired by the leader/organization through his or her "own direction and motivation." That is, she or he is a "leader-light" who needs little or no instruction. A *willing* follower is sufficiently enthusiastic, interested, independent, self-confident, and so on that she or he does not need to be motivated. Leaders can strategically adapt their own behavior in ways that help an immature and/or unwilling follower to be healed (or transformed) into one who no longer needs a leader.

Unfortunately (or fortunately, depending on your perspective), leaders will always be needed. Even mature, motivated followers can backslide – they are inherently flawed beings and cannot resist temptation – and will need to be constantly "developed" in order to master new technologies and work processes. If followers assert themselves in any way – by pushing for enhanced safety measures or for other worker rights, wage increases, collective bargaining, or worker democracy – they not only provide further evidence of their "immaturity," they reduce organizational performance by requiring leaders to spend more time and effort educating and motivating them, and they legitimize stronger forms of managerial domination, undertaken for the sake of the firm's survival.

The second depiction of followers in twentieth-century leadership theory treats them as *resources* or *objects*, like desks, corporate jets, and computers. They may be *"human* resources," but they are *resources* nonetheless (Steffy and Grimes, 1986, 1992; Steffy and Maurer, 1987). In the rhetoric of human resource management, "individuals are presented as numerical objects that can be observed, held over time, retrieved, analyzed and shared by interested parties. [. . .] [I]nformation not measured, often information depicting the employee as unique, dynamic and ever-changing, may be largely discounted and ignored" (Steffy and Grimes, 1992, 191). Most importantly, when the organization faces difficulties, followers are expendable. Like orders for steel or photocopy machines, their numbers can quickly and easily be reduced. Indeed, the best worker resources are contingent workers, hired on short-term contracts, with no expectation of long-term employment. In short, they are like the cabbage growers in Plato's *Republic* – necessary cogs in the wheels of a society or organiza-tion, but expendable, disposable, and easily replaced (Conrad and Poole, 1997; also see Pfeffer, 2007 and Pfeffer and Sutton, 2006).

Although this depiction of non-leaders has been around since the coercive era of the late 1800s, it was revived during the organi-zational downsizing efforts of the 1980s and 1990s. Competition from abroad, primarily from Japan, accelerated after the fall of the Iron Curtain. In order to deal with the realities of globalization, managers had no choice but to create lean, streamlined operations (without reducing the managerial burden). Of course, "having no choice" is itself a crucial rhetorical construction, one that is con-sistent with free-market fundamentalism – the "invisible hand" made me downsize. Leaders in many firms, primarily in Europe, found or developed ways of dealing with globalization that did not involve massive job cuts, an approach that management scholar Richard Freeman has called the "high road" (Freeman, 1994; Deal and Jenkins, 1994; Krugman, 1994; Levinson, 1996). So it would be more accurate to say that devotees of downsizing did not seri-ously *consider* any other option. The rhetoric about downsizing is distinctive in another way: it never suggests that there are *people* involved in the process; advocates of downsizing strategies such as re-engineering "transform a painful, wrenching process into a clin-ical but [purportedly] necessary management strategy" (Conrad and Poole, 1997, 589; see also Keith Grint, 1994; Jackson, 1996; Boje et al., 1997; Cheney and Carroll, 1997; Boje, 1999). Used by almost 70 percent of North American and European firms during the late 1980s and early 1990s, re-engineering targeted more than two-thirds of all employees for elimination, because both professionals in staff positions and non-managerial employees were defined as expendable – only managers were immune.

For executives, downsizing does have some virtues. Typically it creates short-term profit increases and massive rewards for the leaders who carry it out. Between 1980 and 1995 the 500 largest US firms (Fortune 500) eliminated more than 8 million jobs, while their CEOs' compensation increased by 1,000 percent. Anthony Downs found that the number of jobs eliminated by a company is a significantly stronger predictor of executive compensation than the 5-year performance of the company. After job reductions are announced, stock prices quickly jump – when IBM, Sears, Xerox, McDonnell Douglas, and Dupont cut between 4,500 and 6,000 workers, there was an increase of stock value of between 3.4 percent and 7.7 percent the very next day. For executives whose compensation is primarily based on stock price, a group that includes almost everyone who runs a Fortune 500 firm, the personal gains from cutting jobs can be monumental.

However, the positive economic effects of cutting jobs are smaller and tend to be short-lived. Within two years firm performance falls, in part because the employees who are forced to leave take a great deal of the organization's intelligence with them. They are often re-hired, usually as consultants or contract workers, and often at greater salaries than before, but with smaller or nonexistent benefits packages and no job security. For example, during 2009 the Chrysler corporation declared bankruptcy, accepted a $12.5 billion taxpayer bailout, and emerged from bankruptcy as a partner of Fiat. By the end of the year Chrysler's management realized that they had fired the designers and engineers who might have created the new products that the company desperately needed in order to recapture market share. As a result, Chrysler showed up at the January, 2010 North American International Auto Show with no new products, and consequently was the only manufacturer not to hold a flashy press conference to introduce its new vehicles. All that its new management could do was to announce plans to hire more engineers and product development specialists (Krishner, 2010; Whoeriskey, 2010).[6] Over an even longer time frame, of fifteen years or so, companies whose managers choose strategies other than downsizing prove to be stronger than those who opted to cut jobs (Downs, 1996; Boje, 1999). But the strategy of cutting jobs will continue to be practiced as long as it is perceived as involving "streamlined resource utilization" rather than people losing their livelihoods, and as long as it leads to massive rewards for executives.

Positional Constructions of Leaders/Leadership

The simplest definition of the term "leadership" involves a person's position: leaders are located at the top of an organization (which is usually symbolized by their literally inhabiting the space at the top of the building that houses the company's home office); lower-ranking leaders are positioned lower in the hierarchy, but above their subordinates. This conception can be traced to the beginning of recorded history, but it was formalized by the Christian church during the Middle Ages, and subsequently appropriated by political leaders through the concept of the divine right of kings and nobles. Whether secular or religious, positional views of leadership tend to reduce followers to automata. As Adam Smith explained, serfs are completely dependent on their lords and come to accept their subservient roles because of the tangible benefits they obtain; and lords become just as dependent on compliant serfs and on the feudal system. Parishioners become dependent on ecclesiastical institutions for their identity and their salvation, and subordinates accommodate to scientifically prescribed ways of doing their jobs because of the promise of increased financial rewards. The systems are very stable, but only because they rob human beings of the drive to make more of themselves, to develop their natural human capacities (what Smith called our "natural liberty") to their fullest.[7]

Positional definitions of "leader" often contradict everyday experience – everyone has known people in leadership positions who are inept, and everyone has known people lower in the hierarchy who are superbly skilled and highly productive. Because there is no necessary relationship between simply occupying an elevated position and being a competent leader, positional definitions of leadership must continually be legitimized through rhetoric (Gemmill and Oakley, 1992). Common rationalizations of positional views of leadership include:

1 Serfs/parishioners/citizens/workers are mistaken about their leaders' incompetence because they are incapable of understanding the king's/priest's/managers' (*super*human) wisdom.
2 The subordinates may be right that a particular leader is evil or incompetent, but the gods have sent him or her as a way of testing mere mortals' faith in the system as a whole.
3 The gods have a warped sense of humor, get distracted, or are fighting among themselves and the unlucky mortals are caught in the middle.
4 Best of all, when it comes to legitimizing the system, the gods sent a bad leader to punish the humans/subordinates for their disobedience, sins, or incompetence.[8]

Each of these arguments insulates the main assumption – that leaders are ordained to occupy their positions – from the empirical reality that some leaders are inept or worse, and that some followers are more competent and more valuable. The dominance of positional leaders is sustained, and deferring to them continues to seem rational.

Positional views also protect leader dominance by making it difficult to hold them accountable for their actions. This is partly because bureaucratic structures allow people at the top of the organization to shift responsibility for negative events on to employees situated lower in the hierarchy (Mitchell, 2001). From Enron to the Abu Ghraib prison in Iraq or to sexual abuse in the Roman Catholic church, people occupying leadership positions can claim that all kinds of foolish, unwise, or corrupt behavior was the result of subordinates overstepping their orders or acting without the knowledge, permission, or direction of their superiors. It does not seem to matter that supervisors often make it clear to their subordinates that they *do not want* to know what is going on – a process that was labeled "plausible deniability" during the administration of US President Ronald Reagan. Occupying a position at the top of a bureaucratic hierarchy also allows leaders to engage in rhetoric that keeps them safely away from being held accountable. Positional leaders can admit that the person occupying their position is officially responsible for negative events, and they can even apologize for "that person's" actions or negligence, while never accepting *personal* responsibility for them. For example, Secretary of Defense Donald Rumsfeld admitted to the US Senate that the Abu Ghraib atrocities "occurred on my watch as secretary of defense. I am accountable for them. I take full responsibility," knowing that no one in the Department of Defense's chain of command who was above the level of prison commander General Janis Karpinski would receive any form of personal punishment (Banks, 2008, 10).[9] However, holding a leadership position means that, when good things happen, leaders can claim credit and collect extensive rewards, even when it is the leader's followers who originate or develop new ideas or are responsible for the organization's new-found success (Stein, 2008).

Leader Traits and Leadership Behaviors

Later conceptions of leaders and leadership moved beyond occupying a particular organizational position to focus on leader traits and behaviors. Trait theories of leadership effectiveness emerged during the late 1800s and were popular during the first half of the twentieth century. They were a shift away from positional views, in that they claimed that people in leadership positions deserved to be there by virtue of their superior intellects, bravery, or ability to command love from others (the attributes that led the Wonderful Wizard to turn Oz over to the Tin Man, the Scarecrow, and the formerly cowardly Lion just before losing control of his balloon). A large part of the voluminous leadership research literature described earlier in this chapter sought to determine the personal traits that correlate with leader effectiveness. For example, between 1865 and World War I there were thousands of studies about the traits that made Abraham Lincoln an effective leader. Eventually, almost every conceivable attribute, including IQ, head size, and head shape and texture (a "science" called phrenology) was considered.

It probably does not come as much of a surprise that, in general, this Herculean effort failed to discover any traits that are either necessary or sufficient for leadership effectiveness, although the research did a better job of predicting who would be perceived as "leadership material." In other words, researchers found that, if powerholders in organizations *believe* that certain traits predict effectiveness, they are more likely to hire and promote people who *seem* to have those attributes than people who do not. Sometimes this process is a little silly – in the US one of the best predictors of leadership emergence is height, at least for men, although the only evidence showing a relationship between height and leader effectiveness reverses the causality: tall men are *perceived* to be better leaders than short ones regardless of their actual performance. But the *assumption* is so pervasive that people in the United States and in many other countries with a similar cultural profile try very hard to obtain, develop, or display the desired traits through tactics as diverse as plastic surgery and following the dictates of "dress for success" books. Typically these selection processes lead to predictable outcomes – people who occupy leadership positions pick candidates whom they perceive to be like themselves. But, as Ralph Stogsdill (1974) persuasively observed thirty-five years ago, trait theories of leadership effectiveness simply are not supported by the available empirical evidence (see also Cheney et al., 2004; Parker, 2001).

Consequently, leadership researchers eventually shifted their focus away from traits to leader behaviors, or at least they claimed to have done so. The resulting behavioral theories were similar to the earlier trait models in two ways: (1) they included almost as many lists of valued behaviors as there were leadership researchers; and (2) scholars found it hard to link leadership behaviors to organizational effectiveness. In addition, behavioral models found it difficult to explain what leadership "is," although they were more successful at explaining what leadership is not.

Leaders are not managers. "Managers," Abraham Zalzenik (1977) asserted, are people who occupy upper-level positions and strive to maximize organizational efficiency. They evidence a distinctive mixture of traits and behaviors. They are persistent, tough-minded, hard working, intelligent, tolerant, and have good will toward other members of the organization. They react quickly and decisively to organizational problems and opportunities, but, as a result, they tend to protect the status quo. In contrast, *leaders* focus on the "drama of power and politics." They are proactive, successfully manage high-risk situations, are visionary, and focus their attention on what events and decisions mean to participants. In the process they express strong emotions and they elicit them from others. The leader–manager distinction has two important effects. One is that it aggrandizes "leaders." "Managers" are involved in mundane, everyday activities, including listening to their followers. "Leaders," on the other hand, are dynamic, inspirational people who do all, or at least most, of the talking. The second effect is that it makes it much more difficult to assess the impact of "leadership." Mundane, "managerial" activities can be measured, evaluated, and rewarded appropriately. Visionary, inspirational actions are much more difficult to evaluate. Thus "managers" can be held accountable for their actions, while holding "leaders" accountable is a much more tenuous, difficult, and rhetorical process (Burns, 1978; Carroll and Levy, 2008).

By the early 1980s, leadership rhetoric and research was focusing almost completely on creating visions, motivating followers through powerful emotional appeals, and managing the meanings that followers attribute to organizational actions and events. The most popular of these perspectives were labeled "transformational leadership" – a framework initiated by James Burns and popularized by Bernard Bass and others – and "corporate culture," which achieved near-cult status after the publication of Tom Peters and Robert Waterman's (1982) *In search of excellence* and Terrence Deal and Alan Kennedy's (1982) *Corporate cultures*.[10] Both of these perspectives depicted leaders as charismatic "secular saviors" who use symbolic forms – myths, metaphors, stories, rituals, and so on – to persuade followers to view the world in desired ways and to motivate them to exert exceptional effort and performance. A leader (not a manager), Peters and Austin concluded, is a "cheerleader, enthusiast, nurturer of champions, hero finder, wanderer, dramatist, coach, facilitator, builder," someone who influences followers by fostering desirable beliefs, creating trust, and excitedly enacting a particular vision of the future. Leaders use labels, metaphors, stories, and platitudes as building blocks for more complex symbolic forms (Peters and Austin, 1985; Czarniawska, 1997). The key to achieving "excellence" is a particular pattern of leader behavior, one that Peters and Waterman called "wandering around." Most leaders are simply out of touch with their followers and customers. Leadership starts with the recognition that every minute of every day is an opportunity for symbolic action. Seizing the moment cannot be done in the executive suite. It requires leaders to be constantly interacting with their followers – paying attention to them and getting their attention, dramatically enacting the core values of the organization, consciously using key words, metaphors, stories, and so on to normalize a particular way of thinking and talking about organizational issues, as well as constantly preaching the vision of the organization.

In their popular book, *The art of framing* (1996), organizational communication scholar Gail Fairhurst and business consultant Robert Sarr offered a more detailed analysis of how leaders should communicate while "wandering" (see also Gronn, 1983). More than other behavioral theories, their perspective went beyond viewing followers as automata; it recognized that followers actively interpret actively leader actions and communication and strategically choose how to respond. The primary work of leadership, they argued, is to manage meaning, which relies, more than anything else, on the ability to "frame," that is, to persuade followers "to choose one particular meaning (or set of meanings) over another. When we share our frames with others (the process of framing), we manage meaning because we assert that our interpretations should be taken as real over other possible interpretations" (Fairhurst and Sarr, 1996, 3). To be credible and persuasive, framing communication must be genuine – it "must come from the heart." It cannot be impromptu – it depends on a great deal of forethought, both about what the leaders' sense of the mission of the organization and what her or his vision for the organization and its future are, and about how the mission/vision applies to everyday behavioral work. Framing involves strategic rhetoric, as the phrase was defined in Chapter 1. It requires sensitivity to rhetorical situations, to the opportunities and constraints present in every communicative interaction. It simultaneously reveals leaders' "internal compasses" and forces them to test those principles in everyday challenges. It also requires leaders to revise their perspectives in order to cope better with changing situations. Framing also depends on a leaders' mastery of symbolism and symbolic action – metaphors, jargon, contrast, spin, and stories. It is both a cognitive process – a way of thinking and encouraging others to think – and a communicative activity that selects some aspects of a situation for attention or emphasis, and in the process excludes other aspects from awareness (Fairhurst, 2005).[11] If done well, framing allows followers and leaders to make sense out of even the most surprising events, which provides them with a degree of stability and predictability in a chaotic environment.

Of course, these perspectives were very popular among organizational communication scholars, because they suggested that leadership is essentially a persuasive activity. They were even more popular among managers, because they suggested that *they* are the key to making organizations succeed and provided them with some seemingly simple and relatively inexpensive tools, which could be used to control followers' behaviors while raising their morale, commitment, and productivity. Since more traditional models of leadership had increasingly been shown to provide only "marginal returns on performance and productivity," this alternative model seemed like a route to salvation (Barley, Meyer, and Gash, 1988, 31).[12]

Almost as soon as the corporate culture perspective was articulated, it received criticism. Many of the critiques struck a familiar tone: like in the case of trait and behavior theories, its advocates' claims of increased organizational performance simply did not seem to be supported by the evidence they presented. For example, the most popular version of the model was presented in Peters and Waterman's *In search of excellence* series. There is no question about its popularity. During its first two years, *In search of excellence* sold more copies in English than any other book save the *Living Bible*; within a decade 5 million copies had been purchased. When combined with income from sequels, media events, and consulting contracts, it generated for its first author an annual income larger than that of many nations (Kleiner, 1996; Cheney et al., 2004). Subsequent books in the series provided even less data, offering instead illustrations of the model's effectiveness. So critics were not all that surprised when, twenty years after *In search of excellence* was published, Peters admitted that he and Waterman had invented the "data" used to link their leadership advice to organizational performance:

> This is pretty small beer, but for what it's worth, okay, I confess: We faked the data. A lot of people suggested it at the time. The big question was, How did you end up viewing these companies as "excellent" companies? A little while later, when a bunch of the "excellent" companies started to have some down years, that also became a huge accusation. (Peters, 2007, n.p.)[13]

A more fundamental critique involved the way in which the perspective defined "culture." Critics argued that cultures, both natural and organizational, are composed of active, thinking human beings who may interpret and respond to management's messages in completely unanticipated ways. Some employees may even interpret as offensive and manipulative management's attempts to mold beliefs, instill values, and manipulate perceptions and emotions (regardless of how management interprets them). In other cases they may resist even positive changes in their organization's culture, and generally make "culture management" or "planned cultural change" much more difficult than the model suggests. Drawing on research conducted by academics in sociology departments from the early 1950s on, these critics proposed a very different conception of *organizational* cultures (as distinct from *corporate* cultures) and of the role that leaders and leadership plays in them. Both leaders and followers are competent, self-interested, organizational actors who work together to create, sustain, and transform organizations. Organizations do not *have* cultures that can be easily manipulated by leaders, as is suggested in the corporate culture perspective. They *are* cultures – complex, ever-changing collectives that are defined, stabilized, and sometimes transformed by the *mutual* actions of knowledgeable people – leaders *and* followers (see Giddens, 1984; Smircich and Calas, 1987; Conrad and Haynes, 2001).

This *organizational* culture perspective offered a fundamental departure from mainstream models of leadership. Followers were depicted as competent actors, whose decisions to ignore and/or resist "leaders" were a rational response to complicated situations, not the destructive, irrational rantings of flawed but fixable individuals. Organizational success depended on the actions of all employees, not just on corporate saviors. While leader behaviors can have a positive impact on organizations, the unintended and unanticipated consequences of those actions often are more important than the intended ones. It is probably not a surprise that this perspective was less attractive to managers than the corporate culture perspective (Barley, Meyer, and Gash, 1988). As a result, it did not take long for the corporate culture perspective to dominate managerial attitudes, management training, airport bookstores, and the scholarship produced within US business schools. But the organizational culture perspective continued to occupy an important place in the thinking of scholars in US departments of sociology and communication and in European business schools. Eventually it led to the development of the resistance-oriented models of leadership that I will discuss at the end of this chapter. Followers of the corporate culture perspective looked elsewhere for legitimation.

Sustaining the Cult of Leadership

Like all mythical systems, managerialism and mainstream leadership theory can remain dominant only if they are supported by an ongoing rhetoric. From their inception, both have relied on the presumption that leaders possess knowledge that is beyond the ken of mortal followers. Consequently, the creation and dissemination of what appears to be new knowledge is central to maintaining managerial dominance. By the mid-1980s, an entire industry had developed to meet this demand for new ideas.

Fads, Fashions, and Gurus

Managerial fads and fashions, developed and propagated by management "gurus," are diffused through their target population in predictable ways. A new wisdom is introduced and, through effective marketing usually based on testimonials, it is adopted by more and more managers and organizations, until a saturation point is reached. Managers "buy into" the rhetoric articulated by the guru, develop their own versions of it, and then selectively monitor the results of implementing the fad, so that they produce data that can be used to legitimize their adoption of it. Their self-fulfilling interpretations become the basis of their own overly optimistic rhetoric, which allows them to respond to pressures from doubters inside their organizations.

Eventually, promised dividends fail to materialize and managers begin to face increasing dissent within their organizations and from outside stakeholders, who pressure them to adopt the newest "best thing" that "everyone else is using" (Fombrun, 1987; Mitroff and Mohrman, 1987; Abrahamson, 1991). A new fad has become fashionable, and the cycle begins anew. The T-groups of the 1960s were supplanted by matrix management, which gave way to MBWA (Management by Walking Around) and corporate culture, which were replaced by quality circles, Theory Z, TQM (total quality management), one-minute managing, BPR (Business Process Re-engineering), learning organizations, the habits of successful people, New Age spiritualism, servant leadership, The 5 Practices of Exemplary Leaders, and so on. Fads and fashions are characterized by high rates of failure, and implementing them often does more harm than good to the organizations in which they are adopted. They largely re-invent the wheel, but package it in new terminology; old wine in new wineskins, so to speak (Kimberly, 1981; Eccles and Nohria, 1992; Barker, 1993; Grint, 1994; Guest, 1996; Jackson, 1996; Clark and Salaman, 1996, 1998; Zbaracki, 1998; Nadesan, 1999). They are sustained by a carefully crafted rhetoric.

The earliest explanations of the guru phenomenon argued that managers face increasingly uncertain, unpredictable, and threatening environments, and gurus provide simplistic solutions that make them feel secure. In addition, gurus make themselves indispensable by way of "pandering to the egos of corporate executives by equipping them with the secret formulas for achieving saviorhood" (Barker, 1997, 348; see also Alvesson, 1990). Later researchers agreed with this overall assessment, but pointed out that it underestimated managers' very real needs to legitimize themselves, both to themselves and to others. A guru is a shaman, a witch doctor, or a sorcerer, who is summoned by managers partly "for the instrumental effect of his medicine but also for the cathartic satisfaction of emotional pressures, to reassure the manager that he [*sic*] is working in a proper manner" (Cleverly, 1971, 69). Gurus "tell managers why they are important, why they matter, and why their skills are critical" (Clark and Salaman, 1998, 153).[14]

Successful gurus are consummate performers whose rhetoric

is powerful because it articulates dominant cultural myths. This explains why gurus have been especially successful in the US. Their rhetoric is grounded in the traditonal "American values" of optimism, simplicity, focus on a dream, an idealized sense of possibility, and, most importantly, individualism, all of which are threatened by a foreign enemy (Japan during the 1980s; "socialism" since the late 1990s). Moreover, gurus' sagas enact the familiar forms of Western literature and of Hollywood – they present senior managers as heroes/protagonists fighting against the forces of doubt or resistance – these usually being embodied by middle-managers, who play the role of scapegoat. This good-versus-evil mythology focuses attention on a lone, messianic hero, who offers hope that in the future everything will work out for the best and that members of the organization "will be delivered from their anxieties, fears, and struggles" (Gemmill and Oakley, 1992, 119; see also Guest, 1996; Grint, 1994). In the process, a guru focuses attention away from complicated social and economic structures and organizational systems. Like the Jeremiads of Protestant evangelists, their rhetoric begins with "hell-fire-and-brimstone" appeals that create a pervasive fear that continuing the status quo will inevitably lead to ruin (Bercovitch, 1978; Bormann, 2001). However, salvation is possible if members of the organization confess to their failures and convert to the guru's theology. After wandering in the wilderness for a time, the organization and its members will arrive in a well-earned land of milk and honey. Michael Hammer, primary guru for the re-engineering fad of the 1990s, once explained that "you must play on the two basic emotions, fear and greed" (Hammer, 1990, 105) and promise people personal redemption if they quickly convert, make a public declaration of their new-found faith, and pursue its tenets with evangelical vigor. Implementing the guru's magic, which cannot be done properly without continued guidance by the guru or his carefully selected apostles, serves as a consummation of the conversion process.[15] The fads are appealing, and they are sustained over time even without evidence of their positive effects – for a simple reason: gurus sell myths, not data.

Summary: The Effects of Leadership Rhetoric

In spite of multiple studies, carried over decades, which show a weak or nonsignificant link between "leadership" and organizational outcomes, there is no question about the effectiveness of rhetoric supporting the leadership *mythos*. Leaders, followers, and society as a whole largely believe traditional leadership myths and act in accordance with them. For example, Mats Alvesson and Stefan Sveningsson (2003a, 2003b) interviewed a number of supervisors and subordinates in European firms. When they asked supervisors to define the term "leadership," they easily reproduced the rhetoric of mainstream leadership theory. But, when they asked managers to describe the behaviors they engaged in while "leading," the interviewees found it very difficult to do so. When pressed, they mentioned routine activities that would fit the mainstream definition of "management" better than modern definitions of "leadership," or were so mundane that they are rarely even mentioned in leadership rhetoric – listening to followers, informally chatting with them, and being cheerful while around them. The researchers concluded that, when leaders did talk about leadership, their discourse did more to promote their own significance and to support their own egos than it did to describe what they actually did at work.

When the researchers asked *followers* about leadership, people in these groups mentioned the same mundane activities, but they did so in a way that conferred the activities in question symbolic importance:

> The expectation that leaders do special, significant things matters, turning everyday activities into something remarkable. This expectation, based on images of the leader and leadership, gains prominence in the interpretation of everyday acts, and has a greater impact than what managers actually do. Everyday activities such as listening and talking informally become special when exercised by a manager-"leader" but remain everyday and trivial when performed by someone else. (Alvesson and Sveningsson, 2003c, 1452)[16]

Just as a jersey once touched by David Beckham or a T-shirt worn by this week's pre-teen hearthrob no longer are *just* articles of clothing, a smile or an approving comment from a "leader" is more than communication. Like all other cultural myths, the leadership *mythos* provides a sense of security, stability, and predictability, regardless of the empirical effects of "leaders." In the process of "romanticizing" leadership, the leader's influence and power are enhanced (Collinson, 2005).[17]

Resisting the Leadership Mythos

A decade after publishing *The art of framing*, Gail Fairhurst revisited leadership theory and research and observed that framing – and, by extension, every rhetorical strategy or "symbolic resource" described in mainstream leadership research and theory – often functioned to maintain power imbalances in organizations. But it does not *have* to do so. "Followers" could master the skills typically attributed to leaders and use them to pursue their own goals, as well as the goals of their organizations (Fairhurst, 2005, 181). On the surface, this may seem like a minor definitional change, but it has two important implications. First, it focuses attention away from "leaders" and toward "leadership." Followers are no longer depicted as objects, or as flawed but repairable leaders doing what they are told. Instead they are cast as knowledgeable actors involved in complex relationships with other members of their organizations, including the "leaders." Second, by redefining followers as competent individuals, this change revives the possibility of democratic forms of organizing.

Fairhurst's comments mirrored a fundamental shift in the social sciences, which took place during the last half of the twentieth century. Scholars moved away from viewing human behavior as determined by situational factors or personal characteristics to depicting humans as "agents," that is, as active beings who are well aware of the social and organizational structures and rules that constrain their actions, and of the resources they can draw upon to pursue their own goals and interests. Agents differ in their access to, and ability to use, these resources – power is not equally distributed across a population. But all forms of influence, including leadership, are products of ongoing interpersonal interactions – they emerge from constant negotiations among proactive, self-aware, and goal-oriented agents. Even in non-democratic organizations leaders depend on followers to some degree, while followers retain a degree of autonomy and discretion as they maneuver through their organizational lives using a wide repertoire of strategies.[18] In the process, they engage in leadership *behaviors* that contribute significantly to the success or failure of their organizations. Sometimes they even compensate for bad decisions or counterproductive actions executed by people occupying *leadership positions.* These new perspectives also recognized that traditional, pejorative views of resistance – which depict it as perverse and/or pathological behavior by flawed followers who need to be "fixed" – are themselves a rhetorical strategy, one that privileges the interests of supervisors, and that they silence meaningful, principled dissent by other members of organizations (Hardy and Clegg, 1999; Hardy, Palmer, and Phillips, 2000; Piderit, 2000; Symon, 2005).

Speaking Resistance to Power

Traditionally, the term "resistance" has been used to describe blatant, open, sometimes violent confrontations between labor and management – Luddites sabotaging UK, factories during the early 1800s, the Bolshevik Revolution of 1917, or the sometimes violent strikes that took place in the United States during the early 1900s, pitting (usually immigrant) workers against vastly better armed Pinkerton agents, or against the military. Although general strikes still occur, albeit with much lower levels of violence, they have become quite rare in the developed economies. Even peaceful, legal strikes have virtually disappeared in the US since President Reagan used military personnel to break the PATCO (air traffic controllers' union) strike during the early 1980s. Two years later the Phelps Dodge corporation used permanent replacement workers to break a strike at the Morenci open-pit copper mine in Arizona, which initiated a systematic use of the strategy by managers in unionized US firms. A series of court decisions and legislative acts quickly followed, which made it more difficult for workers to unionize and allowed corporations more easily to hire permanent replacements for striking workers (Shostak and Skocik, 1986; Geoghegan, 1992; Rosenblum, 1995).

As a result of these changes, overt resistance in US organizations is usually restricted to local issues and relies on verbal strategies more than on overt confrontation. For example, Prasad and Prasad's study of the introduction of computer technology into a health care organization outlined a number of direct challenges raised by workers to managerial actions and rhetoric (Prasad and Prasad, 2000).[19] Workers interrupted scripted training sessions by asking relevant questions that management had tried to ignore – about the adverse health effects of the new technology (miscarriages or carpal tunnel syndrome), for example – and by asking other questions that revealed management's ignorance of how the system worked or of what effects it might have. Other workers circulated newspaper and magazine articles about problems with the new technology. Others simply refused to use it, relying instead on their old "paper and pencil" technology, or delayed switching over as long as possible. As a group, they carefully documented problems and flaws in the new system and repeatedly reported them to management. In stark contrast to the workers that Alvesson and Sveningsson studied, who romanticized leaders and mundane leader behavior, these workers took responsibility for their seemingly mundane actions and redefined them as brave, oppositional, or resistant. For example, one worker, Georgia, told the researchers: "I'm too old to care about [the effects the technology might have on] miscarriages and pregnancies. But I think it's important that we show them [*sc.* managers] that we are not stupid." In the process of resisting they undermined the rhetorical idea that managers have superior expertise and followers are docile automata.

Micro-Resistance as a Rhetoric of Maneuver

In many organizations, managerial control is so complete that overt resistance is too difficult and risky. As a result, "resistance" takes much more subtle forms and is much more difficult to recognize and understand (Fleming and Spicer, 2003; Cloud, 2005). Through everyday practices of "micro-resistance" workers assert their independence from, or defiance of, their leaders – mechanics who hide under trucks to take a quick nap, clerical employees who do a "little bit" of surfing the web on company time, anyone who takes a "few" office supplies home with them, flight attendants who sometimes "accidentally" spill hot coffee in the laps of especially obnoxious travelers, even though their managers strictly enforce a "customer is always right" policy, and so on. Even seemingly harmless, everyday behaviors *may* be resistant – gossiping, engaging in horseplay, withdrawing/disengaging from one's work and doing just enough to "get by," or even dressing in ways that *barely* violate dress codes (Graham, 1993; Thompson, 1983; Gottfried, 1994).

Employees who are especially creative even disguise resistance as compliance. For example, Czech popular culture celebrates the "good soldier Svejk," an employee who *appears* to bumble through his duties, while also quietly undermining bureaucratic structures and supervisory dominance. One of Svejk's strategies is "flanneling," that is, engaging in exaggerated displays of deference and enthusiasm. It is obvious to everyone that Svejk is being intentionally (and strategically) obsequious, but his behavior places his supervisors in a difficult position, because they cannot legitimately punish him for being enthusiastically obedient. The *Dilbert* comic strip, which is popular in the US, includes a number of characters who engage in some form of covert resistance – Wally, who works very hard to avoid doing any (approved) work, and in the process makes himself invisible to such an extent that the boss never notices, much less reprimands, him; the pointy-headed boss's secretary, who exploits her boss's stupidity even to the extent of having him sign his own dismissal order; and so on (Fleming and Sewell, 2002). Of course, many instances of gossip, inappropriate dress, and the like do not constitute intentional resistance. People gossip about lots of things and for lots of reasons, and some dress inappropriately outside of work as well as at work. But this ambiguity makes it difficult for managers to deal with covert, everyday resistance. If they confront the worker, she or he can deny any intent to resist; if they do not confront him or her, the behavior may spiral. Routine acts of resistance "are the stubborn bedrock upon which other forms of resistance may grow" (Scott, 1995, 273).

In other cases workers simply hide resistance from management's view. For example a flight attendant, Terry, was reprimanded for wearing her Santa earrings on flights during the holidays, and was told never to wear them again. To get around the policy, she took them off when management was around and put them on when she stepped on a plane. Flight attendants learn to fulfill company requirements that women wear makeup by doing so only during their annual performance reviews. On cruise liners and in upscale resorts – in galleys, back rooms, and the tiny employee staterooms on cruise ships – anywhere that is safely out of the hearing of guests and managers, employees talk about anything and everything, including obnoxious or stupid customers and overbearing or incompetent supervisors. With the advent of new electronic technologies, which allow managers to spy on workers in almost any locale, backstage resistance has become more difficult, but maneuvering still occurs, as workers engage in ongoing struggles to find and/or create spaces and times where/when resistance can occur.[20]

When micro-resistance is discovered, it often generates complex negotiations between leaders and followers about the degree and types of resistance that will be allowed. Usually these negotiations are unplanned and spontaneous – people "push the envelope" until they "cross the line" and are reprimanded. Employees learn from the experience as the story is circulated through informal communication networks. In fact, one of the biggest challenges that newcomers to an organization face is learning where the lines between acceptable and unacceptable dissent and resistance are drawn. Learning the ropes of resistance is difficult, in part because the lines and rules are constantly being negotiated and re-negotiated, in part because they are different for some employees from what they are for others, and in part because resistance is often disguised through humor or other symbolic forms.[21] In fact, one of the most important informal tasks played by the "oldtimers" in organizations is to teach newcomers how to maneuver around these ever-changing resistance rules and to teach new supervisors when to confront and when to play the game (van Maanen and Schein, 1979; Louis, 1980).

Resistance as a Corrective for Flawed Leadership

Mainstream views of leadership depict resistance as an evil that must be eliminated or channeled in appropriate directions by positional leaders, lest it damage the organization. Contemporary leadership researchers recognize what "real people" have known for a very long time: so-called resisters are often motivated by a genuine concern for their organizations and its members, and their acts of resistance are courageous attempts to compensate for weaknesses in the design and operation of their organizations. For example, D. K. Kondo's (1990) study of workers in a Japanese factory found that they actively criticized management, usually in "backstages," and openly questioned managerial rhetoric that depicted the organization as a "family." But they also took pride in being part of the organization and worked hard to help it succeed. Pro-organization motives are often present even when resistance involves disobeying orders from leaders (see also Kelley, 1992; Chaleff, 2003; Raelin, 2003; Kelley, 2004). If an employee loves her or his job and organization but fears that some of her or his supervisors' or colleagues' actions threaten the long-term survival of the firm, she or he may choose to accept the risks of speaking out. For example, two of Enron's employees spoke out against the behaviors of the organization's leadership and of their peers, who participated in the complex pattern of fraudulent behaviors that led to the organization's demise. Unfortunately, neither of them succeeded in stopping what was going on in their organization. Sherron Watkins kept her job and was vindicated somewhat when she later was named one of *Time Magazine*'s "persons of the year" for her efforts. Jeff Baxter lost his job and subsequently committed suicide, because he felt that he had not done enough to stop the unethical actions of his supervisors and to save *his* organization. In some cases dissenters whose legitimate concerns are ignored by their supervisors take the even greater risk of "blowing the whistle" to regulators or to the media, virtually guaranteeing that they will be fired and/or punished by the organization they are trying to save.[22] In short, resistance emerges from complicated, multi-faceted motives, and has equally complicated effects, both for the resisters and for their organizations.

Loril Gossett and Julian Kilker (2006) provided an excellent example of the complexities of dissent in their analysis of an oppositional website, radioshacksucks.org (see also Baber and Khondker, 2002). What started out as a website for consumers upset with the products or services provided by the corporation eventually became a sounding board for anyone who desired changes in the organization – consumers, employees, and former employees who had been "promoted to customers" – to use the vocabulary of the website. Half of the comments posted on the website involved people sharing job-related information or offering work-related complaints, information that managers should have provided to employees through formal channels. Other postings told customers how to troubleshoot problems with Radio Shack products, information that should have been provided by the company's customer service department. Other postings offered insightful suggestions for improving operations or the corporate image. Ironically, making this information available provided a valuable service for the organization (for a similar case study, see Orr, 1996).

Many postings constituted resistance in a more traditional sense of the term. For example some postings warned employees not to dissent in public lest they be disciplined, told them to be careful about what they said in their postings because management was monitoring the site, and suggested covert ways to resist – filing change-of-address forms for stores with the US Postal Service, using remote control cars to set off a store's motion detectors after hours, which forced the store manager to return every time the alarm was triggered, and so on. They also advised workers to not believe promises about future job prospects within the organization, and provided advice and contacts needed in order to find employment elsewhere. Some reported illegal activities by management, for example manipulating job categories in order to avoid paying workers for overtime; and some provided contact information for law firms preparing class action suits. Of course, Radio Shack's management could have used the website as a virtual suggestion box and adopted reasonable suggestions about improving organizational operations. Intead, they entered into a series of legal actions designed to shut the site down, and eventually obtained an injunction against its operations. According to the leadership *mythos*, all resistance is bad because it challenges the assumed divinity of leaders, and therefore it must be suppressed. Leaders are trapped in the ideology just as much as followers are (Deetz, 1995).

Resistance Leadership

To this point I have discussed two forms of resistance: overt resistance by groups of individuals, often aided by ties to other institutions (a labor union or political party, for example), and subtle or covert resistance by individuals acting on their own, albeit often with other employees as collaborators or observers/audiences. What I have not discussed is the question of how resistance by one or more individuals is transformed into collective action. Somewhat ironically, the answer involves *leadership* – defined as an activity, not as the mere occupation of a formal position. Resistance leadership begins with communication among workers, often about events in which positional leaders exploit workers in ways that "insult and slight their human dignity" and/ or create strong feelings of injustice. Individual workers respond to these affronts with rhetoric that undermines the key source of the supervisors' domination – their presumed superior expertise. Resisters point out contradictions within organizational missions, ideologies, or values, or they focus attention on contradictions between what leadership rhetoric *says* the organization stands for and what its leaders *do* in everyday actions. Doing so harnesses strong, widely experienced emotions and channels them toward collective action. But shared emotions will not galvanize workers into collectives unless resistance leaders can persuasively make a case that resisting is rational. Since workers are accustomed to social and organizational rhetoric claiming that resistance is never rational – wisdom and power *always* favor docile compliance – resistance leaders face a daunting rhetorical challenge. It can only be overcome by finding ways to frame ongoing organizational practices as irrational. The radioshacksucks contributors did this when they described organizational policies and procedures that made no sense, or managerial actions that violated sensible policies. Often couched in humor, their rhetoric redefined resistance as the rational response to managerial irrationality.

A more complete example was provided by Laurie Graham's (1995) study of domination and resistance at an Indiana Subaru-Isuzu automobile plant. Her account includes an episode that started when a line supervisor (euphemistically called a "team leader" in the Japanese management strategy used in the plant) ordered his subordinates to work overtime at the end of their shift. Two of the workers could not do so. According to existing company rules, the workers could not be required to stay because the overtime had not been announced on the previous day. The supervisor made the conflict escalate by telling them that, if they did not stay, human resources would give them an unexcused absence (no one really knew how important this was). A third member refused to stay. The production manager was called in, and he threatened to discipline the workers. The women stood their ground, and, though some of her team mates were in tears, the woman who was beginning to emerge as the resistance leader advised the other workers to view management's actions as intimidation that had to be resisted, lest management get by with violating established worker protections in the future. In this case, she argued, resistance was both rational and absolutely necessary. Another manager intervened and told her that her job was in jeopardy, but he soon backed down once it was clear that so many workers were planning to leave that the assembly line would not be able to keep operating.

Heather Zoller (2005), and Zoller writing with Gail Fairhurst (2007), explain that this case study illustrates resistance leadership in two ways. First, it clearly shows that followers can engage in "leadership" behavior. By taking a principled stand against multiple efforts to silence her and by articulating a strong case for resistance that was legitimate given existing rules and regulations, a courageous worker–follower found common ground with other workers and by doing so was able to persuade them to act as a group. She drew upon the resources that were available to her and developed a persuasive rhetoric – doing exactly what is recommended in "transformational" or "charismatic" theories of leadership. Some of these resources were located in the taken-for-granted assumptions of US culture – definitions of heroism, for example – others in the formal rules and routines that are a key element of Japanese management, and others still in the communication networks, common experiences, and mutual support that the workers offered one another. Second, this case shows that leadership is a widely distributed capacity and that, in real organizational situations, it moves from person to person. When the overtime episode was over, the worker–leader returned to her previous status as a regular worker. In subsequent episodes of resistance other workers took on the role of leader. The plant continued to experience conflict between management and labor as supervisors attempted to exert power beyond what was sanctioned by formal contracts, and workers continued to resist those efforts. Through ongoing informal interactions, the two groups negotiated a leader–follower relationship that was fundamentally different from the one envisioned in mainstream leadership theory and research.[23]

Recovering the Potential for Democracy

In an important way, the contrast between mainstream theories of leadership and resistance leadership takes us back to the key contrast outlined at the beginning of this book – between the rhetoric used by elites to create a stable society based on their purportedly superior knowledge and the rhetoric used by citizens to maneuver through daily life in a somewhat democratic society. Thomas Cronin summarizes the distinction succinctly:

> In many respects leadership – the process whereby an individual or a few select individuals are in a position to provide the vision and make things happen – is at odds with much of what is implicit, if not explicit, in notions of democracy. These ["leadership" and democracy] have been warring concepts, just as freedom and authority have long been fierce antagonists. (Cronin, 1998, 304)

Leadership, as defined in mainstream academic theory and in everyday rhetoric, focuses on suppressing dissent or channeling it into approved forms and directions. From that perspective, leaders succeed when they take away followers' capacities to pursue their own goals and interests at work, or when they persuade them to sacrifice their own goals and pursue those of their leaders/ organizations. Values of *individual* rights, freedom of expression, and political representation are sacrificed to the promise of social/ organizational stability and economic growth.

In contrast, resistance leadership focuses on the expertise and potential contributions of each worker, and depicts dissent as a necessary element of effective organizational operations. It sacrifices the stability and predictability of autocracy for the flexibility, adaptability, and "messiness" of democracy. Cronin continues:

> More than any other form of government, democracy requires a peculiar blend of faith in the people and skepticism of them. It requires a faith concerning the common human enterprise; a belief that if the people are informed and caring, they can be trusted with their own self-government; and an optimism that when things begin to go wrong, the people can be relied on to set them right. Plainly, however, a robust, healthy skepticism is needed as well. Democracy requires us to question our leaders and never to trust any group with too much power. Although we prize majority rule, we have to be skeptical

enough to ask whether a majority is always right. (Cronin, 1998, 306–307)[24]

But it is this "messiness" that allows human beings to realize their "natural liberty," to use Adam Smith's key phrase. Capitalism provides an opportunity for humans to escape the mutual dependency relationships of feudalism and hierarchical religion, so as to develop their "natural" attributes in the economic realm. Democracy allows us to do the same in the political realm. Moreover, democracy raises a barrier to the revival of feudalism. So it is not especially surprising that the political and economic elites who celebrated Smith's rationale for capitalism quickly abandoned his belief that participatory democracy was a necessary companion. It was much more consistent with their interests to reduce the complex social analysis presented in *The wealth of nations* and in *The theory of moral sentiments* to a simplistic call for free markets/trade, much as it was in the interest of wealthy members of the Athenian elite, like Plato, to depict the complex worldview of the sophists as a handful of manipulative techniques (or "cookery"; see Salter, 1992; Cropsey, 2001; Rothschild, 2001; Perelman, 2006). Two millennia after Plato, we still are dealing with key issues of the classical era, both in our societies and in our organizations.

The concept of resistance leadership takes us back to Chapter 1 in a second sense. It is through rhetoric that the taken-for-granted assumptions of a society are created, articulated, reproduced, and in some cases transformed; and it is through rhetoric that those assumptions are applied to concrete, everyday problems. Organizational rhetors have at their disposal a complex set of taken-for-granted assumptions – from the naturalized and normalized attributes of the American system to the organizational imperative and the tenets of free-market fundamentalism, to managerialist models of leadership and followership. But these cultural assumptions are also available to resisters in any society or organization.

Case Study: Myths, Markets, and Executive Compensation

On January 22, 2010, President Barak Obama once again expressed his disdain for the excessive bonuses being granted to the executives of the bailed-out banks, whose excessive risk-taking had plunged the nation and much of the developed world into the second-worst recession in history. But only a fortnight later he announced that he did not begrudge multi-million bonuses granted to the CEOs of J. P. Morgan Chase and Goldman Sachs, two of the largest players in the financial industry collapse: "I know both those guys; they are very savvy businessmen. I, like most of the American people, don't begrudge people success or wealth. This is part of the free-market system." Within hours, White House spokespersons were scrambling to "clear up some confusion" about the President's remarks. It is easy to attribute the "flip-flop" to the difficulties faced by a centrist president dealing with an emotionally charged issue (a positive interpretation), or to take it as evidence that the "change president" was just another beltway politician stoking populist sentiment on the one hand while accepting the cash and blessings of the Wall Street establishment on the other (a negative interpretation; Calmes, 2010; Cooper, 2010; Kuhnhenn, 2010a, 2010b, 2010c).

It is more informative to view the president's ambivalence as a reflection of the ambivalence of US political–economic culture. On the one hand, we wish – perhaps we need – to believe that rewards, even massive ones, are earned and deserved. There is a bit of Puritanism/Calvinism left in all of us, and within that religious fundamentalism the only viable explanation of inequality is that the elect have curried God's favor in some way, and those who suffer have not. On the other, like Adam Smith, we "know" that greed is a powerful motivator that sometimes must be restrained, hopefully through the invisible hand of market processes or community values and informal pressures. When faced with compelling evidence that threatens those core assumptions – and the 2008–2009 financial collapse and subsequent government bailouts have provided that kind of evidence – our faith is shaken. The easy explanation, consistent with America's individualist values, is that such crises result from the excesses of a few "bad apples," positional leaders who have substituted "situational" values – which represent doing whatever the situation will allow, no matter the wider interests of organizations and communities – for "sustainable values" – which represent the commitment to acting in ways that promise to "sustain – my employees, my customers, my suppliers, my environment, my country and my future generations" (Krugman, 2010a, n.p.). Although the contrast may be apt, defining the problem as one of individual weakness distracts attention away from the structures that allow, and may even encourage, excess (Friedman, 2010).[25] There is something far more insidious afoot.

As I explained earlier in this chapter, two conclusions are consistently supported by the available empirical evidence: US organizations reward their upper management much more handsomely than those in other countries do, and there is only a weak and indirect link between corporate performance and executive compensation. Both "facts of life" are based on a set of taken-for-granted *assumptions* – what Rakesh Kuhrana (2002) has called "a distinctively American cult of the CEO" – and on the creation of a particular *structure*, which lacks the controls that are necessary for free markets to work properly. The assumptions are grounded in the rhetoric of leadership described earlier in this chapter.

The structure of modern executive compensation systems emerged piecemeal over time. At one time, executives were chosen on the basis of their experience in a particular firm and of their performance in the rather mundane tasks of running their organizations. Promotion from within was the norm, and executive compensation was based on comparisons with the wages and salaries of the company's workers. But during the 1980s a number of changes took place. The insider-trading scandals of the mid-1980s made CEO compensation a volatile political issue, and policymakers attributed both the scandal and the escalating gap between executive and worker pay to the secrecy with which compensation was determined. Laws were passed that required corporations to be more open about executive pay. Ironically, requiring organizations to be more open allowed executives to use the incomes of other CEOs as the appropriate standard for setting their own compensation, instead of the pay of their own workers.

At the same time, charismatic/transformational models of leadership became the rage. The view of CEOs as visionary secular saviors, evangelists, role models, and coaches was taught in business schools and sanctified by the business press and by news media alike. Hiring from within became *passé* and having a lifetime of loyal experience within a firm was deemed irrelevant or worse. Selecting a CEO became a public drama, one designed to excite the interest and support of three key external stakeholders: stockholders, especially those from pension funds and mutual funds, financial analysts whose recommendations drive stock prices, and the media. Personality, image, and the "ability to command attention from the media and stock market analysts in a way that will establish credibility for the firm and inspire confidence in both investors and others" became much more important than "firm-and-industry-specific knowledge and experience" (Kuhrana, 2002, 78, 79; see also Chen and Meindl, 1991; Salancik and Meindl, 1984; Meindl, Ehrlich, and Dukerich, 1985).

In this highly public ritual, a search committee that failed to land its "No. 1 candidate" would reduce the organization's credibility. Its stock price would fall, and the eventual hire would be saddled with the mantle of being second-best. Aided by corporate "headhunters" whose own compensation depends on getting as much money as possible for their clients, the preferred candidate is in an enviable negotiating position. Extracting concessions on initial compensation, separating rewards from firm performance, and arranging for lucrative "golden parachutes" to be awarded *when* the CEO fails became legitimate demands. Negotiations during hiring rituals are only the first act of a multiple-act play, but they establish the plot lines for subsequent acts and prepare for the final curtain. In the logic of the play, "obscene" compensation packages are transformed from representing the tangible costs of doing business to being a sort of symbolic evidence that the organization has hired the best possible leader.

Finally, differences in the information available to decision-makers also support a preference for outside candidates, with predictable results. Boards of Directors have a great deal of very specific information available about the strengths *and weaknesses* of internal candidates – every detail of their records is known. But Boards can only speculate about the veracity of the limited and carefully massaged information available about outsiders. Kuhrana continues with an example:

> [H–P directors hired Carli Fiorina as CEO because they] associated Fiorina with the strong performance of Lucent Technologies, her previous firm. Lucent's stock had indeed performed extraordinarily well since the company had been spun off from AT&T. Yet, while the H–P directors had attributed Lucent's success to its executives, much of this "success," it was later revealed, was due to creative accounting and liberal financing of sales to customers. Another relevant factor that these H–P directors seemed to ignore was that investors had bid up almost every technology-related stock in 1999. (Kuhrana, 2002, 109; see also Norris, 2010)

In theory, boards can supplement the information they have available by hiring independent outside consultants. But executive search-services are paid to get jobs for their clients, not to contribute to the rationality of search processes or to the long-term growth of organizations. Furthermore, their degree of "independence" is often questionable. A search firm usually has other contracts with their client organizations, and

> a long and lucrative relationship with the company, maintained at the behest of the executives whose pay it recommends. This is the secretive, prosperous and often conflicted world of compensation consultants, who are charged with helping corporate boards determine executive pay that is appropriate and fair, and who are often cited as the unbiased advisers whenever shareholders criticize a company's pay as excessive. (Morgenson, 2006)

It should not be surprising that the gap between executive compensation and firm performance seems to be greatest at firms that use these not-quite-independent outside consultants. In theory, the checks and balances of the labor market will eventually lead to more rational compensation packages – that is the assumption underlying the second half of President Obama's ambivalence. But the CEO labor market is nothing like the self-correcting markets of free-market theory. Unlike those open markets, which involve a very large number of transactions that occur independently of one another, the CEO market is closed. The attributes that selection committees look for, which largely duplicate those of committee members themselves, mean that there are very few people who are seriously considered. Since Boards of Directors are largely composed of executives at other companies, the applicant pool is further reduced, so as to include only members of those established communication networks. As a result, in most cases the finalists in a CEO search are known to the selection committee long before searches begin. When Boards decide on compensation packages, they do so by comparing proposals to their own compensation, knowing that eventually they will be able to point to the packages they approve in order to legitimize their own requests for increased compensation.

Ironically, the theatrics of executive succession and compensation seem to work, at least in the short term. Yan Zhang and Nandini Rajogapalan's research found that hiring an outside CEO does lead to positive short-term results, at least in terms of organizational image and stock value. Kuhrana explains:

> for example, when computer maker Compaq announced in July 2000 that an insider, Michael Capellas, would become CEO, its stock price immediately dropped 4 percent. By contrast, computer maker Hewlett-Packard's shares jumped 2 percent when it was announced in July 1999 that an outsider, Carly Fiorina, would become the next CEO. (2002, 65–66)

The new CEO placates outside audiences by cutting costs (which usually means cutting jobs) and by divesting under-performing parts of the firm. New CEOs selected from the inside also make major changes, but they are armed with experience in the firm and expertise in the industry. Consequently, "after three years, bold strategic changes under the leadership of an inside CEO are more beneficial to company performance than changes under the leadership of an outside CEO" (Zhang, 2010). But, for the media and many investors, three years is an eternity and long-term growth is both boring and old-fashioned.

Overall, Kuhrana concludes: "today's cult of the charismatic CEO and the closed succession process that perpetuates it are more than just historical curiosities. They are developments that threaten serious damage both to corporations themselves and to the society that they increasingly dominate" (2002, 187).[26] Ideas/rhetoric and structures combine to obscure processes that increasingly separate pay from performance and rewards from merit. And they do so to such an extent that even presidents can be fooled.

Discussion Questions

1 Compare all of the numbers you found during the Weekend Fun exercise. How have stockholders fared under your company's current leadership? How does this number compare to the overall stock market, or to stocks in that sector of the economy? How does this number compare to CEO compensation in comparable firms? To jobs created or lost? Should stockholders be happy with the performance of their CEO? With his/her compensation? Why or why not?

2 How difficult was it to find the information that you needed in order to answer these questions? What does your experience suggest about the possibility of investors making rational decisions about which stocks to buy? About rational employees' decisions concerning which organizations to join?

4

Organizational Rhetoric and Public Policymaking

Governments create corporations, much like Dr. Frankenstein created his monster, yet, once they exist, corporations, like the monster, threaten to overpower their creators. [...] That is, after all, what many business leaders want: replacement of government regulation of corporations with market forces. [...] In this scenario, corporations get all the coercive power and resources of the state, while citizens are left with nongovernmental organizations and the market's invisible hand – socialism for the rich and capitalism for the poor.

Bakan (2004, 149, 151)

Core Concepts

- Organizational rhetors both respond to rhetorical situations and create them through the strategic management of legislation, litigation, policy implementation, and regulation.
- Policymaking inherently involves conflict, competition, and compromise. Elites, including organizations, prefer to have public policies made in private. Non-elites, including citizen advocacy groups, prefer making policy in public.
- Lobbyists are important to organizations. Campaign contributions (monetary and otherwise) give them access to policymakers and help elect candidates who are sympathetic to their positions on key issues. The impact of lobbying on the enactment of new policies often is exaggerated, but lobbyists do block change efforts, especially those advocated by citizen groups.

- Lobbyists engage in public rhetoric only when they have lost control of the political process, or fear that this may happen.
- The extent to which the costs and benefits of a policy proposal are concentrated or diffused, and the degree to which different advocacy groups are organized, combine to influence policy-making processes in important ways.
- Sometimes problems, proposals, and politics combine to open policy windows. During ensuing debates organizational rhetors can draw upon a number of *topoi*, the most important of which were discussed in Chapters 2 and 3. The primary issues raised in policy debates involve *equity*, *efficiency*, *security*, and *liberty*.
- A crucial strategy for organizational rhetors is to close policy windows as quickly as possible, to re-privatize policymaking.

Traditionally, organizational rhetoric has been viewed as the art of *reacting* to rhetorical situations – rhetors draw upon the structural and symbolic resources that are available to them in order to respond to the challenges they face. In the preceding chapters I suggested that rhetors not only respond to situations, they proactively and strategically mold them. The advent of globalization has made it even more important for organizations to anticipate the challenges they will face, to plan for them, and to actively try to create favorable political and economic structures and cultural assumptions. Many organizations have approached this challenge by increasing their size (and thus their power) and the geographic scope of their activities. As a result, today many multinational corporations are wealthier and more powerful than all but a handful of nations. The only institutions with sufficient economic and political power to influence or constrain them are the governments of four or five nations, in particular the United States. Consequently, influencing public policymaking, especially in the world's largest economy, is a crucial strategy for multinational organizations (Cheney and Christensen, 2001; Stiglitz, 2002).[1]

In this chapter I will present a model of public policymaking that focuses on the concept of strategic maneuvering, which I introduced in Chapter 1. To this point I have used the concept primarily to describe the efforts of people who resist organizations or their managers. But organizations also can "maneuver" within policymaking processes in an effort to achieve their goals and to solidify their power. Public policymaking is an especially complex process, much more complex and much less rational than the models typically presented in high school civics classes. Policies emerge over lengthy periods of time, through multiple phases, and in multiple venues. Organizations can influence policymaking at each stage and in each venue, sometimes through private "backroom" discussions and/or deals with policymakers or government bureaucrats, sometimes through rhetoric that is in full view of the public, and usually through both.

Organizational Maneuver and the Strategic Selection of Venue

The first strategic choice that organizational rhetors must make involves the optimal audience(s) and venue(s) for their rhetoric. A corporation may begin a persuasive campaign in a state legislature. If it loses there, it can take the issue to the US Congress or to the state courts. If it fails there, it can appeal to the federal courts, and eventually to the US Supreme Court. In both state and federal courts, the company is able to "shop" for the most sympathetic courts and/or judges. For example, when Eastern Airlines, once the largest carrier in the free world, filed for bankruptcy, it did so in Delaware. Eastern had no operations in Delaware, it did not fly to any airports in Delaware, and it flew over the state only rarely. But Delaware had judges who, historically, had been very favorable to management's requests during bankruptcy proceedings. When lawsuits over the explosion and oil spill at British Petroleum's (BP's) Deepwater Horizon started, BP requested US District Court Judge Lynn Hughes *by name*, a request that was granted. Even if a corporation cannot select its preferred judge, it has wide latitude to have cases heard in courts that have favorable rules – for instance about the kinds of evidence that can and cannot be introduced. Therefore choosing the proper venue can largely determine the outcome of litigation before it begins. Of course, the organization's opponents can contest these strategic choices, but those challenges rarely succeed.

If court decisions do go against them, organizations can appeal them to a higher court or move to another state legislature and begin the process anew, over and over again. Over a twenty-year period, ExxonMobil repeatedly appealed state court findings that it owed aggrieved Alaska citizens millions of dollars in punitive damages as a result of the Exxon Valdez wreck. Eventually it found a sympathetic majority on the US Supreme Court, one that was willing to reduce the award from $2.5 billion to $287 million. As Chapter 1 pointed out, the "American system" was created by court decisions as much as by federal legislation, and by states competing against each other for corporate investments and taxes. Having a "federal" system means that policymaking is distributed across multiple levels of government – federal, state, and local – rhetors have an extensive number of venues in which they can construct or resist public policies (Banting and Corbett, 2002). In sum, organizational rhetors influence public policymaking by strategically selecting the optimal time and place to engage in rhetoric; they devise and implement the best strategies for managing the rhetorical situations they select and/or construct; and then they move on to other venues if they fail to get their way.

Organizational Rhetoric and the Policymaking Process

During the years following World War II, US political scientists focused a great deal of attention on public policymaking. Out of that research came a number of complex, multi-level views on the nature of social and organizational models of power, and a lively debate over the processes through which public policies are made (see Conrad, 1983; Conrad and Ryan, 1985; Clegg, 1989; Mumby, 2001; Conrad and Poole, 2005). Each of the models that were developed assumed that public policymaking in modern democracies is defined by conflict, competition, and compromise.

They focused on the role that interest groups, including formal organizations, play in policy formation and implementation.

Making "Public" Policy in Private

Elites, including corporate executives, draw on a reservoir of private information, interpersonal connections, and political skills to ensure that policymaking fosters their individual interests. Sometimes corporate interests coincide with broader public interests; sometimes they do not. Since citizens usually have learned to defer to people who occupy leadership positions (recall Chapter 3), elites usually are able to dominate the political decisions made in the communities in which they operate and to influence significantly the policies made by elected bodies (Vogel, 1989; Greider, 1992; Berg, 1994; Stone, 2001).

Even with these advantages, elites still prefer to construct public policy in private. Public debates are risky for them. They can lead to the creation of citizen advocacy groups, or to the formation of coalitions among low-power actors. The ensuing conflict may even persuade citizens to quit deferring to elites. For example, in 1987 Congress enacted an immigration reform bill including a provision that President Reagan kept calling "amnesty" for immigrants currently in the US illegally (much to the chagrin of the Republican sponsors of the bill, who were very careful to avoid using that emotionally loaded term). The bill *seemed* to include strict barriers designed to stop further illegal immigration. But, at the last minute, its primary enforcement mechanism – a provision requiring employers to use a secure system for checking job applicants' identities – was removed because business lobbyists persuaded Congress that the provision would be expensive to implement. During the next twenty years, illegal immigration increased five-fold, largely because a series of Republican and Democratic administrations chose not to implement consistently or rigorously the barriers included in the 1987 law. Fines and forfeitures levied on businesses fluctuated from $37,514 in 2003 to $15.8 million in 2005, to $234,000 in 2006, and to $31.4 million in 2007. Although a number of advocacy groups opposed strict enforcement, the most important lobbyists represented corporations whose managers wanted a supply of workers who were willing to work for low wages and were not likely to claim protection under state and federal labor laws because they feared being deported. In 2008 President George W. Bush upset this quiet, largely private arrangement by proposing reforms of US immigration law that were very much like the changes enacted in 1987. His proposal was met with a firestorm of protest by anti-reform citizens, who used the internet to organize and activate what turned out to be a very influential opposition. These anti-reform groups not only prevented the enactment of any new legislation, they forced Congress and the administration to produce at least a symbolic effort to enforce existing restrictions. Moreover, their success encouraged other groups, some of which eventually took the label of "Tea Parties," to challenge political elites over other issues (Preston, 2008; Carroll, 2009; Skerry, 2009; Windes-Munoz, 2009; Harrop, 2010). It was enough to make organizations who employ large numbers of illegal immigrants – and the politicians who represent them – long for the days of making immigration policy in private.

Making policy in public also forces elites to justify their preferences. Although they have a number of influential rhetorical strategies available, public rhetoric is inherently risky. It may fail to persuade key audiences, who actively interpret messages in terms of their own perceived interests, and it may magnify tensions within coalitions of elites. Historically, US immigration policy has pitted citizens who oppose immigration on economic and/or cultural grounds against a coalition made up of (usually) Republican owners/CEOs and (usually) Democratic politicians who want to attract the votes of newly naturalized citizens and their supporters. During time periods in which immigration policymaking remained private, the pro-immigration coalition was stable. But, when the debate went public, the resulting conflict revealed splits within the coalition, making it more vulnerable.

Fortunately for corporations, there are many means of keeping public policymaking private. The simplest strategy is to press for laws and political structures that allow them to hide information about their operations. This can be done directly, as when the petrochemical industry persuaded the US Environmental Protection Agency (EPA) to allow firms to release up to 5,000 pounds of toxic chemicals – DDT, PCBs, and so on – into the environment (a ten-fold increase over the previous limit) without disclosing their actions, or to allow the industry to use dispersants to fight oil spills without revealing their chemical composition; or as when the US financial industry persuaded the federal government to endow it with billions of dollars of "bailout" money without its having to reveal what it used the money for – and so on (Gormley, 2006). Issues can also be privatized indirectly – as when companies choose to fight policy proposals in court – and then arrive at out-of-court settlements with plaintiffs that seal the information gathered during legal proceedings from public view. Negotiated settlements with regulators whose terms are not divulged have the same effect.

However, the primary way of exercising private influence is through lobbying. Lobbyists create and maintain communication networks that link corporations to policymakers, connections that can be activated at a moment's notice. In spite of the public perception that lobbyists are constantly wining and dining the policymakers in an orgy of influence, they actually spend most of their time and energy in "watchful waiting," husbanding their resources for an unlikely moment during which change seems imminent. In general corporations are satisfied with the status quo, largely because they have been successful in influencing policies enacted in the past. So they stay in contact with policymakers through lobbyists, especially the chairpersons of legislative committees, who control political agendas. Sometimes lobbyists, like the think tanks described in Chapter 2, furnish policymakers with research that supports their employers' positions on key issues. But most of their time is spent in discussions designed to make policymakers fear change. This private rhetoric usually deals with abstractions – how a proposed policy would undermine the sanctity of the free market, or threaten the "American way," or how it will interfere with corporate activities and damage the economy, and so on. When lobbyists discuss specifics, they do so in rather mundane terms – the feasibility and costs of proposed policies, or the ways in which the current system achieves desirable goals. But all of these discussions establish the groundwork needed to block future proposals for change.

Somewhat surprisingly, lobbyists do not spend much time discussing politics. Politicians are well aware of the political realities in their districts or states, and of how difficult it would be to get re-elected in the face of concerted opposition from well-funded corporations, particularly if they employ large numbers of the politicians' constituents. Lobbyists "go public" only when they lose control of the private policymaking process (Baumgartner and Leech, 1998; Baumgartner et al., 2009). However, it is important to realize that the relationships formed between lobbyists and policymakers are, like any other interpersonal relationships, *mutually* beneficial. Politicians need the help of lobbyists in pursuing their own agendas, something they must to in order to get re-elected. Lobbyists offer them the contacts, expertise, and goodwill that they need in order to do so. By strategically meeting one another's goals, lobbyists and politicians also achieve their own objectives.

Rousing the Rabble (Motivating Action by Non-elites)

In contrast to elites, non-elites generally prefer that public policies be made in public. Open debate gives them an opportunity to receive inexpensive media attention for their causes and to attract support from other non-elites, perhaps creating a coalition that is powerful enough to pressure successfully policymakers into action or inaction. To do so, advocates must locate each other, develop communication networks that link like-minded people together, develop a persuasive rhetoric, and sustain the expenditure of energy and political pressure over time. But mobilizing people is harder than it sounds. It is easiest when the perceived costs or benefits of a proposal are *concentrated*, that is, if its impact is focused on a small number of people and touches a significant part of their lives or resources. It also seems to be easier to mobilize people to oppose a proposal than to support one. Conversely, if the costs or benefits of a proposed policy are *diffused* over a large number of people and/or are only relevant to a peripheral part of their identities or lives, those people have much less incentive to act.

This difference between concentrated and dispersed interests has predictable outcomes. If a proposal has diffused effects on everyone, no one will act. When a proposed policy has concentrated effects on one group and diffused effects on another group, the first group has a lot of incentive to act, while the second group has little incentive to do so. If a proposal promises concentrated benefits to multiple groups, they will have incentives to collaborate with one another, support the policy, and negotiate with their allies over an acceptable division of the spoils once the proposal is enacted. If the proposal imposes concentrated costs on multiple groups, they have incentives to form an alliance in order to defeat the policy. Finally, if a proposal imposes concentrated costs on one group and offers concentrated benefits to another, both will have incentives to act and the outcome will be determined by the relative political power and rhetorical skills of the two groups. This is the primary reason why lobbyists' efforts to enact policies often fail. Corporate lobbyists sometimes oppose each other. For example, one of the key issues in the 2010 debate over regulating the US banking industry involved the fees that merchants are required to pay whenever a customer uses a debit card. The battle pitted the banks and credit card networks, which wanted large and unregulated fees, against retailers such as Wal-Mart and Target, which wanted to reduce the $20 billion in fees they pay to the banks every year. It was obvious that consumers (you) would be affected by the outcome of this battle among lobbyists, and some pro-consumer lobbyists were involved in these secret deliberations; it is also clear that some corporate lobbyists would lose (Kuhnhenn, 2010c).[2]

However, *incentives* to act are not sufficient in themselves. They have to be supplemented by an organizational structure that makes it possible to act in a coordinated way. In general, this puts non-elite groups at a disadvantage. Organizations usually have these structures in place. Through campaign donations they forge links to policymakers, help elect people who share their values and are sympathetic to their positions on key issues, and hire former politicians or government bureaucrats as advisors and/or lobbyists. For example, literally hundreds of people who worked for the federal agencies that regulated the financial industry quit their government jobs during 2008–2010 to join firms that were lobbying their former colleagues about new banking regulations (Lichtblau and Pear, 2010).

The resulting communication links are supplemented by massive campaign donations. For example, the US financial industry, whose members received at least $3 trillion in taxpayer "bailout" money during 2008 and 2009, contributed $99 million to Congressional candidates running for election in 2008, and millions more to Congresspersons who were not running. Between 1989 and 2009 financial giant AIG (American International Group) contributed more than $9 million (50 percent to Democrats and 49 percent to Republicans), Bank of America contributed almost $16 million (47 percent Democrats and 52 percent Republicans), and Citigroup donated more than $25 million (50 percent Democrats and 49 percent Republicans). In contrast, donations from citizen groups opposed to the bailouts were too small to be counted, giving corporations an advantage during the public phase of policymaking.

Other industries are less balanced in their donation strategies, and the precise amounts vary across different administrations and different issues. About three quarters of oil company donations go to Republicans and one quarter go to Democrats, for a total of $169 million during 2009 – eight times the amount spent by all environmental groups combined ($15.9 million). In addition, contribution patterns shift as corporations attempt to reward their allies and/or to punish their opponents over specific legislation. For example, once Congress increased regulation of the financial industry during the summer of 2010, donations shifted markedly, 75 percent going to Republican candidates and 25 percent going to Democrats. As readily available data show (see for example the website of the Center for Responsible Politics and the links it provides), almost all corporations use their constitutional rights as persons to contribute millions to reward their political allies and punish their political foes.

Weekend Fun 4

Choose an industry that interests you. Find out how much money it spends on campaign donations and lobbying (the website of the Center for Responsible Politics is a good place to start your search). It is also interesting to compare the donations of different companies in the industry – sometimes smaller firms give most liberally because, "when you're number 2, you [have to] try harder," as the Avis Car Rental Company has proclaimed in its US advertisements for decades. Then choose a policymaker who interests you, preferably your own representative, senator, governor, or state legislator. Find out how much money she or he received from the industry/ companies that you chose. Now, find out how he or she voted on a key issue involving the industry. To what extent were you able to explain voting behavior by observing campaign donations? What other factors might be involved? (For example, is political party membership or avowed political ideology a better predictor than money?) How can you find out? If you want to have even more fun, try to figure out how cheap/easy your politician is compared to other policymakers. As I will explain below, politicians' votes are not a perfect indicator of corporate influence, but they *are* correlated highly. By the way, don't you feel sorry for readers outside of the US who cannot do this exercise because their countries do not allow corporate funding of political campaigns?

Defenders of this system argue that campaign contributions do not "buy" politicians' votes, they only ensure that contributors will have access to decision-makers. There is research evidence to support this conclusion, but it must be interpreted carefully. Having access means that corporations are able to influence which proposals are considered by policymakers, how those proposals are structured, and how the related issues are framed (recall Chapter 3). This is why lobbyists are most active at the very beginning of the policy formation process. If they can control the policy agenda (that is, if they can kill a proposal they oppose before it is discussed in public and/or elevate a proposal they support) or determine how an issue is framed, the debate is likely to play out in ways they prefer. Since this kind of influence is exercised long before any votes are taken, tracking a legislator's voting record provides only an indirect indication of corporate influence over his or her decision-making. In general, citizen groups lack this kind of access and do not have the structures and networks in place that are necessary to influence agendas or the framing of policy issues. So, even if they can mobilize and become organized, they usually become involved in the policymaking process only *after* the most important decisions have already been made (Baumgartner and Leech, 1998; Baumgartner et al., 2009; Jones and Baumgartner, 2005).

In sum, these factors combine to create situations in which it is highly unlikely that non-elites will be able to influence public policymaking significantly. This is true for policies in general and for the specific provisions of those policies. For example, in 2008, large majorities of US (and UK) citizens opposed taxpayer bailouts for the financial industry (as much as 80 percent in some polls). They were enacted anyway, although the resulting uproar led the Obama Administration to aid the industry quietly through operations by the Treasury Department and other government agencies rather than through the very public process of legislative action. However, as the demise of the Bush Administration's immigration reform proposal indicated, popular pressure sometimes does succeed. Significant policy changes are proposed, some are enacted, and a few are implemented in ways that frustrate the goals of organizational rhetors. Explaining those instances requires the introduction of another framework.

Windows, Streams, and Making Policies in Public

Two metaphors dominate theories of how public policies are enacted – streams and windows. During normal times three streams – problems, proposals, and politics – flow along independently of one another. Social *conditions* exist, and they may even be getting worse in the eyes of many observers. But conditions alone do not prompt policymakers to act. Something must happen to persuade them that those conditions constitute *problems* that demand action. One way this happens is through the efforts of policy entrepreneurs (the mass media usually calls them "wonks") in government, education, think tanks, and the private sector. These professionals constantly advocate in favor of pet *proposals* that they believe would be beneficial to the stakeholders whose interests they represent. *Political* trends ebb and flow, and every now and then the three streams come together – rhetors persuade policymakers that existing conditions are *problems* that need to be dealt with, entrepreneurs successfully argue that their pet *proposals* will solve the newly defined problems, and for some reason *political* dynamics support taking action. Policy "windows" open and the problem and/or proposal catches the attention of policymakers. Of course, rhetors who represent interest groups that are satisfied with the status quo and oppose change will spring into action, in an effort to keep the issue off of the policymakers' agenda (they try to "slam the window shut," if I can extend the metaphor). All of this activity attracts the attention of the media, and the issue suddenly reaches their agenda. Sometimes policy windows remain open long enough for the struggle over ideas – meanings, classifications, evaluative criteria, and ideals – that makes up *public* policymaking to begin. Some windows even stay open long enough for major policy changes to be proposed; a few stay open long enough for action to be taken; but many close so quickly that little substantive change occurs (Baumgartner and Jones, 1993; Kingdon, 1995; Jones and Baumgartner, 2005).

How and Why Policy Windows Open

There are two other ways in which policy windows open: (1) conditions reach a *critical mass* and concerned interest groups persuasively argue that they constitute a *crisis* that demands action; and/or (2) an external event captures attention and activates the pressure for a policy response. For example, every fifteen years or so since the end of World War II, the number of US residents without health insurance has combined with rapidly escalating health insurance costs to create an opportunity for advocates of health care reform to define the situation as a crisis. There was no startling revelation that suddenly put the issue on the policy agenda. Instead, the number of uninsured steadily increased, and health insurance costs for corporations and individuals steadily climbed, until a critical mass was reached (Quadagno, 2005).

Issues can also reach the policy agenda because of sudden, external events. The grounding of the Exxon Valez forced maritime safety onto the policy agenda, and some new regulatory policies were implemented. For a decade before the accident, regulation of the petrochemical industry had steadily declined in rigor and effectiveness. After the Exxon Valdez accident regulation became much stricter for a time, and then started to relax once again. This was partly because the agency overseeing the industry (the Minerals Management Service, or MMS) was charged with two incongruent responsibilities: collecting royalties and tax revenues from oil wells, refineries, and transportation systems, *and* ensuring safe operations for those facilities. Denying a permit, closing a mine, or shutting down a well because of safety problems reduced the funds going into the federal treasury. So-called "activist" regulation also alienated policymakers, who receive millions in campaign contributions from the industries being regulated and prompted hostile messages from constituents whose livelihoods depend on the facilities continuing to operate. None of this is hidden from industry insiders or interested policymakers, who often complained about the agency's "excessive" regulation. Deteriorating regulation did not become a problem, much less a crisis, until a fatal explosion at BP's Texas City refinery and the April, 2010 explosion and sinking of BP's Deep Water Horizon drilling rig, which released thousands of barrels of crude oil into the Gulf of Mexico. Suddenly the dangers and regulation of petrochemical operations in general and of deepwater drilling in particular became a crisis that required policymakers to act. The director of the MMS was fired and the agency was broken into three parts, each with a single mission (DeParle, 2010).

However, opening a policy window is only the first of many steps that must be taken before policy change takes place. Only two of the five presidents who attempted major health insurance reforms – Truman, Johnson, Nixon, Clinton, and Obama – succeeded. Opponents of change were able to close the policy window before major reforms were enacted. Even if advocates are able to open a policy window and to keep it open for a time, they must also successfully link their proposals to the core values of the public *and* to the interests of policymakers. For example, President Johnson knew that, during the mid-1960s, many Americans held pervasive biases against "welfare," especially for "undeserving" citizens, and that they were opposed to government interference in the free market. He also knew that they were suspicious of government's ability to operate large programs successfully (recall Chapter 2). Advocates of health care reform managed this situation by focusing on people who the public thought deserved special care: senior citizens. They were especially vulnerable to bankruptcy from health care expenses and/or death from having to forego treatment that they could not afford. Advocates carefully structured Medicare so that it would be similar to Social Security, an *earned* benefit that enjoyed strong popular support and was *not* viewed as a welfare program (Kingdon, 1995; Marmor, 2000). Since all Congresspersons had needy seniors among their constituents, the proposal was also politically viable. Opponents vowed to repeal or roll back the act, but, once Medicare was in place, popular support grew so quickly that doing so was politically impossible.

At other times advocates successfully appeal to the public's values, but fail to satisfy the interests of policymakers. For example, restraining the cost of government and eliminating government waste is a highly visible issue for the public, which makes it an attractive issue for policymakers. But much of the cost of government and a great deal of so-called government "waste" benefit powerful political constituencies. Of course, the organizations and the people who receive government funds never label their gains as "costs" or "waste";" they reserve those pejorative terms for monies received by *other* people and organizations. One of the policymakers that John Kingdon interviewed provided a pithy summary: "[E]conomists somehow think that waste is a politically potent issue. But they get to the Hill and discover that

143

Congressmen [*sic*] favor waste. [. . .] *For a politician, the costs are the benefits"* (1995, 137).

Organizational Rhetoric while Policy Windows Are Open

Making policy in public involves a web of dilemmas and para-doxes, enigmas that are constructed, revised, and reconstructed through rhetoric. Political structures, economic systems, and cultural assumptions combine to create the sites within which public rhetoric takes place. The tensions and contradictions that exist within cultural ideologies, and between those assumptions and existing structures, create ambiguous situations, in which rhetoric becomes crucial. Centuries ago Aristotle realized that rhetoric is the art of choosing the best out of the many *topoi* that are available in everyday situations. Today policy debates in the US focus on four primary issues – *equity, efficiency, security,* and *liberty*.[3] When politics involves organizations, these debates are often reduced to a conflict between the simple, uncluttered claims of free-market fundamentalism and the organizational imperative on the one hand (recall Chapter 2) and more complex, commu-nitarian concepts on the other. In general the simple claims are more persuasive, not because they are more rational, but because they are easier to cast in emotion-laden bi-modal terms – us vs. them, good vs. bad, freedom vs. slavery, socialism/communism vs. capitalism/democracy, and so on. Through these simple appeals, organizational rhetoric activates passions and achieves organiza-tional goals.

Contesting Equity The simplest definition of equity is equality, treating members of the same group in the same way. But even this simple mode of distributing something is more complicated than it seems. First, every individual is a member of multiple groups simul-taneously. For example, consider a recent graduate of a US high school who, along with his or her parents, is in the US illegally. Should that student be eligible to pay in-state tuition and fees at a state university? The distinction is important for tangible reasons – out-of-state students pay thousands more than in-state students, sometimes ten times as much – and for philosophical reasons – the monies paid by out-of-state students usually more than cover the costs of their education; the monies paid by in-state students do not, the difference being paid by the state's taxpayers. If the state's tax system is regressive (and many are), the taxpayers paying the bills tend to be in middle- and lower-income levels. It is possible for the child of illegal immigrants to receive the benefit of in-state tuition even though his or her family income is much higher than that of the taxpayers who will pay for a part of her or his education. Making tuition policy for this student is complicated, because he or she is part of at least three relevant groups: illegal immigrants (citizens of a country other than the US); an in-state resident who has this status for tuition purposes; and a member of a particular economic category. State laws currently say that membership in the second group takes precedence over membership in the first group – the student gets in-state tuition because she or he has lived in the state for a certain period of time and/or has graduated from a high school in the state, *even if* he or she is in the country/state illegally, and *even if* his or her family is wealthy enough to afford out-of-state tuition easily. Conversely, a student who graduated from high school in the student's country of origin and who is in the US legally, on a student visa, will pay out-of-state fees regardless of his family's ability to pay, because she or he does not fulfill the legal definition of "resident." The system is *equal* – all members of each group are treated the same. Its *equitability* is a very different, and far more complicated, question.

In other policymaking episodes equity issues are even more complicated. Some complications involve the potential beneficiaries of proposed policies – does the recipient *deserve* the benefit (which raises even more complicated questions about what it means *to deserve* or *not to deserve* something), either as an individual or as a member of a particular group? Other complications involve the item itself – should the waiver of out-of-state tuition apply only to undergraduate education, or only to graduate school, or only to students training for professions that are understaffed in the state? Other issues may involve the process through which the benefit is distributed. Basing benefits either on the results of a "fair and open" competition (itself a contestable concept) or on chance is a culturally legitimate mode of distribution in US society, but it produces very different outcomes in each case. Or should the distribution be made through voting, which privileges members of majority groups? Or should it be done by the courts, a process that sometimes favors members of minority groups?

Contesting Efficiency A second issue that can legitimately be raised in policy disputes is efficiency. The concept is supported by almost everyone, but the devil is in the details. First of all, there may be circumstances in which citizens and consumers actually prefer economic inefficiency. In general, parents prefer to place their children in schools with high teacher–student ratios or place their elderly relatives in nursing homes with high staff–patient ratios, even though those institutions are economically less efficient. Subjective considerations such as quality of care overwhelm objective, output-per-input considerations.

Second, definitions of the concepts may themselves be problematic. Efficiency is a *means* that often is treated as an *end* – as a decision criterion, it tells us the best way to go somewhere, but not whether or not the destination is worth the effort. Treating efficiency as an end in itself ignores that very important issue. In contrast, treating efficiency as a means to some other end immediately raises value-laden questions. For example, answering questions such as "what level of environmental damage is our society willing to sustain in order to maximize profits?" or "what proportion of a firm's profits should be re-invested in the publicly funded infrastructure (roads, education systems, and so on) that the organization uses to make its profits?" (the positive externalities described in Chapter 2) is more a function of abstract values than of simple cost–output computations (Jehenson, 1984; Gowler and Legge, 1996).

If policymakers do opt for broader, ends-oriented definitions of efficiency, policymaking becomes very complicated (which is one reason why simplistic means-only definitions are attractive). Policymakers must decide what the optimal outputs/goals/objectives of a policy are. If more than one output is valued, their relative importance must be ranked. They also must determine which interest groups are likely to benefit and/or be penalized by a particular policy proposal. Then they must decide whether the likely impact on various interest groups is deserved, which takes us back to thorny issues of equity. The result may be a policy that, on the surface at least, makes very little sense; a good example of policymakers' convoluted efforts to answer these questions is the US income tax code (and we all know how popular that is). Every deduction, every tax credit, every limit imposed on deductions or tax credits, indeed every decision that helped make the tax code what it is today, was the result of policymakers' efforts to balance competing interests. Hence "tax simplification," which in the abstract is supported by every US politician, would require the reversal of thousands of public policy decisions that were, and still are, supported by influential interest groups. Ironically, such calls (which presume a simplistic definition of "efficiency") are so attractive and so emotionally involving that rhetors cannot resist the temptation to use them to justify changing every part of the tax code that does not favor them and the interest groups they represent.

Other questions involve inputs: how should a given expenditure be defined – for example, are wages paid to workers "costs," are they "income from meaningful employment," or are they "the impetus for economic growth?" If they are costs, it is easy to argue that they should be minimized; if they are defined as either "honest income" or "the source of economic growth" it is easy to argue that they should be increased. Furthermore, what activities count as "work?" Should policymakers count the economic value of unpaid labor performed by "full-time housewives" as "wages?" Should income from gains on no-load mutual funds (which require little or no actual work or expertise on the part of investors) be treated as labor and taxed the same as working hour after hour in dangerous jobs in the hot sun (the federal tax rates on investment income are currently less than half that of real labor)? How should opportunity costs be incorporated into decision-making? For example, companies that rely on illegal immigrants for low-cost production have little reason to develop (or purchase) more efficient technologies for completing those tasks. Should fines for employing illegal immigrants take into account the negative effects that doing so has on innovation, on the development of related scientific expertise, and on the loss of high-tech jobs that would be produced through innovation?

Contesting Security The simplest definition of "security" involves the expectation that one's "needs" – the minimum requirements for the survival of an organism – will continue to be met. Because needs are so fundamental, policy debates about them are even more conflicted, and the related rhetoric more powerful, than debates about desires or deservingness (the under-lying issues in conceptions of equity and efficiency). When this issue is cast in its simplest terms – should innocent people be allowed to suffer grievously and/or die when the society has sufficient resources to prevent it – most people would answer "no," and "security" is not terribly controversial. But are societies also responsible for fulfilling non-biological needs, such as self-respect or dignity? For example, by almost all accounts, the process of applying for "welfare" programs is demeaning, frustrating, and time-consuming. If policymakers use a simple definition of "security" as including only material needs, these considerations are either irrelevant or positive, because they give potential recipients additional incentives to do whatever is necessary to not wind up on the dole. But, if "needs" include dignity, the application process should be changed. Alternatively, should "need" be defined in fixed and absolute terms (for example, food assistance is only made available to a family of four earning less that $12,000 a year, not to a family earning $12,001) or in relative terms (adjusted to the income norms of a community)? Should food aid for the indigent include "prestige" items such as "store bought" ice cream, or should it be limited to raw ingredients (low-fat milk and sugar) that recipients are expected to process on their own?

Or should "security" be defined as encompassing only immediate needs, with no guarantees for the future? Advocates of this position usually justified it by arguing that long-term commitments will encourage people to become dependent on the dole.[4]

This concept explains why US and European unemployment insurance programs are so different. In the US benefits are highly restricted in terms of size, duration, and eligibility. For example, if someone "voluntarily" quits a job regardless of how good or bad the pay and working conditions are, he or she is not eligible for unemployment benefits. During extended recessions, Congress *may* choose to extend unemployment benefits to eligible workers, but it may not do so, providing very little security over the mid- or long term. During late 2010, a proposal to extend unemployment benefits for "99ers" (the term given to people who had been unemployed for more than 99 weeks during the Great Recession) was debated in precisely these terms. In the other OECD (Organization for Economic Co-operation and Development) countries benefits are larger, extended over longer periods of time, and less dependent on the politics of a particular moment. As a consequence, they provide greater security.

The unemployment insurance example also illustrates the way in which efficiency and security are interconnected. Sometimes the link is very specific. A simple, free-market perspective assumes that, for a society to have "winners," it must also have "losers." Without a very real possibility that one will become the latter and in the process lose security and psychological comforts, the argument goes, people have no motivation to work at all, much less to work hard enough to create a productive economy, or the innovations that are necessary for an efficient society. The counter-rhetoric claims that, without a measure of security, people will be unwilling to take the risks involved in becoming more productive, innovative, or efficient.

The inter-relationship between security and efficiency is also illustrated by health care policy. For example, some very new anti-cancer drugs cost hundreds of thousands of dollars, but only extend patients' lives by a few months. Should government health care or (private sector) health insurers pay that much money for the security that comes from knowing that one's life will be extended for as long as it is scientifically possible? Or, alternatively, should a system that is designed to ensure security be limited by considerations of efficiency (since the economic or other return achieved by extending a terminal patient's life by a month or two is so small, the drug would not be covered)? In both cases – unemployment insurance and expensive prescription drugs – efficiency and security are interconnected through culturally legitimized assumptions about human motivation and need.

Contesting Liberty The simple, potentially most persuasive definition of "liberty" is "the freedom to do what one wants, providing it does not harm others." Like with the other core constructs, one's conception of liberty depends on one's answer to a host of other questions. Some questions involve the definition of "harm." Should it be defined as an individual attribute, consistent with individualistic cultural assumptions? Or is it an attribute of groups – communities, organizations, or sub-cultures? The latter definition legitimizes laws that stipulate greater penalties for "hate crimes" (that is, those that are motivated by the victim's membership in a protected group) than for crimes that are motivated by other considerations; the former definition does not.

Do only material harms count, for example bodily injury or death, loss of income, decline in the value of one's possessions, or increased taxes? Does "quality of life" count (a neighbor builds an ugly fence, or a developer clear-cuts a woodland in order to build a subdivision more cheaply/efficiently, or a cattle feedyard creates an inescapable stench for miles around)? Do psychological losses count (the stress from having a half-way house for drug addicts or sexual offenders, or a noisy elementary school, built in one's neighborhood)? For example, should the Klu Klux Klan (KKK) and neo-Nazis be allowed to sponsor an otherwise legal march through a Jewish neighborhood whose residents include survivors of Nazi concentration camps? Do spiritual harms count? (For example, a town near my own allows bars to be built in a particular area, but not a Hooters, because its scantily clad waitresses offended some citizens' moral/religious beliefs.) Should *potential* (but not actual) harms to groups be sufficient to deny liberty? Should everyone be forbidden to park their vehicles on a narrow street, even though doing so does not create a significant barrier to movement unless a large number (critical mass) of people do so? Should people be required to render aid to accident victims even if they did nothing to cause the accident (a sin of "omission" rather than a sin of "commission")?

Summary All of these complications place issues regarding human values and conceptions of what it means for a group of people to be a "community" at the center of public policymaking. Every position that one might take on them raises additional issues, none of which can easily be resolved through the application of some seemingly objective "scientific" criterion – they create far more loose ends than they tie up. In short, taking them seriously generates a style of rhetoric that is diametrically opposed to the "realist" style of free-market theory (recall Chapter 2) and to the certainty, security, and predictability of managerialism and the organizational imperative (Chapter 3). Such issues move the "messiness" of democracy center stage, and in many cases make the simplicity of Plato's *Republic* seem all the more attractive. They create complications, which cause confusion and necessitate compromise. The passion that opens policy windows and keeps them open for a time begins to dissipate, and the windows begin to close.

Influence beyond Rhetoric

Open windows provide opportunities for rhetoric. They also invite the use of other forms of influence. Earlier on I described the impact that professional lobbyists have on the early stages of public policymaking – influencing the sites (private or public) in which policy is made, the issues that make it to the policymaking agenda, and the ways in which these issues are framed. But lobbyists also play an important role during the public phase of policymaking. Consider three examples. On a single energy bill debated in 1997, a handful of advocates from citizen groups and environmental organizations faced a coalition composed of the Petroleum Institute (270 full-time paid lobbyists costing $42 million), the Nuclear Energy Institute (125 lobbyists costing $34

151

million), and the Electricity Institute (200 lobbyists, $50 million). In a six-month period between March and September 2008, the US financial industry spent more than $200 million in an effort to persuade policymakers to bail out the "toxic assets" they had accumulated. At the height of President Obama's efforts to reform the US health insurance system, there were six times as many full-time registered health care lobbyists as there were policymakers involved in the process (100 senators, 435 Congresspersons, and 3,300 lobbyists). The health care industry was spending $1.4 million *per day* lobbying Congress. During the final two weeks before the bill was passed, it spent more than $30 million lobbying thirty-seven recalcitrant Democratic Congresspersons (Barrett, 2009; Krugman, 2009).[5]

In short, when any major bill is being discussed, legislators are literally inundated with lobbyists. The number has grown substantially because of the US Supreme Court's 2010 *Citizens United* v. *Federal Elections Commission*, which invalidated key provisions of laws that limited campaign contributions, and this number will continue to expand in the future: "the Supreme Court has handed a new weapon to lobbyists. If you vote wrong, a lobbyist can now tell any elected official that my company, labor union, or interest group will spend unlimited sums explicitly advertising against your re-election" (Kirkpatrick, 2010a, n.p.; also Kirkpatrick, 2010b).[6] With unequal resources, even the most persuasive messages from non-corporate rhetors are likely to be lost in the flood.

If direct influence on policymakers is insufficient, organizational rhetors can also "go public." Doing so is risky, but it can pay major dividends. The now famous "Harry and Louise" ads were an important factor in the defeat of President Clinton's health reform efforts – the complexity of the bill, combined with the simple questions that Louise asked, created a level of confusion and insecurity that pro-reform rhetors were not able to overcome (Hacker, 1996; Skocpol, 1997).

PUPPY SALE

SOMETHING TO DO WITH FREEDOM TO CORRUPT.

THE SUPREME COURT HAS RULED THAT CORPORATIONS MAY NOW BUY AND OWN AS MANY CONGRESSMEN AS THEY CAN AFFORD.

Houston Chronicle 1/31/10, B12

How and Why Windows Close

Policy windows eventually close. If the impetus for action comes from citizen groups, they will eventually exhaust their tangible resources and the passion that motivated them to act. When policymaking shifts from an analysis of problems to the consideration of alternative proposals, differences within coalitions may begin to split the groups. Conversely, if the pressure for change comes from an external crisis, memory of crisis events will begin to fade. The public has a limited attention span; that of the media is even shorter (Downs, 1972; Iyengar, 1991; Kingdon, 1995). Time is on the side of established, well-funded, well-connected rhetors, which often means corporations. In addition, rhetors interested in preserving the status quo have a number of blocking strategies

153

available that can be used to help close policy windows.

One blocking strategy involves manipulating the structure of government – to foster and/or encourage turf battles among various committees, between different houses of Congress, between the executive and legislative branches, and/or between the federal and the state governments. For example, rhetors representing the tobacco industry have been able, historically, to play the Department of Agriculture, which subsidized the crop, against the Department of Health and Human Services, which wanted to limit its use. Blocking action has become easier in recent years because of changes in the structural configurations within Congress, especially in the US Senate. When the United States was created the ratio between the least populous state and the most populous one was 13:1. Now it is 68:1. A group of only forty-one senators, representing as little as 11 percent of the US population, can use a filibuster to keep a bill that is supported by 89 percent of the population from even being considered.[7] If a proposed change has a great deal of popular support, politicians do face significant pressure to act and the interest groups who prefer maintaining the status quo face a significant challenge. But, if the public is apathetic, confused, or ambivalent about an issue (or can be made to feel apathetic, confused, or ambivalent), popular pressure will be weaker and it will be easier for organizations to manipulate legislative structures.

Sowing confusion is an important strategy in itself – one that presents very low risk for organizational rhetors because it involves merely asking questions, not making arguments that might be discredited or attacked. It is especially useful when advocates of change have high levels of social legitimacy, which makes them very difficult to discredit. Other low-cost strategies include refusing to acknowledge that a problem exists – an approach commonly used with environmental issues: acid rain during the 1960s and 1970s and global warming today – because scientific research rarely provides absolute conclusions. Supporters of the status quo can also refuse to recognize the legitimacy of advocacy groups (for instance by calling them "silly tree-huggers" or "well-meaning but uninformed extremists"). One of the most sophisticated low-cost strategies is "anti-patterning" – that is, arguing that a problem is an isolated incident or resulted from the actions of a "rogue" individual, and thus does not warrant making a major policy change. The strategy is most effective when media coverage of an issue is "episodic," in other words focused on individual events, rather than "continuous," focusing on the systems that created a problem or allowed it to persist. In a highly individualistic society, anti-patterning is especially persuasive. For example, the Bush Administration strongly argued that the 2002 "corporate meltdown" (scandals at Enron, WorldCom, Adelphia, and other companies) resulted from the actions of a "few bad apples" in an otherwise adequately regulated system. The strategy succeeded in minimizing reform of the overall regulatory system (Ibarra and Kitsuse, 1993; Cobb and Ross, 1997; Conrad, 2004; Cheney et al., 2010).

If low-cost blocking strategies fail, defenders of the status quo can shift to moderate-risk strategies. If advocates of change are viewed positively by the society as a whole, defenders of the present system must attack their proposals, not them. To do so, they can focus on procedural or logical flaws in the proposals. Opponents of change can also raise jurisdictional issues, claiming that a problem should be left to the states or to the private sector. They can challenge the proponents' evidence, too, or sponsor studies that draw contradictory conclusions (one of the most important activities of industry "think tanks"). Or they can issue warnings about possible unintended consequences of adopting a proposal. Even if these predictions are not credible – and they often are not – they sow confusion, which helps block change. On the other hand, if the proponents of change lack social legitimacy, the defenders of the status quo can attack their patriotism, competence, motivation, and/or morality.

However, the most effective middle-risk strategy is *symbolic placation*: offering an illusion of change without taking substantive, meaningful action. Placation always involves a symbolic affirmation of the advocates' claims and experiences. It usually involves highly emotional, ritualized expressions of outrage or pride. For example, CEOs in firms whose stock value has plummeted along with the overall market often promise to work for a salary of only $1 per year, plus stock options. The move *appears*

155

to make executives *seem* to be willing to risk their own future as well as that of the companies they run. But executives who make this "ultimate sacrifice" can almost always rest comfortably in the knowledge that (1) when the overall market recovers, so will the company's stock values, regardless of the executive's performance, or (2) if the market does not recover, the Board of Directors will re-negotiate his or her compensation package to protect his or her income (recall the case study at the end of Chapter 3). Or corporate rhetors can express heartfelt regret that a negative event took place, promise to "make things right," and create an internal investigating committee that is charged with "getting to the bottom" of the controversy. Typically, these internal reports take time to create (and time is on the side of the status quo), and eventually conclude that actors other than the corporation were at fault. Sometimes the results of these internal reports are later contradicted by independent analyses, but, once the issue is reduced to a battle of competing charts and graphs, the passion for change begins to fade.[8]

Policymakers friendly to corporations that are under attack also can engage in symbolic placation. They too may sponsor investigations and/or appoint committees, both of which *appear* to be taking action. If the public is so outraged that these procedural steps would be viewed as insufficient, policymakers may hold their own hearings. These events often deteriorate into contests of comparative outrage as politicians compete with one another to display their disdain, as corporate executives are pilloried after taking the 5th Amendment. In very, very rare cases, policymakers may use hearings to announce that they are returning campaign donations they have received from the offending parties. Similarly, if demands for strong action continue, organization-friendly (or industry-friendly) regulators may suddenly embark on a flurry of activity, but make no fundamental changes. For example, the Securities and Exchange Commission (SEC) has repeatedly responded to instances of corporate malfeasance by increasing the number of reports that organizations are required to file with the agency: "although this activity did not deal with the main concerns of critics, it gave the impression that the SEC was an activist agency pursuing solutions to problems in the financial marketplace" and undermined popular pressure (Cobb and Ross, 1997, 215). If popular pressure continues, policymakers may enact "hollow laws" – which make only cosmetic changes to current systems, lack viable enforcement mechanisms, or will be implemented by the same regulators whose inaction helped create the crisis in the first place.

For example, the Obama Administration has regularly used the symbolic placation strategy, sometimes quite effectively, although aides have found it difficult to train the president to *look* emotional while *saying* he was enraged, pleased, and so on (Blow, 2010; Dowd, 2010; Kuhnhenn, 2010a, 2010b). During the administration's "battle" with Wall Street, the president repeatedly attacked the CEOs of bailed-out firms for their excesses and irresponsibility, while Secretary of Treasury Geithner quietly arranged a multi-trillion dollar aid package for the industry, an amount many times larger than the Troubled Asset Relief Program (TARP) bailout passed during the waning months of the Bush Administration. Geithner's quiet activities led Neil Barofsky, Congressional monitor of the bailouts, to complain that these actions left the bailout programs "open to fraud," and prompted economist William Cohan to exclaim:

> So the Obama administration, which has repeatedly pilloried banking executives in an effort to build support for its financial reform package, has in one step reduced exponentially the chances of actually holding people on Wall Street accountable for the financial crisis, which was an utterly preventable self-inflicted wound. This is simply incomprehensible. (Cohan, 2010, n.p.; see also Andrews, 2009; Conrad, 2009; Dash, 2009; Labaton and Dash, 2009; Norris, 2009a)

Of course, from a rhetorical perspective the decision is easy to comprehend – the combination of "bad apples" rhetoric and symbolic placation is a regular part of policymaking in the US precisely because these elements successfully undermine pressure for meaningful reform. Placation diffuses the emotional intensity underlying advocacy groups – it is very difficult to mobilize people to keep fighting after it appears that they have won.

Re-privatizing Policymaking: Conference Committees and Policy Implementation

If a bill does pass both houses of Congress but does so in a different form, it will be referred to a "reconciliation committee," which will operate in private. Typically advocates from both ends of the political spectrum call for open and public deliberations by conference committees, but they rarely take any action designed to ensure openness. For example, when bills designed to reform US banking regulations went to a conference committee in 2010, rhetors on both sides of the reform issue warned the public about the dangers of private policymaking. Heather Booth, head of a coalition of liberal interest groups, warned that "the battle now moves to conference, where the big banks will look to weaken or kill the bill behind closed doors," and House Republican leader John Boehner complained that "this subject is too important [. . .] to be written in its final stages by a select few Democrats and lobbyists behind closed doors" (cited in Chan, 2010; see also *NYTimes on the web*, 2010; Johnson, 2010b; Superville and Raum, 2010). But the committee's deliberations were conducted in private, where elites prefer public policies be made. The resulting bill strengthened regulation in some ways, but left in place the incentive system that led to the crisis and bailout (Blake, 2010; Johnson, 2010c).

Once a bill is signed into law, organizations can shift their focus to the government employees who will implement it. Especially at the federal level, legislation is incredibly complex and bills are amazingly long, 1,000 pages or more. They would be much longer if the included details about their implementation. Those decisions are left to the executive branch, primarily cabinet departments, which operate largely outside of the public's view. Of course, the simplest way to undermine the impact of the new legislation is for its opponents to persuade government agencies to implement it in ways that undermine its intent (see Reinhardt, 2010; Lichtblau and Pear, 2010).

If strong implementation rules are written, organizations can quietly negotiate arrangements with regulators that minimize their impact – a process that political scientists have labeled "regulatory capture" (Wilson, 1974; Ritti and Silver, 1986; Baker et al., 2009). Most US citizens perceive that government regulations and regulatory agencies are created in order to protect citizens from misdeeds perpetrated by corporations or other actors. In a few cases this assumption has been accurate: popular pressure leads to policy debates that focus public attention on a moral "evil," personified by a corporation or industry and illustrated through the evocation of "horror stories" that stress the virtue of victims and the venality of perpetrators. The industries to be regulated have strong economic incentives to fight these bills, but they often cannot do so in public, lest they inflame popular indignation even further (Cobb and Ross, 1997; Baumgartner and Leech, 1998; Conrad and Millay, 2001; Stone, 2001; Conrad, 2004). Instead, they quietly negotiate with regulators about enforcement mechanisms and appropriate penalties. Congressional allies are enlisted to pressure regulators to be more compliant. For example, a decade before the scandals at the turn of the century (Enron, WorldCom, Adelphia and the rest), US Securities and Exchange Commission (SEC) Chairman Arthur Levitt realized that the existing system allowed corporations to award lucrative consulting contracts to the accounting firms that they hired to perform supposedly "independent" audits of their books. Levitt concluded that this arrangement created an obvious conflict of interest, one that invited fraudulent audits. His proposal to separate the consulting and the auditing functions met stiff resistance from the accounting industry – primarily from Arthur Andersen, who was serving as auditor of a number of firms that later declared bankruptcy and from their allies in Congress. Senator Joseph Lieberman, then chairman of the Government Affairs Committee, which oversees the SEC, threatened to cut the agency's budget if Levitt continued his efforts, and Andersen's allies in the House Commerce Committee – Tom Bliley, W. J. "Billy" Tauzin, and Chairman Michael Oxley – increased the pressure by demanding that the SEC provide time-consuming answers to a number of unimportant questions, thereby bogging them down in paperwork. Levitt got the message, backed down, and resigned, something he later admitted was the most shameful thing he had done during his lengthy career (Reinert, 2002; Levitt, 2002; Conrad, 2004).[9] Eventually, these quiet multi-party negotiations reduce the regulatory burden that corporations must bear. Privately negotiated arrangements remain stable until a crisis makes the public aware of the process, and pressure for reform escalates once again.

When the new crisis occurs, anti-government rhetors proclaim that regulation failed because the regulators had been incompetent, or because the agency had been "captured" by the industry they were supposed to regulate, undermining popular faith in government regulation. These claims create further outrage, which in turn creates another episode of outcry, public debate, legislation, and negotiation (Conrad and Abbott, 2007; Llewellyn, 2007).[10] For example, in 2000 (under the Clinton Administration) the federal agency that oversees offshore oil drilling (known as the MMA) required companies to install multiple levels of back-up safety systems, including one that long had been required for wells in the North Sea and off of Brazil's coast. The industry, led by BP, quietly lobbied against these restrictions on the grounds that they were expensive and unnecessary, since free-market processes would discipline the companies and be sufficient to ensure safety. In 2003 (under the Bush Administration), the agency reversed its policy and abandoned the stricter requirements, in spite of more than 1,400 documented offshore accidents between 2001 and 2007. In 2009 the Obama Administration waived a requirement that BP file a detailed environmental statement, which would have revealed the weakness of the well's safety systems, and ignored agency scientists' warnings that BP's single-level safety system was too risky (the scientists were prophetic – the blowout preventer failed in April, 2010). When the Deepwater Horizon exploded and sank, critics attacked the agency and its "cozy relationship" with the oil industry (Broder and Cooper, 2010; Urbina, 2010).

However, throughout US history it has been much more common for regulation to emerge in response to pressure from industries themselves (Wilson, 1974; Baker et al., 2009; Llewellyn, 2007).[11] The organizations' goal usually is to obtain regulatory protections for themselves and/or to impose legal burdens on competitors, actions that typically are justified through a rhetoric of "reining in excessive competition" or of rescuing the economy or some industry, from "chaos."[12] In a sense, these agencies are "pre-captured," since from their creation their mandate has been to serve the industries they regulate, not to protect consumers or other stakeholders. Corporate beneficiaries maintain a strong influence over the agencies, and both the companies and the regulators try to keep a low profile. Of course these arrangements are risky, because future crises will inevitably make them public, and they are highly offensive to a public which believes that regulators should regulate in the public interest (Perrow, 2002).[13]

Consequently, regardless of the origins of particular regulatory agencies, regulators and the organizations/industries they regulate face complex rhetorical problems. In order to legitimize themselves, regulators must appear to be sufficiently activist to forestall accusations that they have been "captured," but sufficiently responsive to industry needs to keep anti-regulation, free-market advocates at bay.[14] Conversely, corporations in regulated industries must appear to be sufficiently law-abiding and socially responsible to undercut calls for increased regulation. The solution to this dilemma is for regulators occasionally to impose minor punishments on the companies they regulate (recall the list of fines in Chapter 1) and for target companies to complain loudly about regulatory excesses, but to comply with the penalties in order to "put the issue behind them." Ironically, it is because regulators and regulated companies enact this ritual so successfully that Americans are surprised and outraged whenever regulatory breakdowns do occur. While the outrage is often appropriate, they should not have been surprised.

Conclusion

Throughout this book I have argued that organizational rhetoric is strategic in many different senses of the term. It involves the creation, reproduction, and transformation of social, political, and economic structures and the creation and legitimation of

161

complex webs of taken-for-granted assumptions. It also involves the strategic maneuvering within those structures, and using these assumptions as the basis for rhetorical appeals. The present chapter has added another layer of strategizing: managing processes of making, blocking, implementing, and modifying public policies. For organizations, the ability to influence public policy involves tangible advantages – it means that the power of government can be enlisted to facilitate concrete organizational goals. It allows organizational rhetors to construct organizational identities as socially responsible actors and legitimate members of society. These processes will be the focus of my final chapter.

Case Study: Dealing (Legal) Drugs, the Rest of the Story

I concluded Chapter 1 with a case study about the role that rhetoric plays in one sector of the "American system": prescription drug pricing. Some readers, especially "twenty-somethings" who consume few prescription drugs, may have finished the exercise wondering: "Why is this important to me?" At the end of this extension of that case, you will be able to answer the question.

Prescription drug spending is concentrated among a politically organized group: senior citizens, who repeatedly pressured Congress to add a prescription drug benefit to Medicare. Bills were introduced in 1990, 1994, 1999, and 2000. They placed Congresspersons in a difficult position. Given current drug prices and inflation, adding a drug benefit would be prohibitively expensive, unless it included a form of government-negotiated pricing like those used in every other industrialized country. But price controls were vehemently opposed by another organized and influential group, PhRMa (the drug firms' lobbying group). Consequently, none of the bills passed. Indeed most died in committee, which kept the issue private and spared Congresspersons from having to vote against the proposals in public thereby risking the ire of the senior lobby.

But costs continued to skyrocket. Some states, tired of waiting for the federal government, acted on their own (Conrad and Jodlowski, 2008). For example Maine, led by state Senator Chellie Pingree (now a US Congresswoman), sponsored bus trips to Canada, where seniors could purchase prescriptions at around half their US price. She eventually introduced a bill in the state legislature, nicknamed "Maine Rx," which limited drug prices charged to Maine's citizens to Canadian levels. The bill used negotiations between suppliers and the state's Medicaid program, which bought nearly one quarter of the drugs sold in Maine, as an enforcement mechanism. PhRMa immediately dispatched its lobbyists to Augusta, who used the standard strategies (a mix of campaign contributions, threats, and the rhetoric described in Chapter 1) to kill the bill. They failed, and on May 11, 2000, Maine Rx passed with near-unanimous support. But on October 26, the day before the bill was to take effect, PhRMa shifted its efforts to another venue, the federal courts, and obtained a temporary injunction that stopped Maine Rx in its tracks. The federal appeals court soon ruled in favor of the state, and PhRMa appealed to the business-friendly US Supreme Court. On March 5, 2001, the Supreme Court heard the case and PhRMa got nervous. Maine is a small state, but bigger states had noticed what was going on and had started to act. So, while continuing its litigation, PhRMa suddenly abandoned its decades-old opposition to a Medicare drug benefit and started supporting it, as long as the bill did not include price controls. In May the Supreme Court made a surprising 6–3 decision to allow Maine Rx to proceed. Soon the media became involved – through Peter Jenning's 2002 ABC News broadcast, "Bitter Medicine," and the 2003 PBS "Frontline" episode entitled "The Other Drug War" – and made the crisis a public crusade. By 2003, a Medicare drug benefit was once again a hot topic.

The benefits of a Medicare drug benefit would be concentrated on two stakeholder groups – seniors, and corporations which currently pay for their retirees' prescriptions. If the bill included some form of price controls, its costs would be concentrated on pharmaceutical firms; if not, the potential costs would become concentrated benefits for the industry. In that case, the costs of the proposal would be diffused over a large and unorganized group – taxpayers, especially future ones. Drug companies have a very effective organizational structure in place through their lobbying group PhRMA, which brought 946 full-time paid lobbyists to Capitol Hill for the Medicare prescription drug debate. They also have close ties to policymakers via campaign contributions – an average of $15 million each year between 2000 and 2006 ($10 million of which went to Republicans, whose party controlled Congress and the presidency during the debate over the prescription drug benefit). The business lobby is just as well organized, and gives even larger campaign contributions. It hired more than 1,000 full-time lobbyists to work the bill. Seniors and consumer groups have some very effective lobbying organizations, but limited resources (they were able to fund only 6 full-time lobbyists during the debate). Taxpayers, the interest group for whom costs would be much more widely diffused, and who have little/no organization or history of campaign donations, have little influence. This is especially true of future taxpayers (e.g. current college students), who usually don't even vote, and (according to most polls) could not care less about health policy issues (Wilson, 1973; Fouhy, 2009). Given this configuration of costs, benefits, and organizational structures, anyone who can add and subtract should be able to predict the outcome: no price controls on drugs, substantial benefits to corporations, and greatly improved access to life-saving drugs for seniors, with the costs paid by taxpayers, especially future taxpayers.

But legislative processes are never easy. The key debate was between a Democratic bill that was relatively simple and a more complicated Republican alternative. In the Democrats' bill, each senior would pay an annual deductible of $100; the federal government would cover 80 percent of his or her drug costs if she or he spent between $100 and $2,000 in a year, and 100 percent of her or his spending above $2,000 per year. The estimated cost of the bill was $700–800 billion over the first ten years of the program. The bill anticipated significant costs savings (which meant profit reductions for PhRMA's members) as a result of Medicare negotiating with drug companies, as the US Office of Veterans' Affairs currently does. PhRMa strongly favored a Republican version which supposedly would cost only $385 billion over the first ten years of the program (less than the $400 billion cost that President Bush had authorized in his 2003 budget), because it was less generous to seniors (and much more generous to the drug companies). Most frustrating for retirees, the bill included a "donut hole" within which drugs would not be covered at all (about

25 percent of seniors reach the donut hole; about 5 percent have catastrophic costs that exceed its upper limit).

However, Republican leaders knew that the bill would cost much more than $385 billion. Bill Foster, the chief actuary of the Medicare and Medicaid programs, had told them so. They threatened to fire him if he told anyone in Congress that his cost estimate was $534 billion, very close to the cost estimate made by the Congressional Budget Office in early 2004 ($558 billion) after the bill had been signed into law. Many recalcitrant Republican House members suspected that the numbers were inaccurate, and they had to be persuaded to vote for the bill. For example, Nick Smith (R-Michigan), who had announced his retirement, was told that the party would fund his son's efforts to succeed him in office if he would vote "yes." He declined; his son lost. The House Republican Study Committee had requested on October 29 that the bill itself be made available to House members three weeks before the vote, so they could read it and actually know what they were voting for. But on the final night a single copy of the bill, with last-minute amendments hand-written in the margins, was circulated among House Republicans. At some point during the process, someone inserted a provision that *forbade* Medicare administrators from negotiating with drug companies over prescription costs or using a drug's cost as a reason for not paying for it. As far as I know, the identity of the author of that provision has never been divulged in public, but many observers give the credit/blame to "Billy" Tauzin (D-LA – you will remember him as one of the Congresspersons who harassed SEC Director Levitt into dropping his proposal to separate auditing and consulting), who abandoned his Senate seat soon after the bill was passed, in order to take a $2 million per year job with PhRMa. Eventually these steps and the additional arm-twisting were sufficient to change enough Republican votes to ensure passage of what former Reagan Administration staffer Bruce Bartlett called "the worst legislation in history," with five votes to spare.

In 2004, Medicare estimated the long-term cost (its first decade and beyond) of the program at $10.8 trillion; in 2005 it increased its estimate to $18.2 trillion. It is a little difficult to comprehend a number this big, but Mr. Bartlett helps:

> [I]n 2005, this [the cost] would have come to $232 billion – more than
> all of the corporate income taxes collected by the federal government
> and [plus] 26 percent of all personal income taxes. In other words, the
> individual income tax would have to rise by 26 percent immediately
> and forever just to pay for the drug program. (Bartlett, 2006, 116)[15]

But even these numbers significantly *underestimate* the total cost of
the program to taxpayers. In order to get support from the nation's
governors, the bill shifted 6.4 million "dual eligibles," people who
are both elderly and poor, from Medicaid programs, which are
largely funded by the states, to the federal Medicare program. This
made governors happy because it reduced their Medicaid costs,
but it invalidated the lower prices that many states had negotiated
over time with drug companies. The increased costs, 30 percent
on average, provided an additional $3.7 billion windfall for the drug
companies (Wilson, 2009).[16] Most importantly, the bill was carefully
crafted to hide a massive additional cost. Lobbyists representing
large corporations had made it clear that they planned to end their
own (usually much better) prescription coverage for their retired
employees if the legislation passed. This would have driven up the
costs of the plan significantly. So the bill's authors included a provision to reimburse corporations for their drug costs through a 28
percent tax subsidy, one that increased corporate profits by at least
$8 billion per year. Since tax reductions are not "costs," this amount
would not have to be included in the program's cost estimates. So
the bill gave corporations an additional tax break by not requiring
them to pay federal income taxes on this $8 billion gift from the
federal government (that is, from the taxpayers). And that, young-
sters, is how "A Bill Becomes a Law."

Why is all of this important to you? Not only will the bill cost future
taxpayers hundreds of billions of dollars, it increases the likelihood
that they will wind up paying for other bills too. Medicare Plan D
frees up billions of dollars in extra profits that corporations and drug
companies can use to increase their campaign contributions and lobbying efforts. In addition, millions of baby-boomers will soon retire,
massively increasing both the costs of the program and the size and
potential political influence of the seniors' lobby. Given the model of

diffused and concentrated interests that I introduced earlier in this chapter, who would you predict will wind up paying the bill? Got a mirror?

Discussion Questions
In 2009 President Obama attempted to fulfill one of his major campaign promises: to provide affordable health insurance coverage for all Americans. It was not an especially new idea – Presidents Roosevelt (both of them), Truman, Nixon, and Clinton had done the same, and failed. Only Lyndon Johnson had succeeded, and then only for the elderly (Medicare) and the poor (Medicaid). In spite of a number of adverse events – including the death of Senator Ted Kennedy, long-term proponent of health care reform, and his replacement by a moderate Republican who had voted for a very similar plan for the state of Massachusetts but made his opposition to nationwide health reform quite clear – President Obama succeeded. Using your internet research skills, find out:

1 what "Obamacare" did for/about prescription drug coverage and costs; and
2 what position(s) were taken by PhRMa during the 2009–2010 debate over health care reform. Then explain why.

5

Rhetoric and the Management of Organizational Identities, Images, and Crises

Did you ever expect a corporation to have a conscience, when it has no soul to be damned, and no body to be kicked?

Edward, First Baron of Thurlow (cited in Llewellyn, 2007, 177)

PR is really about selling an idea, a product, a personality, a government policy, a candidate, maybe even a war. PR is always selling. Sometimes these days we are even selling the idea that our corporate chief is not a crook, or that the church is not really a haven for sinful priests, or our glorious leaders have feet of clay, or that our own PR agency is as transparent as Saran Wrap and as pure as Ivory Flakes.

Pederson (2006, 3)

Core Concepts

- Like research on leadership, research on organizational identity, image, and crisis management is extensive but atheoretical. The key terms refer to audience members' perceptions of an organization, but they differ in terms of time. *Identity* encompasses perceptions of the organization's central, enduring character, which includes expectations about how its members will act in the future. It is sufficiently stable for people to link their own identities to that of the organization. *Image* reflects impressions people have of the organization in the present, given current issues and activities; and *reputation* is composed of audience members' reconstructed memories of the organization's past.

- Organizational identities guide and constrain rhetors' selection of image/crisis management strategies, and stakeholder's interpretations and responses to that rhetoric.
- Identity crises occur when external events or organizational actions threaten to damage, or otherwise alter, an organization's identity. Organizational rhetoric during crises can protect an organization's identity, harm its identity, or become a source of crisis in itself.
- Academic research and practitioner experience draw similar conclusions about managing identity crises, both in terms of the process that should be used and in terms of the strategies that are available. However, a number of factors, including the potential for litigation, complicate strategy selection.
- Because organizations have such a powerful influence on society and on the lives of its members, there are many interest groups that wish to influence organizational actions and/or resist organizational power. Although they have access to far fewer material resources than multinational corporations, resistance groups are able to engage in sophisticated rhetorical campaigns that influence organizational identities, policies, and actions.

In this chapter I examine two tightly inter-related processes: the creation and modification of organizational *identities* and *images*, and the strategic management of identity-related *crises*. It took a long time for professional managers to recognize the importance of these processes, and some firms still do a poor job of integrating corporate communication experts into strategic decision-making (Marchand, 1998). But, by the 1980s, more than 90 percent of large (Fortune 500) firms had implemented programs of some type (Bucholz, 1988).[1] The delay happened partly because organizations are generally resistant to change, but mostly because executives tend to rely on advice from people like themselves. Since few CEOs have backgrounds and expertise in corporate communication or public relations, they tend to exclude those specialties from strategic decision-making, unless (or until) they are forced to deal with serious reputational crises.

Although scholars have yet to find an overall theoretical framework that makes research on organizational identity/image/crisis management fit together, some general principles have emerged. First, like any of the forms of rhetoric that I have discussed in this book, organizational rhetors face complicated, multi-faceted situations and must make strategic choices based on an assessment of them all. For example, Robert Rowland and Angela Jerome's (2004) survey of research on just one type of strategy, apologies, concluded that rhetors need to consider four variables simultaneously: (1) the extent to which various audiences perceive the organization to be guilty of wrongdoing, which is influenced by their perceptions of the organization's history; (2) the magnitude of the harm caused by the organization's actions and the nature of the people who were harmed by them (whether they are innocent and/or similar to the audience being addressed); (3) the presence or absence of third parties onto which blame might be shifted; and (4) the ways in which the organization's actions violate or affirm the audiences' moral standards. Of course, strategic adaptation of this kind is very complex; if executives are interested in simple "cookbook" solutions to these complex rhetorical problems, they are likely to be disappointed (Leeper, 2001; Botan and Taylor, 2004).

Researchers do know that identity/image/crisis management is like the other forms of rhetoric I have examined in this book. First, it is intimately tied to the taken-for-granted assumptions of the cultures within which the organization operates. Rhetors draw upon those assumptions in order to devise persuasive campaigns designed to legitimize the organization and its actions, as well as to create potentially effective persuasive appeals during crises. In the process of using cultural assumptions, identity/image/crisis managers reinforce them. Second, contemporary models of identity/image/crisis management assume that audiences are composed of active, thinking beings, whose responses to organizational rhetoric are influenced by their individual beliefs, values, and ways of making sense out of experiences and rhetoric. As a result, they may interpret even the most carefully crafted persuasive messages in ways that organizational rhetors did not expect or intend, may reject those appeals outright, and may even use the rhetors' words to challenge or undermine the organization's identity, image, or efforts to manage crises.[2] Consequently, identity/image/crisis management may be the most complicated and unpredictable form of organizational rhetoric.

Defining Key Constructs: Organizational Identities and Image Management

When a topic is as atheoretical as this one, it is important to start with key definitions. It is clear that there are four key terms that must be defined – identity, image, reputation, and crisis. The number of existing definitions of these terms is almost as large as the number of researchers and practitioners in the respective areas. But their definitions do tend to cluster together into groups that focus on an organization's future, its present, or its past.

Organizational Identity

An organization's identity expresses its "central, enduring, and distinctive" character. In that sense it encompasses its past, present, and future. The key feature of an organization's identity is its stability and predictability. This stability allows various stakeholders to connect their own, personal identities to the identity of the organization. An organizational identity also provides a frame of reference (recall the discussion of "framing" in Chapter 3) for stakeholders to use in making sense out of an organization's actions and rhetoric. But, this does not mean that an organization's identity is either simple or internally consistent. Identities are like the taken-for-granted assumptions of cultures – complex and filled with tensions and contradictions. For example, McDonald's "identity" is a combination of its being a US firm and its serving, quickly, food that has very predictable ingredients and taste, regardless of where stores are located. Each component of its identity carries different associations for different stakeholders – fast food is viewed as modern, functional, unhealthy, culturally subversive, a threat to (or mechanism for enabling) meaningful family interaction, and so on. Both organizational insiders and outsiders – customers, suppliers, and members of the communities in which an organization has operated for a long time – will identify with some parts of an organization's identity while ignoring or rejecting other parts. Or, they can accept (or reject) the identity, and the organization, altogether.

A paradigm case of customers identifying with an organization probably is that of college/university alumni. At one point in their lives, alumni were customers who purchased an education, or at least a diploma, from the organization. But, fortunately for university fund-raisers, many alumni have constructed a very different view of their relationship with the institution – they come to define themselves in terms of their link to their alma maters. Long after their mandatory economic transactions were completed, many of them voluntarily donate additional funds to the organization, either directly through contributions or indirectly, through paying inflated prices for licensed clothing and paraphernalia that bear the university's logo. Some even vow that their unborn children will purchase their educations/degrees from the same organization. In many cases identification is so complete that students and/ or alumni forget that they were customers of their universities and instead act more like docile servants. They proclaim (often quite loudly) the virtues of the organization, would never dare to try to influence organizational policies or actions, and never ask themselves if they would have obtained a better return on their investment by purchasing an education/degree from a different university.[3]

Customer identification is important for other organizations as well. After September 11, 2001, when most US airlines were lining up for taxpayer bailouts, thousands of customers of Southwest Airlines demonstrated their identification with the organization by sending monetary donations to its Dallas headquarters in order to keep their airline flying. (So did some of its employees.) Even though Southwest's management had strategically cultivated customer identification from the organization's beginnings, they were momentarily befuddled by this customers-become-benefactors behavior. (For those of us who have been repeatedly abused by

172

Southwest's competitors, it was easy to understand.) Eventually Southwest returned the donations, along with a heartfelt thank you and a note indicating that, unlike most of their competitors, which were on the verge of bankruptcy, Southwest was a profitable airline with millions of dollars in the bank. US automakers relied just as heavily on customer identification during the 1950s and 1960s, when every good American was a Ford person or a Chevy person or a Dodge person or a Cadillac person (and some fringe elements were even Volkswagen or Honda people). "Everyone" knew what the identification said about the owners' values, patriotism, socio-economic class, emotional stability, and so on (Ewen, 1994). High levels of customer–organization identification make organizational decision-makers' lives much simpler, because they allow them to focus their attention on satisfying other stakeholders.

Of course, insiders and outsiders alike also may dis-identify with an organization, and do so just as strongly. Employees who dis-identify are likely to leave the organization as soon as alternative employment becomes available. Customers, too, will "vote with their feet" if they can. A complicated set of organizational identities and identifications eventually emerges. While there may be a "core" identity that is shared by all or almost all stakeholders, each potential audience may also hold "peripheral" conceptions of what the organization is "really" like. As a result, different stakeholders and different stakeholder groups may hold somewhat different expectations for the organization and may feel betrayed if organizational rhetors adapt their messages and appeals to a different stakeholder group.

Organizational Images

A second key term is organizational "image" – that is, the impressions about an organization that operate in a particular rhetorical situation. These are congruent with the organization's overall identity, but usually they highlight some elements of that identity and de-emphasize others. For example, when McDonald's introduced vegetarian burgers for its stores in Hindu communities, it created a local image. For some members of those local audiences the image was that of a US capitalist organization shamelessly exploiting local traditions; for others, it was that of a multinational firm making wise strategic adaptations. Both interpretations were credible, because they are part of McDonald's identity. But neither interpretation threatened core elements of McDonald's identity as a US organization whose essence is predictability and homogeneity. Because images are located in the "here and now," they are directly influenced by the conscious, strategic manipulation of symbols. Organizational rhetors may construct different images with different audiences and rhetorical situations, just as twenty-somethings (and other people) strategically construct different images for the audiences they encounter on the internet, in a college bar on a Friday night, among the crowd around them at a college basketball game on Saturday afternoon, or amidst the participants in a religious service they attend some time on the weekend (Schenkler, 1980; Tedeschi, 1981).

In all of these cases, image management involves legitimizing one's self by forging symbolic links to the dominant values of the culture and sub-culture from which each audience is drawn, as well as creating one's identity. The more diverse the set of rhetorical situations that a person (individual or corporate) faces, the more complicated image management becomes. For multinational corporations operating in multiple cultures, or for twenty-somethings who have a rich and varied social life, simultaneously maintaining a coherent central enduring character (an identity) while strategically adapting their images to the demands of local audiences can be challenging.

Organizational Reputations

An organization's *identity* is projected into the future; its *image(s)* is (are) constructed and enacted in the present; and its "reputation" is composed of memories – the symbolic recreations of relevant past experiences that audiences bring with them to their encounters with the organization and its rhetoric. Memories are not literal histories; they are moderated by complex interpretive processes. Like the taken-for-granted assumptions of a culture, they are usually stored below conscious awareness, but they can be activated (raised to a conscious level) by crisis events or image managing rhetoric in specific rhetorical situations. Some memories are shared by almost all members of a culture. For example, every US citizen "remembers" that NASA (National Aeronautics and Space Administration) landed men on the moon; beat the Soviet Union in the space race; and got the Apollo 13 astronauts home against insurmountable odds (and they "remember" these events even if the were not yet alive when they happened). Millions remember the gasps produced by their elementary school classmates when they watched a space shuttle that was carrying the first teacher–astronaut exploded before their eyes. Others remember that NASA crashed spaceships on various celestial objects (sometimes accidentally, sometimes intentionally); and a few share my memory of watching the shuttle *Columbia* streak across a cloudless Texas sky after being turned into a flaming coffin by falling foam (Kauffman, 1997; Berger, 2010; Manber, 2010). Some people recall parts of NASA's history that did not involve space flights – as an organization that became involved in an awkward romantic triangle among astronauts; provided employment for rocket scientists from the Third Reich; and helped create Tang (an artificial, powdered citrus drink that helped astronauts in space ingest adequate levels of vitamin C) and Corningware (a kind of cookware that can be taken directly from a freezer to a hot oven, or vice-versa, without breaking). Still others recall that the organization spends more taxpayer money ($18.69 billion in fiscal year 2010) than the federal school breakfast and lunch program for low-income, nutritionally at-risk children ($16.9 billion in fiscal year 2010); or that taxpayer monies have given the organization a massive competitive advantage over private sector organizations that would like to be involved in space exploration and research. Every rhetorical situation involving NASA, and every message produced by the organization's rhetors and by its critics, will activate some of these memories and repress others. The scope and complexity of such memories and the degree to which they vary across audience members guide and constrain the range of rhetorical strategies available to rhetors, while creating complex, multi-dimensional challenges for them.

Finally, while organizational identity, image, and reputation are important, their inter-relationships are also significant (Kuhn, 1997; Cheney and Christensen, 2001; Coombs, 2007, 2009; Coombs and Holladay, 2010). For example, an organization's identity influences its reputation. Memories do not make sense by themselves. They are connected and thus given meaning when audiences interpret them in terms of the organization's identity. For most audiences, the memory of an astronaut's death means something different from the death of a worker at a BP refinery or in an offshore drilling rig, not because one death is more or less tragic than the other, but because NASA's identity is different from that of BP. If an organization has a positive identity, which is solidly based upon many supporting memories, it is easier for organizational rhetors to persuade stakeholders to overlook or forgive a negative event. Rhetors can claim that the event is an aberration, an exception to the organization's normal way of doing things, and has no larger significance. Similarly, if the organization's identity is negative because it is based on a series of unfortunate events, or if it is unstable because stakeholders can recall few relevant memories, or if it is untrustworthy because they hold a number of inconsistent or confusing memories, creating a positive image during a reputational crisis will be very difficult. It is the combination of identity, image, and reputation, that guides and constrains crisis management.

Key Concepts in Crisis Management

In Chapter 4 I explained that a condition can exist for decades before rhetors are able to define it successfully as a *problem* that demands action on the part of policymakers. Similarly, adverse events may turn into identity crises for organizations; but then they may not. Or some stakeholder groups may perceive an event in ways that create an identity crisis, while other groups view the same event in very different terms. The meaning of an event is, by itself, ambiguous – its significance, who is responsible for it, and what should be done in response to it all are contested concepts. Whether an event becomes the source of an identity crisis or not will depend on the nature of the event and, especially, on the rhetoric that it generates.

Pre-Crisis Identity Management

One factor that influences the likelihood that an event will start a crisis is the organization's prior image and its communicative relationship with stakeholders. In general, having a coherent, positive identity with key stakeholders is helpful, but there are no guarantees. First of all, developing a positive identity with *most* stakeholders may not matter to *some* powerful stakeholders. For example, Malden Mills, a Boston-area textile firm, was the "poster child" for positive relationships with stakeholders for a long time. It was a model corporate citizen, and its owner, Aaron Fuerstein, had developed a very clear image as a tough but fair member of the local community. When the company was forced to declare bankruptcy during the Reagan recession of the early 1980s, Fuerstein was forced to lay off many of his employees. But, instead of moving the company's operations to Mexico or Southeast Asia, as almost every other US textile firm had done, he innovated, brought his employees back to work, and ensured that Malden Mills would continue to be a pillar of the community. During the mid-1990s, when a fire destroyed the mill, Fuerstein drew on his private fortune to pay his workers' salaries while the plant was being rebuilt, which earned him a permanent place in the annals of corporate social responsibility and prompted the media to anoint him as a "saint" (a label that embarrassed him to no end). As a result, everyone with whom Malden Mills had an ongoing relationship went out of their way to support the firm and its leadership during the event. Suppliers delayed collection of owed monies; retailers patiently waited for orders to be filled; community members, workers, and so on praised Feuerstein and his organization. But, when the (second) Bush recession forced the organization back into bankruptcy, Feuerstein was forced to go to the capital markets for funding. He suddenly found that local goodwill, carefully developed over decades, was irrelevant. General Electric (GE) Capital, which had gained control of the company through the bankruptcy process, refused to grant him an extension he needed in order to secure additional funding, and other concessions. Feuerstein was ousted, and the new owners quickly closed the mill and shipped all of its operations to Southeast Asia (save a contract with the US Department of Defense, which, by law, has to be filled by firms located in the United States). In short, having a strong relationship with almost all stakeholders is of limited value when an event makes the organization dependent on one powerful stakeholder, which could not care less about the organization's positive image/ identity. For this reason some management-oriented models recommend that, during crises, organizations should focus only on those stakeholders that are positioned in such a way, and sufficiently powerful, so as to do significant economic damage to them. In short, stakeholders are not created equal, and for some of them – like GE Capital in this instance – a firm's identity, the CEOs' reputation, and a history of positive relationships and social responsibility matter little when money is involved (Marcus and Goodman, 1991; Barton, 2001; Ulmer, 2001; Seeger and Ulmer, 2002).

Second, and ironically, having a positive pre-crisis identity can actually increase an organization's vulnerability. Organizational identities entail expectations, and, if the organization acts in ways that violate those expectations, its credibility will suffer. For decades, the US nuclear power industry engaged in rhetoric claiming that its product would eventually be so inexpensive that electricity would be "too cheap to meter" – a prophecy that never came to pass. It replied to critics' questions about reactor safety by claiming that the superior scientific expertise of its designers and the extensive training of its operators combined with complex, multi-layered safety systems to make major accidents impossible. The good news for industry rhetors was that employees, policymakers, and the general public largely believed these claims and came to trust the industry. The bad news was that they made the industry's identity especially vulnerable to an accident, as it discovered during the 1979 partial core meltdown at Three Mile Island. Members of Western societies have long been enamoured with the power of science, and they have accepted their own increasing dependency on the miracles that high-tech organizations provide. But they have also retained a fear of science-gone-wrong – a concern so brilliantly articulated in Shelly's novel *Frankenstein*. For all organizations, trust is a crucial element in a positive identity. But, like in interpersonal relationships, building trust is a difficult and time-consuming process; destroying it is easy and quick; and feelings of betrayal can last a very long time (Farrell and Goodnight, 1981; Perrow, 1984; Dionisopoulos and Goldzwig, 1992; Dionisopoulos and Crable, 1988).

Finally, an organization can change in ways that create a gap between its identity and its capabilities. Like cultural myths, identities are stable because they form the frames of reference that stakeholders use in order to make sense out of everyday events. Information that might disconfirm an identity is often ignored, obscured, or treated as an unimportant aberration. Organizational rhetors may encourage this de-coupling process by managing crises successfully. By crafting a series of positive images, they ensure that stakeholders' expectations about the organization's capacity to deal with potential crisis will continue to be positive, but also unrealistic. So, at some point, a major crisis will come as a surprise. With surprise comes doubt and suspicion, further complicating the rhetorical situation that the organization faces.

For example, the American Red Cross had been in disarray for some time prior to hurricane Katrina. Slow responses to hurricanes Hugo and Andrew revealed internal communication problems, which were largely forgotten by outsiders once the organization "got its act together" and successfully responded to the storms. Insiders and stakeholders who were tightly connected to the organization knew that the slow response was a symptom of bigger problems that had not been solved. Infighting among members of the Board of Directors and instances of corruption had produced a new CEO almost every year for an extended period of time. Controversy over the organization's handling of donations collected after the September 11, 2001 attacks had generated a great deal of criticism and had weakened the standing of the Red Cross among other stakeholders. The deteriorating climate had prompted a number of key employees to leave the organization, taking a great deal of organizational intelligence with them.

Overall, the organization's rhetoric had successfully minimized the impact of these problems on the organization's identity. Most stakeholders still viewed the Red Cross positively, and as a result expected a highly competent response to Katrina. Perhaps more importantly, many of the remaining employees had come to believe the organization's "our problems are behind us" rhetoric, which made it impossible to take corrective action before Katrina hit. When the storm created challenges that exceeded the organization's capacities, these hidden weaknesses suddenly became very clear to everyone concerned. Ironically, successful crisis/image management had made the organization's identity more vulnerable to external threats (Williams, 2001; Atkinson, 2002; Meisenbach, 2006).[4]

Transforming Events into Crises

Regardless of how vulnerable a given organization's identity might be, events themselves will not threaten that identity unless they are perceived as both significant and the organization's fault. When a serious, objectionable event occurs within an organization, the transformation to a reputational crisis is almost automatic. For example, the sexual abuse of children by adult leaders of organizations, whether secular (the US Boy Scouts) or religious (the Roman Catholic Church), is perceived as significant, indeed horrendous, by all stakeholders. The only question in such cases is who or what is to blame: is it the organization's responsibility, or is the fault of a few "bad apples" (recall Chapter 4)? This is why evidence that the organizational hierarchy "covered up" the events was so damaging – evil perpetrated by individuals was transformed into an *organizational* crisis. Conversely, when members of Royal Dutch Shell's management were caught lying about the size of the organization's proven oil reserves, the event was highly significant for Shell's stockholders, but less salient to the human rights and

180

environmental groups that had long criticized the organization. Shell rhetors quickly argued that the falsehoods were produced only by a handful of upper managers who were punished by the organization as soon as their actions were discovered. As I pointed out in Chapter 3, the combination of bureaucratic structures and the ideology of managerialism often allows managers to shift responsibility from themselves to the organizational hierarchy. While these strategies may allow corrupt *individuals* to escape responsibility, they do not protect the *organization*'s identity. Stakeholders typically view upper management as the embodiment of the organization, and their actions provide concrete evidence of the organization's operant code of ethics (see Fombrun and Rindova, 2000; Livesay and Graham, 2007; Boys, 2009).

If an event is external to the firm, there is more room to maneuver. Its impact on the organization's identity will depend on how well its rhetors manage the event and/or on their rhetoric during it. In some cases, potential crises may even allow organizations and their rhetors to enhance their standing in the eyes of key stakeholders. For example, consider the effects that hurricane Katrina had on the identities of the Salvation Army, American Red Cross, and Federal Emergency Management Agency (FEMA). Some of these organizations acted in ways that actually enhanced their images and strengthened their identities; others did the opposite.

Long before hurricane Katrina struck the US gulf coast, the Salvation Army had developed a positive identity, albeit a somewhat vague and incomplete one. Most US residents knew the Army as a charity that helps people in need. Relatively few knew that it is the second largest charity in the US, one that in 2004 helped 32 million people to the tune of $2.6 billion. Even fewer realized that it is a religious organization – a Protestant denomination with a particular theology and ecclesiastical structure: it does not celebrate the Christian sacraments of communion or baptism, because those rituals distract from the core belief in redemption through grace; and it demands certain behaviors from its members, imposing prohibitions against gambling and the consumption of drugs (including alcohol and nicotine). As a result of the attention paid to the organization and its superb performance during its Katrina-relief efforts, its identity became clearer and more widely understood. This does not mean that the added attention was wholly favorable – some audiences found its exclusion of homosexual members to be objectionable, for example. But, overall, the Salvation Army's actions and the honest and unassuming rhetoric of its spokespersons enhanced its identity as an organization defined by selfless service to others. At the same time its overall identity was clarified, which bodes well for the future. The National Weather Service and the National Hurricane Center also garnered accolades for their efforts, in spite of some complaints that they failed to predict a sudden strengthening of the storm and a change of direction just before landfall. Similarly, the US Coast Guard's response efforts were praised, and its identity as an emergency-response organization was revived after years of being subordinated to its role in the war against drugs.

However, for other organizations, Katrina became the occasion for an identity crisis. From landfall on, FEMA, like the Red Cross, was vilified for its inept response to the storm. The organization's no less inept rhetoric made things even worse. FEMA rhetors argued that no one could have anticipated a storm of Katrina's magnitude. But it soon became public knowledge that one year earlier the organization had conducted a simulation involving state, local, federal, and volunteer organizations in which a fictional hurricane Pam, almost identical to Katrina, struck New Orleans. After the simulation, FEMA Director Michael Brown implied that the action plans that had been developed as a result of the exercise would be implemented within 60 days, but one year later none had been implemented. FEMA's efforts to shift responsibility for its problems also failed. When asked, on September 26, to explain why Louisiana parishes had not been declared to be in a state of emergency (which would have led to increased aid), while coastal counties of Mississippi and Alabama had, Brown claimed that Democratic Governor Katherine Blanco had not requested the designation. The governor's office immediately produced a copy of a letter asking for the designation and for aid to all of Louisiana's southestern parishes, including the New Orleans metropolitan area. Even potentially positive rhetoric – President Bush's appearance with Brown, which produced the infamous "you're doing a heck-of-a-job Brownie" congratulation while life for thousands of people at the New Orleans Superdome declined into barbarity – further complicated the organization's image.

The US Army Corps of Engineers' identity crisis developed more slowly. For months its rhetors had managed to separate the organization's identity from the events of Katrina by asserting that the flood control systems it had constructed were designed for a much smaller storm. But in June, 2007, a report by the American Society of Civil Engineers concluded that two-thirds of the New Orleans flooding was caused by failure of the city's floodwalls, which led to widespread loss of life. Subsequent research concluded that much of the system was badly designed and poorly constructed, and attributed some flooding to the Corps' decision not to close the flood gates. In sum, external events do not in themselves create identity crises; they merely create opportunities for them to emerge (Strom, 2006; Ghose, 2007).

Weekend Fun 5

Choose a motorized vehicle that interests you, preferably one you drive or ride in frequently. Be sure you know its manufacturer, model, and year. How safe is it? An easy way to answer this question is to find out how many "stars" the National Highway Traffic Safety Administration (NHTSA) gave it for front, side, and rear impacts, and for its tendency to roll over. But be careful – the ratings are adjusted for the type of vehicle, which means that they tell you how safe one mid-sized sedan is compared to other mid-sized sedans, for example, not how safe it is in comparison to a Mack Truck. Another handy source is the ratings given by the Insurance Institute. Then find out how many times your vehicle has been recalled by its manufacturer and what problems were identified that led to the recall. Finally (and this one will be harder, but websites such as Edmunds.com and cars.com are a good place to start), find out how many complaints about life-threatening problems have been reported in connection with your type of vehicle. What effects has your research had on your image of your vehicle, on your view of the identity of the company that produced it, or on your expectations about your future with it? Why?

Strategies of Crisis Management

Once events become crises, organizational rhetors must deal with the immediate rhetorical situation. Researchers and practitioners agree on the *process* of crisis management:

1 respond *quickly* and *clearly*, so that the organization defines the event instead of allowing other parties to frame it for key stakeholders;
2 be *consistent*, both in terms of the claims that are made and in terms of the rhetorical strategies that are used, in order to maintain the organization's credibility; and
3 be *open* and *honest*.

Unfortunately, like every other aspect of organizational rhetoric, life is rarely this simple. An organization's identity and the nature of the event complicate crisis management by making some kinds of responses obligatory and rendering other responses strategically unwise. In addition, each potential response strategy has its own strengths and weaknesses.

Denial

The simplest crisis management strategy is *denial* – asserting that a potentially troubling event did not happen, was insignificant (as in "only a tiny percentage of air travelers get stuck in planes for hours with human waste flowing down the aisles"), or was not out of the ordinary, given current behavior standards (as in "every company is being forced to eliminate its employee's pensions or health insurance"). Even children realize that denial only works if the rhetor (1) responds clearly and immediately; (2) can produce overwhelming, credible evidence to support claims of innocence; (3) has developed an identity as a trustworthy, truthful source;

184

and (4) faces an audience that shares the values that are implied in the message. Of course, the strategy is easier to implement if the organization (or child) actually *is* innocent, or if the event actually *is* trivial. The paradigm case of successful denial was the response of Johnson and Johnson (J&J) to two instances in which someone tampered with Tylenol capsules. By quickly notifying all stakeholders, by removing products from store shelves, by absorbing related financial losses, and by quickly devising enhanced safety measures, J&J not only defused the crisis, it also strengthened its own identity as a responsible corporate citizen (Benoit and Lindsay, 1987; Benson, 1988). Although the perpetrator has never been found, J&J quickly demonstrated that the guilty party was not one of its employees or the organization.

Denials are an especially foolish strategy when they can easily be exposed as false. At one point during the Three Mile Island crisis, utility rhetors persuaded the Lieutenant Governor to announce that no radioactivity had escaped the plant, something that everyone near that plant who was holding a clicking Geiger counter knew was not true. In one fell swoop the company undermined its own credibility and that of the state government, and destroyed a relationship that, up to that point, had been cooperative. In a modern, mediated Wikileaks world in which information and symbolically powerful images are available to anyone with an internet connection, untrue denials are especially foolish. For example, in 2005 activists accused Walmart, Inc., then the world's largest company, of training its US "associates" to manipulate state welfare and Medicaid (health care for the indigent) programs in order to compensate for the company not paying its workers a living wage and not offering them affordable health insurance. Walmart immediately denied the charges; but, within minutes of the official public denial, a 27-page internal document written by Human Resources officer Susan Chambers and entitled "Reviewing and Revision: Walmart's Benefits Strategy" appeared on the internet. Not only did it substantiate the critics' charges, it outlined additional steps being taken and/or considered by the organization to reduce employee benefits even further and/or to shift an even larger percentage of benefit costs to them. Like Radio

Shack's management (recall Chapter 3), Walmart's management immediately took legal action to remove the document from the World Wide Web, but in the meantime thousands of people around the world, including almost every news organization, had downloaded copies. As a result, the organization exacerbated the immediate crisis by reducing its trustworthiness and increasing the credibility of its critics, while creating a new problem for itself. Its management had long garnered support from the business community through an unabashed free-market, anti-government rhetoric, all of which was undermined by evidence that it was strategically manipulating the "socialistic" programs that the business community despised (Bailey, 2006).

Knowingly using false denials is foolish, but there are instances in which organizational rhetors simply do not know the "facts of the case." Their ignorance can result from the events themselves. For example, utility spokesmen at Three Mile Island did not have direct, accurate evidence available about what was happening inside of the plant (in fact it took months to determine whether or not the uranium core had actually melted down). Accidents at petrochemical plants usually result from a completely unanticipated combination of factors, which can only be understood in retrospect. As the events are occurring, no one really understands what is going on. In other cases, particularly those involving indiscretions committed by upper management, spokespersons may have been intentionally kept in the dark or misled. Enron's executives called the firm's corporate communication staff to a meeting in the middle of the night and instructed them to prepare statements for the morning news shows announcing that Enron had filed for bankruptcy protection and expected indictments to follow. Although some members of staff had suspected malfeasance, they did not know the details until long after the crisis started. In short, as your mothers probably told you, (1) lying is not a good crisis management strategy, and (2) if you don't know what you're talking about, quit talking (or at least be very ambiguous).

Confession and Apology

If an organization actually is guilty of wrong-doing, or if denial is not a viable strategy, that organization may choose to apologize for its actions. The key characteristics of *full apologies* are well established in major religious traditions. In the Judeo-Christian tradition, apologies begin with confession and a heartfelt expression of regret for one's actions, and include an admission that the confessant knew that the actions were wrong, a repudiation of the actions and of the "person" who committed them, a promise to behave properly in the future, and the payment or promise of some form of atonement or compensation (see Burke, 1970; Benoit, 1995; Hargie, Stapleton, and Tourish, 2010).

Among organizations, full apologies are rare for two reasons. First, they require that upper management admit to failure. No one believes the myths of managerial superiority and/or infallibility described in Chapter 3 more than managers, and as a result their egos get in the way of admitting mistakes. Second, managers may fear litigation, and legal staffs typically advise them to do almost anything but confess, especially if the organization is actually guilty. The potential economic costs of lawsuits are greater and more immediate than the potential long-term economic costs of a weakened identity. Besides, in many cases the potential costs of litigation have already been included in profit and loss computations. For example, Ford Motor Company's executives made a strategic decision to market the company's Pinto vehicle with its fuel tank knowingly placed in a position which increased the likelihood that it would explode in a rear-end accident. The projected costs of using a safer design (less than $20 per vehicle) were greater than the likely cost of litigation. There are many strategies available to limit the costs of litigation: arranging of out-of-court settlements that include "gag orders," which keep identity-threatening facts secret; ensuring that lawsuits will be filed in states that have passed "tort reforms," which limit corporate liability, in courts whose judges have demonstrated pro-corporate orientations, or in districts that have a history of having plaintiff awards reversed or reduced on appeal; or delaying legal proceedings until a plaintiff dies. (The latter strategy works especially well in medical malpractice or drug side-effect lawsuits – no testimony is as powerful as the one made by an aggrieved, severely injured, and/or dying victim – and dead victims do not testify; see Egan, 2010).[5]

As I explained in Chapter 1, organizational rhetors' first strategic choice is among the many venues available for them. The court of public opinion may be a less wise option than a law court, especially if the corporation has contributed substantial funds to a judge's election campaigns in the past. As a result of these processes, research by Sydney Finkelstein, management professor at Dartmouth University, could find only one instance in which the CEO of a Fortune 500 firm offered a full apology in the more than 100 cases he studied (cited in Martin and Maynard, 2010). Love may not mean that you don't have to say you're sorry, as the old movie suggested, but position power certainly does.

Consequently, it is more likely that organizations whose management chooses to apologize will offer partial apologies, a kind of "nuanced regret," in which the organization expresses its willingness to accept financial "responsibility" for losses. They also commit themselves to compensating victims out of their goodwill and social responsibility, and to investing whatever is necessary to ensure that similar events do not happen in the future. They admit that the event took place and was significant, but they claim that it was accidental, completely unintentional, or could not possibly have been anticipated given the information available to the organization (a strategy generally labeled as *defeasibility*). But, they decidedly do not offer a full confession or use the term "apologize," nor in any way accept blame for the event itself. In most cases partial apologies are combined with efforts to shift blame onto other parties (Benoit, 1995).

Evading Responsibility and/or Shifting Blame

The simplest form of evading responsibility for an event is to assert that it resulted from some impersonal force which is outside of the organization's control. This strategy is quite commonly used, and some uses of it are downright silly. For example Texas Governor

Rick Perry, one of the strongest supporters of the oil industry among US politicians (and one of the primary recipients of industry campaign contributions), claimed that the BP Deepwater Horizon well explosion and fire was an "act of God," an explanation that led a *Houston Chronicle* editorial cartoonist to quip that "the oil companies *are* God in Texas" (Blanton, 2010). Other efforts are horribly misguided, as when Boston's Cardinal Bernard Law asserted in a court deposition that parents of sexually abused children should bear some of the responsibility because they left them alone with priests. In industries that often encounter natural events, stakeholders generally expect managers to make adequate contingency plans for dealing with them and to act quickly and professionally when they do occur. BP's image problem surrounding Deep Horizon resulted from their having done the opposite – steadfastly claiming that the well did not provide a significant risk, persuading regulators to allow them to reduce their safety precautions, and not having a response plan in place until weeks after the explosion.

As I explained earlier in this chapter, it is almost as unwise for management to blame its lower-level employees or contractors (Conrad and Poole, 2005; Acosta et al., 2009; Hoffmeister, 2010a, 2010b; Blanton, 2010). The strategy simply does not succeed, especially with audiences outside of the company. For example, President Obama described Congressional hearings in which the CEOs of the three firms that had been involved in the Deepwater Horizon event (BP, Transocean, and Halliburton) attempted to blame one another while accepting none of the responsibility themselves "a ridiculous spectacle." Audiences outside of the firms agreed, and late-night comedians dubbed the event "The Three Stooges Drill and Oil Well" (Dlouhy, 2010).[6] In short, blame-shifting usually requires an external scapegoat, although not just anyone will do.

To be a good scapegoat, a target must be sufficiently powerful to be feasibly responsible for an event. Such people must also be suspect in terms of some legitimized cultural values. Usually this means that they are "different" from "normal" people in some way. For example, Kenneth Burke's (1941) analysis of the rhetorical appeal of Hitler's *Mein Kampf* examines the ways in which the author constructed an image of the Jewish people (and other suspect groups) as both powerful and alien. Historian Richard Hofstadter (1965) has persuasively argued that US society is especially susceptible to a kind of "paranoid style" that, historically, has cast Mormons, Masons, Catholics (especially immigrants), African–Americans, intellectuals, and a host of other groups as powerful/alien threats to the body politic. But, for rhetors working for the world's largest and wealthiest companies, it is difficult to depict any group of outsiders as sufficiently powerful and alien to be responsible for their plight.

The prevalence of free-market rhetoric and the taken-for-granted assumptions that it has created (recall Chapter 2) make government a handy scapegoat in most cases. Consider two examples. Richard Crable and Steven Vibbert (1983) studied the Mobil Oil Company's responses to the industry's declining image during the late 1970s (see also Porter, 1992). Oil shortages combined with skyrocketing industry (and company) profits to damage seriously the company's/industry's identity with many US stakeholders. Industry lobbying had failed to derail legislation designed to tax the industry's "windfall profits," and additional proposals threatened to force oil firms to open their books to federal regulators and/or to force them to "roll back" their prices. The popular ire, which initially had been vented in the direction of the Organization of the Petroleum Exporting Countries (OPEC), started to focus closer to home.

Mobil embarked on a PR campaign designed to shift popular attitudes. Subtly cast as "observations" rather then "advocacy" or "rhetoric," Mobil's full-page advertisements critiqued every relevant government action or proposal. The energy crisis had resulted from the government's failure to develop a viable foreign policy in the Middle East and/or a comprehensive energy policy at home. Suggestions to break up the oil company trusts were compared to the decision to break up the old New York Yankee dynasty (evidently Mobil was not concerned with Red Sox fans in their audience). Most environmentalists are well intended, Mobil admitted, but they are too naïve to realize that radical environmentalism threatened the jobs that Americans needed. Industry profits were large, but they paled in comparison to the federal budget. Like most issues, energy policy should be left to the "common sense" of citizens and to the discipline of the market, not to some government bureaucrat. Mobil did not limit its ire to government and environmental groups, but also criticized other oil companies which had been willing to cooperate with those villains – a "Quislings in the midst" strategy (Dionisopoulos and Crable, 1988).

A second study examined the California cattle industry's responses to criticisms about the industry's record on issues related to health, the environment, and animal welfare. Kimberly Elsbach (1994) found a somewhat more subtle use of the government as scapegoat. "Institutional appeals," in which a corporation or industry claimed to have followed all existing regulations and to have cooperated with regulatory agencies, were effective, at least with audiences that had a direct financial stake in the organization or industry. Similarly, "technical" claims – arguments that the processes or practices that are being attacked are necessary for the efficient operation of the organizations in a particular industry – are also effective with these "affiliated" audiences. Links to government regulators were especially successful when combined with "acknowledgments" – claims that the event was not the organization's fault, was motivated by legitimate concerns, or had a positive outcome in the long run. Other studies have found similar results (for example Allen and Caillouet, 1994).

However, there are two risks involved in efforts to shift blame onto government regulators. The first is that some audiences may remember that organizations exercise substantial influence over regulations and regulatory agencies – which is expressed through the concept of "regulatory capture" described in Chapter 4. Shifting blame to regulators can remind audiences of this cozy relationship, and in some cases may force the regulators to attack the company's credibility, in order to protect their own legitimacy (Baker et al., 2009; Conrad et al., 2010). The second risk is that anti-regulatory rhetoric may inadvertently encourage policymakers to increase regulation of the industry. Corporations are usually able to block increased regulation (recall Chapter 4), but doing so may become expensive, both in terms of lobbying costs and in terms of maintaining an image of social responsibility. From a rhetorical perspective, organizations have good reasons to prefer being in a lightly regulated industry. Weak regulators cannot significantly impinge on the organization's operations, but they are handy scapegoats when things go wrong (Posner, 2009, 2010; Dunham and Powell, 2010; Johnson and Kwak, 2010; Maynard, 2010).

Restoring/Restorying Organizational Identity

Much as organizational identities guide and constrain the rhetorical strategies used during crises, crisis management potentially influences organizational identities. Organizational rhetors have two inter-related goals during crises – to manage the immediate situation and to insulate the organization's identity from any negative effects. In order to achieve both, organizational rhetors often ramp up identity management efforts at the same time as they are dealing with specific crises, creating two parallel rhetorical campaigns.

A useful model for understanding identity management strategies used in conjunction with crisis management was proposed by psychologist Robert Abelson and his colleagues (Abelson, 1959; Kaplan and Crockett, 1968). Abelson's research team investigated the cognitive processes that audiences use in order to resist persuasive appeals. Their research indicated that people actively resist persuasive messages in four characteristic ways. The simplest resistance strategy is to ignore them, refuse to believe them, or de-value their source (a strategy labeled denial). Or, when we are faced with persuasive messages that threaten our beliefs and behaviors, we may attempt to bolster them by seeking out information, arguments, or appeals that confirm them. Conservatives bolster their beliefs by watching hours of Fox News and by reading every issue of the *Wall Street Journal*, making sure they are only exposed to messages that confirm their existing beliefs and values, while they disparage the "liberal media." Similarly, progressives may voraciously consume MSNBC (NBC News' internet and cable television network) broadcasts, read every page of *The Nation*, and use parental control technology to keep Fox News from invading their homes, comfortable in the knowledge that, by doing so, they will only be exposed to rhetoric that supports their existing beliefs. Through bolstering, we resist persuasive messages by way of overwhelming them.

We may also use more complex cognitive strategies. Through transcendence we re-frame an issue to be about abstract rights rather than concrete circumstances – for example, we tell ourselves that the issue really is not whether or not a specific tax break for the wealthy should be limited or repealed, but about the survival of the free-market economy, which is necessary for the survival of democratic governance and of Western society. Or we differentiate acceptable or tolerable instances of an action from morally reprehensible examples – innocent children killed by missiles fired by the unmanned drones used by "our" side are defined as tragic but necessary "collateral damage" that is unavoidable during warfare, whereas the killing of children by the "other side" is an unnecessary violation of everything that is right and decent.

There is no question that these four strategies are widely used – by individuals, politicians, and organizations – both in general and during identity crises. It is also true that they appear during events that could herald identity crises. But their primary function is not to manage specific crises. Instead, they strengthen the positive aspects of an organization's (or individual's or politician's) identity and/or obscure the negative aspects. They accompany crisis managing rhetoric, because crises have the potential to undermine an organization's identity, but they are not logically or even persuasively dependent on crisis management strategies.

More importantly, these strategies set the stage for restoring and renewing the organization's identity. Eventually crises pass and the attention of stakeholders, including the media, will move on to other topics. At some point the organization will be able to tell its own story, outside of the glare of immediate publicity. The post-crisis period also provides organizations with an opportunity to collect and analyze data about their crisis management, to assess the strategies they used and the options they might have chosen, to evaluate the short and the long-term impact of the crisis, and to make changes necessary in order to manage crises better in the future (Pauchant and Mitroff, 1992; Pearson and Mitroff, 1993; Coombs, 2007). For example, once the leadership of the Red Cross stabilized (months after Katrina), it learned to use new media – websites, Flickr, YouTube and so on – to tell its story, focusing on its overall identity and mission. The combination of the Red Cross' regaining control of its identity and the organization's effective performance during the mid-western floods of 2008 and during the Red River of the North's flood in 2009 allowed the organization to begin the process of restoring a positive identity. If an organization can emerge from a crisis with a positive reputation, or quickly rebuild it, it is likely to benefit financially and will be better positioned to deal with future crises (Dowling, 2001; Davies et al., 2003; Coombs, 2004; Fombrun and van Riel, 2004).

Resisting Corporate Identity Rhetoric

As I indicated at the beginning of this chapter, contemporary identity management research and theory casts stakeholders/audiences as active agents, whose own rhetoric helps create the rhetorical situations that organizations face and influences the impact of organizational rhetoric. Identity management becomes an ongoing dialogic process, in which organizational identities emerge and sometimes are transformed through communicative interactions among multiple parties (Grunig and Grunig, 2000; Grunig, 2001; Tyler, 2005).

Speaking Resistance to Power

At a number of points in this book I have described instances in which individuals or groups challenged the cultural assumptions that underlie organizational rhetoric or critiqued the practices that are legitimized through that rhetoric. In some cases resistance is spontaneous and focused on specific, local issues (as in the case of the worker resistance at Subaru-Isuzu or in the travel and leisure industry, both of which were described in Chapter 3). But resistance is sometimes planned, organized, sustained, and rhetorically sophisticated. Of course organizations have massive advantages in comparison to dissidents, both in terms of tangible resources and in terms of political and economic influence. Thus the likelihood of successful resistance is rather low. Indeed, if resisters thought like the utility maximizers envisioned in free-market theory, they would never become resisters – taking on a multinational corporation simply is not a rational act.

However, resisters do have some advantages (Janeway, 1988). Most importantly, they are motivated by abstract values and taken-for-granted assumptions, both of which may encourage people to act even when the odds are against them (or often because the odds are against them). Their commitments endow them with energy and allow them to identify with other groups or people who share their beliefs and values. Their limited resources allow them to "take the moral high ground" in David and Goliath (underdog vs. behemoth) morality plays, much like the anti-slavery, women's rights, and anti-child labor advocates of the nineteenth century (Brooks, 1900). The advent of high-speed communication technologies also allows them to find each other and to organize their resistance (Maffesoli, 1996; O'Neill, 1999; Bennett, 2003; Kendall, Gill, and Cheney, 2007).

Resisters can draw upon the same cultural assumptions that organizational rhetors use, but employ them to criticize organizations for violating widely held pro-social values of justice, fairness, human dignity, and social responsibility. Embedded in each of the dominant social myths that I discussed in Chapters 2 and 3 – upward mobility, the organizational imperative, free-market fundamentalism, managerialism, and positional models of leadership – are emotions and ideas that can serve as the basis of counter-myths. Thus, it is not accidental that the primary themes of resistant rhetoric are corporate greed and illegality (the dark side of the free market), the creation and/or exploitation of human misery (the hidden effects of mobility), and unfair or unjust treatment of workers (the organizational imperative gone bad). Potential resisters concerned with any of these issues can find solidarity with others, and become unified by their opposition to a concrete, powerful, corporate enemy. A paradigm case of coalition-forming rhetoric was Robert Greenwald's 2005 documentary film *Wal-mart: The High Cost of Low Prices*.[7] Regardless of what an audience's values and concerns might be, there was a segment of the film that graphically demonstrated Walmart's violation of them – the destruction of "mom and pop" businesses, the mistreatment of Chinese (and US) workers, the manipulation of local, state, and national political systems, environmental degradation, even the abandonment of founder Sam Walton's socially responsible vision. The vignettes that made up the movie amplified "viewer indignation [and] identification, which creates common ground among viewers [constituting] [. . .] an anti-Walmart identity [allowing a variety of viewers to] collectively express and unite over their disapproval of the Walmart corporation" (Stokes and Holloway, 2009, 348).

Ironically, resisters also have a structural advantage. Contemporary organizations are interconnected with stakeholders in complicated ways, both within their home countries and around the world. Each of these network links offers a point at which resisters can pressure the organization. A target corporation may be too powerful to be attacked directly, but its operations may rely on a cozy relationship with regulators, or on a key line of credit from a financial institution that is vulnerable to pressure from customers, or on the goodwill of a religious organization whose leaders and members would be embarrassed by revelations about some of the corporation's activities, and so on. Through careful research, all of the relationships that exist between an organization and its key stakeholder can be identified, their strengths and weaknesses assessed, and pressure points and appropriate rhetorical strategies chosen. By attacking at these points, preferably simultaneously, resisters can create situations in which "the stakeholder group in question will be motivated to pressure the target [. . .] out of its own self interest" (Manheim,

2004, 108; see also Manheim, 2001; Ganesh, 2007; Peterson and Norton, 2007). Once these attacks begin to bear fruit, the organization's competitors may find ways to exploit the situation, institutional stockholders may become upset with the economic costs of resistance, and either abandon the firm or exert pressure on its management. Jarol Manheim concludes:

> The specific selection of pressure points will vary, but the logic is always the same: Find the most cost-effective means of using [the target organization's] dependency on various stakeholders to threaten or do actual harm to the target company. Increase the pressure until management yields. (Manheim, 2001, 196)

For example, in 1972 workers struck Farah (jeans) Manufacturing's El Paso, Texas plant, seeking increased wages and the right to unionize. Going on strike was risky, because Farah had ready access to immigrant workers from nearby Juarez, Mexico, who could be used as strikebreakers. Realizing this, the workers supplemented their strike with a multi-pronged rhetorical campaign. Sympathetic people in major US cities started a boycott around stores that sold Farah's products. Media coverage encouraged US Congresspersons to join the resistance, and Bishop S. M. Metzer joined the cause, encouraging other Catholic Bishops to follow his lead. Eventually the boycott was supported by the National Council of Churches, the United Church Board for Homeland Ministries, and several Catholic bishops. Workers filed formal complaints with the National Labor Relations Board (NLRB). Local religious leaders depicted the case as an example of the wealthy Anglo business establishment acting to keep local Latino workers poor and powerless. Other stores and unions joined the campaign – even Santa Claus joined in when a worker at Cleveland, Ohio's largest retailer, walked off the job, in support of the boycott. Farah stock fell from $49 a share to $5, which generated shareholder pressure. Twenty-two months after the strike began, Farah settled with its workers. As I will explain in the following section, this case illustrates each element of corporate campaigns.

Corporate Campaigns as a Rhetoric of Maneuver

Two developments led to the development and refinement of corporate campaigns. One involved changes in the US (and, to a lesser degree, in other countries influenced by Reagan/Thatcher-ism) that made direct resistance by organized labor virtually impossible. The second involved changes in progressive politics. The New Left that developed in the US during the 1960s as a means of reviving participatory democracy had been deeply hostile to corporate power. But its leaders were deeply suspicious also of organized labor because its leaders seemed all too willing to sacrifice the needs of their members to their own personal gain, as well as of politicians, who seemed increasingly dominated by corporate interests. The New Left movement generated the three elements that eventually would become central to corporate campaigns: a commitment to careful strategic research about target organizations, the development of alliances with other change-oriented groups, and a set of tactics. Codified in Saul Alinsky's *Rules for radicals* (1989), these three elements turned into an advocacy for a kind of social and economic judo against a target company, whereby its political and economic power was to be used as a weapon against it.

An excellent example of "judo politics" is the confrontation between Nike and the anti-sweatshop movement that started during the 1990s. Encouraged by Reagan Administration tax breaks and other policies, US textile and shoe manufacturers shifted their production to Asia. By 1984 Nike opened seven factories in China and South Korea and later on shifted much of its production to Indonesia and other southeast Asian countries, in the search for even lower wages and even more favorable labor and environmental laws. Almost immediately, an anti-sweatshop movement began in the US and Europe that criticized these organizations for paying poverty-level wages, often in violation of local minimum-wage laws, or not paying workers at all; for demanding excessive overtime, for allowing sexual harassment of women workers, for showing little or no regard for workplace safety, and so on.

Throughout the 1990s the Nike corporation's rhetors had produced advertising and identity management campaigns that sought to associate the organization with "the rights, needs and aspirations of the socially disadvantaged and excluded, including African-Americans, women, and the disabled, by promoting a discourse of self-empowerment and affirmation through sport, fitness, and physical activity" (Knight and Greenberg, 2002, 548; also see Boje, 1999, 2000; and Stabile, 2000). As a result of Nike's efforts, stakeholders started to expect the company not only to treat relatively powerless people fairly, but actively to help them improve their lives. Where the ethical treatment of all stakeholders was concerned, Nike claimed to lead the industry. This identity combined with three other factors to make Nike an optimal target for a corporate campaign: Nike was large enough for its critics to successfully cast it in the role of Goliath; it was wealthy enough to be able to pay higher wages and to improve working conditions, and it dominated the industry, which meant that changes Nike made would be adopted by its competitors. Nike may or may not have been the worst offender in the industry, but it was uniquely hypocritical, which made it the optimal target.

Labor, religious, and human rights groups sent investigators to Nike's Asian factories. Their combined reports created an appalling picture of Nike's subsidiaries' treatment of their workers – including women and children. In 1993, CBS' (Columbia Broadcasting System) newsmagazine Street Stories featured a story on Nike that focused on the gap between the poverty-level wages paid to its workers and the lucrative contracts the company offered celebrities such as Michael Jordan. The publicity began a drumbeat of pressure on the company. Nike's initial responses – attacking its critics, issuing denials, trying to shift blame, and trying to use internal "audits" to counter critics' claims – confirmed critics' claims of hypocrisy and further weakened Nike's credibility. Compounding matters was its announcement, with great fanfare, of a new workplace "Code of Conduct" which on closer inspection did not contain a single reference to worker rights and did not include any provisions for implementation. A generally favorable report by GoodWorks International was quickly discredited and contradicted by an internal Ernst and Young audit which was leaked to the press by a Nike employee. This audit found serious

199

threats to worker health and safety in Vietnamese plants con-
tracted by Nike. A series of essays by *New York Times* columnist
Bob Herbert, a series of Doonesbury comics, and a Michael Moore
film, *The Big One*, in which Nike CEO Phil Knight "found himself
saying unbelieveably callous, stupid, and uniformed things,"
all made the situation worse. When Nike offered customers the
chance to personalize their new sneakers, customer Jonah Peretti
ordered a pair with the term "sweatshop" printed on them. Nike
refused, and the ensuing email exchange was circulated widely
on the internet, reaching an audience of more than 10 million
people.[8] Eventually a student anti-sweatshop movement began at
Duke University, which seemed the optimal target because sales of
its licensed products generates income of more than $25 million
per year. Eventually the movement spread to more than 100 other
universities, including Georgetown, Wisconsin, Michigan, and
Arizona. Students used a wide variety of strategies, including sit-
ins, to pressure administrations into ensuring that licensed goods
are not produced in sweatshops.

Eventually Nike's competitors – including Reebok, which had
been taking market share away from Nike even before the sweatshop controversy exploded – announced new steps to ensure that
their products were not made in sweatshops. Reebok actively
sought to ally itself with anti-sweatshop activists. Faced with sustained pressure from corporate campaigners and new economic
pressure from competitors, Nike changed course and followed
Reebok's lead – joining the Fair Labor Association, a voluntary
organization established during the Clinton Administration to
monitor and report sweatshop conditions and creating the Nike
Foundation, whose espoused goal is to give "the world's most disadvantaged girls an opportunity to participate more fully in life."
However, the extent to which these actions have been accompanied by significant changes in Nike's factories is still a matter of
substantial debate. For example, Nike's much-ballyhooed decision to increase wages in its Vietnamese factories by twenty cents
an hour was helpful to its workers, but it still left those workers
below the local poverty level. It is, however, clear that activists
forced a change in Nike's rhetoric and identity.[9]

The Nike saga is representative of corporate campaigns through-out the world. Through a complex rhetoric of maneuver, by using simple strategies of creating "David vs. Goliath" narratives and of revealing damning information about ongoing organizational practices and duplicitous organizational rhetoric, critics can bring events and standing conditions to a point of organizational iden-tity crisis. By pressuring various stakeholders through a variety of strategies, some of which involve very creative symbolic action, they can stimulate economic pressures that they could never create on their own. If critics can sustain pressure over time, they may even prompt organizational rhetors to shift away from situationally appropriate identity/crisis management strategies to inappropriate and counter-productive ones (Allen and Caillouet, 1994; Fombrun and Rindova, 2000; Livesay and Graham, 2007). But maneuver is exhausting and advocacy groups have very limited resources, especially in comparison to large, multinational organizations.

Conclusion

In an important sense, the activities, successes, and failures of corporate campaigns take us back us to the very first issue raised in this book. Some people view rhetoric as a synonym for lies, as a substitute for objective analysis, and/or as a group of meaning-less adornments that are used to make bad ideas seem to be good (Foss, Foss and Trapp, 1991; Heath, 2009). It is clear that many organizations around the world engage in socially responsible policies and practices and produce rhetoric that appropriately cel-ebrates those actions. It also is true that, in spite of having vastly inferior material resources, corporate campaigns and community advocates often compel organizations to make changes in their activities and/or in their rhetoric. But it is also clear that many of these celebrations and many of the purported organizational reforms *are* "mere rhetoric" in the pejorative sense of the term – symbolic acts designed to confuse critics or to mislead stakeholders into believing that there is substance underlying the symbolism.[10]

My goal in this chapter, and throughout this book, has been to provide readers with the ability to differentiate one from the other.

Epilogue

One of the most important figures in the history of rhetorical studies in the US was a diminutive, somewhat quirky, man: Kenneth Burke. He dropped out of two colleges, Ohio State and Columbia, because he was frustrated by having to take so many required courses and because classes diverted so much of his time and energy away from what he loved – writing. A theorist who reveled in abstract ideas, he was constantly in touch with the world around him – he referred to rhetoric, indeed to all symbolic action, as "equipment for living." Like almost everyone else of his generation, Buke was traumatized by the massive economic dislocation of the Great Depression and by the subsequent rise of global fascism. During those times he wrote in order to keep from falling apart. Much of his work during the 1930s focused on a distinction between "tragic" and "comic" orientations. In the former, people become trapped in their own symbol systems – their "taken-for-granted assumptions," to use the phrase I have employed throughout this book. They come to believe their own rhetoric and the rhetoric of others who uncritically accept the same beliefs, treating it as absolute truth rather than as a strategic attempt to make sense out of life and to maneuver through everyday experiences. In the process they lose sight of where their rhetoric is taking them, both as individuals and as members of their communities. In extreme cases they produce only polemics, "us vs. them" diatribes. Other people adopt fundamentally different, "comic" perspectives, not in the sense of failing to take their surroundings and experiences seriously, but in the sense of understanding that every view of reality and every person's rhetoric should be interpreted through an ironic frame of reference. This means that people who take "comic" perspectives realize that the taken-for-granted assumptions of their societies, and the frames of reference that dominate those societies, are in some sense arbitrary and often even capricious. They emerge from choices that human beings make and legitimize through rhetoric. People taking a comic perspective also recognize that, when people identify with some individuals and institutions, they sever links to other individuals and institutions. They try to remain conscious that *they* chose to accept a particular set of beliefs and values, and a particular way of viewing the world, and that *they* can change those beliefs, values, and perspectives if they choose to do so. Moreover, they realize that *their* choices determine the paths that their lives will follow. In short, they revel in irony, and reject polemic.

Our current Great Recession is in many ways like the rhetorical situation that Burke confronted during the Great Depression. Indeed, media rhetoric in the US today always seems to begin with the observation that today's data reveal conditions that are worse than they've been any time since the 1930s. In other developed countries, media introductions note that the current situation is in some ways even worse than the Great Depression. Economic dislocation and global threats from different versions of "fundamentalism" have generated the same kinds of doubt about the viability of democratic institutions and the same kinds of threats to the rule of law and commitment to individual/human rights that characterized the 1930s. Whether or not our current challenges are marginally worse or somewhat better than they were then, the appropriate "comic" response is the same: (1) to understand that societal assumptions are created through rhetoric, that they guide and constrain subsequent thoughts and actions, but that they can be transformed through rhetoric; (2) to recognize that managing the tension between the certainty and predictability promised by Plato's ideal society and the "messiness" of democracy is an inherent part of human experience; and (3) to be ever wary of the human tendency to become trapped within our own symbol systems, to view the paths that we have chosen as the only viable, moral, or rational options. The choices that we make today, the kinds of organizations and societies that we create and tolerate, will influence the kind of world we will spend the remainder of our lives in, and the kind of societies that we will leave to our children and our children's children. Make good choices.

Case Study: The Attack of the Killer Toyotas[11]

The case studies that concluded Chapters 1 through 4 were rather detailed, in part because the concepts I was presenting were so new and so complicated that I thought it wise to give you quite a bit of structure. But, you have come far and mastered a large number of complex concepts, so this case study will be shorter, less structured, and more open to your own analysis and interpretation.

During the early to mid-1980s a number of troubling reports became public about the Audi 5000, a favorite vehicle of yuppies (young urban professionals). "Sudden accelerations," in which the car took off on its own, led the New York Attorney General and a couple of consumer watchdog groups to demand that the NHTSA force Audi to recall and repair the vehicles. This pressure culminated in a November, 1986 segment of the CBS news show "60 Minutes," which featured the death of a 6-year-old son of a minister, Joshua Bradosky, whose parents' Audi suddenly accelerated, crushing him against the garage door of his home. The standard litany of events followed: sales of Audi vehicles went into a sharp decline, as did the price of its stock; late-night comics poked fun at the car ("The Audi 5000 – Don't let it leave home without you"); Congresspersons expressed outrage and introduced legislation to ban sales of the car until the problem was adequately investigated and solved; consumer groups created an "Audi Victims Network" through which traumatized Audi owners could share their stories and receive legal and emotional support, etc., etc.

For the company itself, much of this was old news. The acceleration problem had first surfaced in 1979, and Audi had taken a number of steps to deal with it. In 1981 the company recalled its cars in order to replace their floor mats, which it claimed were jamming under the cars' accelerators, causing them to accelerate out of control. Complaints continued, and critics claimed that the problem was much more serious than misplaced floormats. In 1983 Audi issued another recall, this time to install new brake pedals and move them further away from the accelerator pedals. Sales increased – 1984 was the Audi 5000's best year in the US – but so did the number of complaints. Audi quit installing cruise control in its turbocharged models because the events seemed to be more common in those vehicles, thereby undermining its overall claim that there was no fundamental engineering or production problem with the vehicle, and the problems resulted from operator error. But, in order to protect its customers from themselves, Audi argued, it initiated a "service campaign" (carefully avoiding the term "safety recall") to install shift lock devices on the cars. After the criticism had peaked, the company received some relief in a *Detroit News* report, which concluded that the problems actually had been more likely to occur among a particular group of drivers – those who were older, unfamiliar with the car, under 5' 6" tall, and female. But almost immediately the National Highway Traffic Safety Administration (NHTSA) reported that there had been 5,800 incidents involving the car, leading to 56 deaths and 2,043 injuries. The incident rate for 1978–1986 models was 645.4 per 100,000 vehicles – a small figure, perhaps, but significantly higher than General Motor's 4.37 incidents per 100,000 vehicles during the same time frame.

In March, 1988 Audi (finally) engaged in a more aggressive defense of its reputation. It denied that there was anything fundamentally wrong with the vehicles, and admitted that they had handled the crisis badly:

> as an engineering company [. . .] we felt that the facts would speak for themselves. Our silence not only offended our loyal customers but also prejudiced potential customers against us. Our lack of a vocal response to our accusers was perceived by many as a sign of weakness, or worse yet, as an admission of guilt. Neither could be farther from the truth. (Cited in Hearit and Courtright, 2003, 92)

At the same time, they trumpeted the success of the brake locks (complaints had fallen by 90 percent), and changed the name of the cars. In early 1989 the crisis ended when both the Canadian auto safety agency and the NHTSA concluded that the incidents actually had resulted from operator error.

Discussion Questions

1 What lessons should automobile manufacturers have learned about managing identity crises from the Audi experience? Be sure

205

you adapt your advice to two possible situations:

- the company's management has no idea what actually is causing the fatal accidents, but the company's engineers have come up with some hypotheses;
- management knows what is causing the fatalities, but it also knows that fixing the problem will be much more expensive than dealing with the victims' heirs on a case-by-case basis (recall the Ford Pinto experience).

2 Given your answer to question 1, what advice would you have given Toyota when it encountered an almost identical crisis during 2008 and 2009? Why would you have given that advice?

3 Quickly summarize what Toyota actually did. Finding this out will not be difficult. If you drive a Toyota, you probably remember the events. If you don't, virtually every major newspaper website has an archive devoted to the Toyota experience that you can easily access. Now, evaluate Toyota's management of its identity crisis.

Notes

Chapter 1

1 Anne Goldgar (2007) provides an extended analysis of similar actions taken during one of the greatest economic crashes in world history, the Dutch tulip crash of the early 1600s.

2 For a relevant and highly readable analysis of Plato's opposition to democracy and the ways in which leaders in modern organizations operate from "Platonic" assumptions about truth, dominance, and superior–inferior relationships, see Takala (1998).

3 This link was carried over into Judeo-Christian theology. For example, read the traditional account of creation in Genesis 1, the first verse of the Gospel of John, and the miracles included in the Gospels. Note the role that speech and speaking played in each (Burke, 1970).

4 See Gramsci (1992); Mumby (1988); Therborn (1980).

5 Richard Barker (2001) applies this concept to organizational leadership research and theory, a topic that I will discuss at length in Chapter 3.

6 This may be among the most widely misinterpreted of Aristotle's ideas. *Pathos* (literally, "what is suffered") does not refer to the fleeting, superficial emotions – anger, lust, and so on – that a person feels in response to everyday events, and certainly not to the rhetorical presentation of those emotions by a speaker. Instead it refers to the fundamental desires that make us human (Rorty, 1996). For an extended analysis of the relationship between human ontology and rhetorical theory, see Campbell (1970).

7 Unfortunately, the parts of Aristotle's *Rhetoric* that developed in detail his view of the links between rhetoric and politics were lost in antiquity and have never been recovered (Rorty, 1996). A number of modern scholars have attempted to fill the gap. For an overall re-interpretation and updating, see Perelman and Olbrechts-Tyteca (1991); for an analysis of the role that cultural assumptions play in argument, see Toulmin (1972; 2003); and for

a treatment of the complications involved in conceptualizations of "justice," see Perelman (1963, 1967).

8 For excellent analyses of the development of assumptions and ideologies, see Orren (1995) and Deetz (1992a, 1992b). For treatments of the power of ideology, see Therborn (1980) and Mumby (1988). Psychologist Eric Fromm (1970) explains the role that cultural myths play in feelings of security.

9 Aristotle's rhetoric is ironic in a second sense. He returned to Athens for a second time in 335 BCE from Macedon, where he had been tutoring Alexander the Great and apparently writing the *Politics* and the *Rhetoric*. He then founded his own school, the Lyceum. In order to attract students in a highly competitive market that was dominated by the sophist Isocrates, he decided to focus on popular topics such as poetics, rhetoric, ethics, and politics. Only later did he revise the curriculum to emphasize science and metaphysics (Aristotle, 1962).

10 This phrase should probably be "the most recent phase of globalization," since there have been multiple times in world history when world economies became interconnected in ways that had never been experienced before – from the ancient Phoenicians and the ancient Chinese to the empire of Alexander the Great, the Roman Empire, and the European hegemony of the seventeenth to nineteenth century.

11 Some corporations actually fight these tiny fines. For example, Walmart has spent at least $2 million fighting a $7,000 fine levied against it over the death of a worker trampled by customers who surged into a store on "Black Friday," the unofficial first day of the Christmas shopping season (Greenhouse, 2010a).

12 Prior to the Pfizer case, the largest fine on record was levied against Archer Daniels Midland in 1996. The agricultural giant was fined $100 million by the US Justice Department for illegally fixing the prices of citric acid and lysine (an additive in animal feeds). Since the company made extra profits of $200–$600 million by engaging in these illegal activities, the crime was worth the fine.

13 The entire report from which this data was drawn is available on the GAO website. Data on the effective corporate tax rate are available on the website of Citizens for Tax Justice (www.ctj.org) and are summarized in an article on that website by Bob McIntyre. A summary of the tax-minimization strategies of the three companies involved in the 2010 BP Deep Water Horizon explosion and oil spill is available in Kocieniewski (2010).

14 US residents could save an additional 25–30 percent by purchasing prescriptions in the European Union. For example, a study conducted for the PBS series *Frontline* found that a group of four commonly prescribed drugs would cost $367 USD in the US, $145 in Canada (39.5 percent of the US price), and $103 in the EU (28 percent of the US price and 71 percent of the Canadian price: Frontline, "The other drug war," 2003, transcript at www.pbs.org).

15 For an excellent summary of the battle over the national bank, with an application to the 2008–2009 financial crisis, see *Wall Street Journal* columnist David Wessel (2009).

16 Conservative economist and Judge Richard Posner (2010) recently pointed out that the concept of limited liability inevitably creates a "moral hazard" in which organizational leaders are encouraged to take on excessive risks because they can benefit handsomely from making correct bets but can completely shift the costs to others if things go badly. I will examine the concept of moral hazard in more detail in Chapters 2 and 4.

17 In many cases the policies resulted from blatant power politics. For example, in a related action, Henry Clay, faced with a populist Kentucky House of Representatives that was ready to close down the Bank of Lexington (in which Clay held stock and served as legal counsel), threatened to have the state Senate immediately foreclose on all state-backed loans to small farmers (Perrow, 2002, 46–47). Kentucky Progressives capitulated. Each of these decisions were heatedly debated, but in every case advocates of increasing corporate power prevailed.

18 The classic treatment of this issue is Charles Beard (1986).

19 The concept of a financially poor, weak federal government is somewhat implausible to today's US citizens, but the power imbalance continued until the New Deal (Mann, 2003; Perrow, 2002).

20 Two excellent examples of these difficulties are provided by Vaughan's (1983) analysis of fraud at the Revco Drug Company, and the saga of Arthur Andersen (Brewster, 2003; Toffler, 2003).

21 Academic research on the statistical relationship between contributions and policymakers' votes is mixed, largely because different studies measure political influence in different ways. These methodological problems were managed effectively in Peoples and Gortari (2008) and in Peoples (2009). See also Baumgartner and Leech (1998). My own interpretation of this causal relationship is that it runs in both directions: corporations contribute to those candidates they think will favor them (and sometimes they help recruit sympathetic candidates); their contributions help those candidates get elected; this influences their votes, especially in less public venues such as committees; and that attracts further contributions, which are necessary to ensure continued favorable votes. To use the old adage, contributions both "buy Congresspersons" and help ensure that they will "stay bought."

22 For similar analyses of the US, see Baumgartner and Leech (1998), updated in Baumgartner et al. (2009). Also, see Berg (1994); Biersack, Hernson, and Wilcox (1999); Ginsberg and Green (1986); Goldstein (1999); Grossman and Helpman (2001); Rich (2010).

23 For extended analyses of resistance, see Breen (2007); Cox (2004); Kendall, Gill, and Cheney (2007); LaNuez and Jermier (1994); Maignan (2001); Munshi and Kurian (2007); Ozen and Ozen (2009).

24 For excellent summaries of industry rhetoric and critics' attacks and responses, see the materials available on the pbs.com website in conjunction with the Frontline episode, "The other drug war," and Angell (2004). For the debate in Canada, see Fuller (1998); Grieshaber-Otto and Sinclair (2004).

25 Somewhat ironically, quasi-market forces are leading companies to shift more of their R&D activities to small-market drugs. Managed care plans and pharmaceutical middlemen are increasingly refusing to pay higher prices for "me too" drugs than for older drugs. As a result, firms have increased their own R&D spending (up to an average of 6 percent in 2006) and they are focusing on niche conditions with small patient populations, and thus with smaller clinical trial requirements.

Chapter 2

1 For a summary of de Tocqueville's observations and their applicability today, see Cawelti (1974) and Deetz (1992a).

2 Tuohy (1999) makes similar observations about Thatcherism in the UK.

3 More extensive analyses of the overall trends since 1970 have been published by authors from across the political spectrum. At one pole is conservative economist Kevin Phillips (1990, 2002); at the other is James K. Galbraith (1998) and a series of reports issued annually by the liberal Economic Policy Institute: Mishel, Bernstein, and Bousley (2003).

4 For analyses of the rhetoric of "getting a good job," see Clair (1996) and Clair et al. (2008). The concept of "significant others" was introduced by George Herbert Mead (1967).

5 Critics of this research have argued that its findings are inconsistent and sometimes even contradictory, and the authors' conclusions often over-generalize their results (Strauss and Howe, 1991; Howe and Strauss, 2000; Zemke, Raines, and Filipczak, 2000).

6 Soros argues that free-market economists are like religious fundamentalists in two ways. First, they have developed a belief system that cannot be undermined by empirical evidence. Market failures and the social ills that stem from them are interpreted in ways that can only confirm the tenets of the faith (Krugman, 2010b). Moreover, when events do undermine the perspective, as in the economic collapse of 2008 through to the present, the believers respond by holding even more tightly to the tenets of their faith (Posner, 2009, 2010).

7 For an analysis of Iceland's experience that includes both cultural factors and an assessment of free-market rhetoric, see Jonsson (2009). The 2008–2009 meltdown started in the US because of a combination of de-regulatory policies pursued by multiple administrations since 1979 and creative financiers' ability to capitalize (personally and, to some extent, on behalf of their

organizations). When this phenomenon combined with multi-trillion dollar bailouts using taxpayer money, the US economy was so weak by the middle of 2009 that it would not have been eligible for loans from the International Monetary Fund and the from World Bank, at least using the debt-to-income requirements that those US-dominated institutions have long imposed on developing countries. But the dominant economic rhetoric claimed that punishing the US for its irresponsibility would have destroyed the entire world economy. In short, like the financial institutions that were bailed out in the US and in the UK, the US economy was considered to be "too big to fail." Iceland's was not, although it eventually did receive a $6 billion USD bailout package from the International Monetary Fund (IMF).

8 The economic distortions imposed by US bankruptcy laws eventually led the chief executive officers (CEOs) of Southwest and Continental Airlines to call for at least a partial re-regulation of the industry (see Hensel, Jr., 2009; Steffy, 2009a).

9 Ostas (2001) has persuasively argued that all of these advantages occur independently of anything that managers do. This raises a number of interesting questions about managerial power and rewards, all of which will be examined in Chapter 3.

10 For an application to the minimum wage debate and an excellent analysis of the rhetorical power of free-market fundamentalism, see Aune (2001).

11 Tuohy (1999) examines the lack of medical data in the US, UK, and Canada. Stone (2001, esp. Ch. 10) provides a compelling explanation of why policymakers do not want useful data to be collected and made available to consumers. Thanks to the internet, information about the cost-effectiveness of various drugs is available from other sources, which lie outside of legislative reach (e.g. aarp.org and familiesusa.org). Since this is simple information, most consumers can use it to make rational decisions. Deciding whether to choose drug treatment (or surgery) over alternative modes of treatment is a very different story.

12 By the late 1960s these problems created an entire new school of economic thought, usually called "behavioral economics." An excellent introduction is Wilson (2008); a very brief overview is available in Brooks (2010). For more technical presentations, see the classic book in the area, Kahneman and Tversky (1982), as well as Comerer and Lowenstein (2004); Hogarth and Rader (1987).

13 For extended critiques of the "efficient market hypothesis" (the economic phrase for the assumption that markets are rational), see Aune (2001) and Kuhn and Ashcraft (2003).

14 Economists across the political spectrum have reacted to the Great Recession with a third reason for regulating the financial markets tightly: they are positioned in such a way that their collapse can bring down the entire world

economy, something that is not true of other sectors (see Krugman, 2009; Posner, 2009, 2010; Stiglitz, 2010).

15 This very, very brief summary of Smith's very complex ideas is based on my reading of Smith's work and on five secondary sources: Heilbroner (1982); Werhane (1991); Peters (1995); Cropsey (2001); Gore (2005). For an analysis of the tragedy of the commons, see Hardin (1968). In a superb little book, Sennett (1998) has traced the processes through which reasonably ethical, "normal" people, turn into reprobates by participating in modern capitalism.

16 For overall analyses, see Ralph Nader at www.nader.org (on the political left) and the essays by Stephen Slivinski at the libertarian Cato Foundation's website, www.cato.org (on the political right). Free-marketeer criticism of food subsidies is available at the Heritage Foundation (www.heritage.org); leftist critiques are provided by the Environmental Working Group (farm. ewg.org) and by Winders and Scott (2009).

17 For an extended analysis of "second-best" markets, see Lancaster and Lipsey (1956).

18 Landes and Posner (1978); Posner (1987). For a brief treatment of the subject, see Posner (1992, 139–143).

19 As Judge Posner's quotation at the beginning of this chapter suggests, the events leading up to the collapse of the US financial industry in 2008, and the subsequent government bailouts and Great Recession, have led him to take a much more positive view of government regulation (the kind that is designed to protect consumers and other stakeholders) than he once did, and to distinguish explicitly his own positions from those of free-market fundamentalists (see Posner 2009, 2010).

20 In the US there are informal guidelines for pricing eggs, but there is no way of enforcing them, and they often are unrealistic when compared to the actual market. See for example Tuller (2010).

21 Manga (1987); Canadian Press (2007a); Johnson and Porter (2009); Marchione (2009).

Chapter 3

1 As noted in chapter 2, there was zero net job creation during the Bush, Jr. administration: "no previous decade [2000–2008] going back to the 1940s had job growth of less than 20 percent. Economic output rose at its slowest rate of any decade since the 1930s" (Irwin, 2010, n.p.).

2 Management scholar Jeffrey Pfeffer (1998) effectively critiques arguments claiming that high executive compensation, low worker wages, and large gaps between the two are good for organizations and economies.

3 Kuhrana (2002) attributes the shift from "promoting home-grown talent" to hiring outsiders to the content of MBA (Master of Business Administration) programs and to the "dramatic rise of the MBA as a professional creden-

tial" (p. 125). See also Kuhrana (2010), DiTomaso, Parks-Yancy, and Post (2003), and the special issue of the *Academy of Management Executive* on teaching ethics in business schools (vol. 16, no. 2, 2002).

4 Thus the key question is: "When does leadership matter?"

5 There are very good recent works that focus on followers and followership from a "non-mainstream" perspective. See the work of Barbara Kellerman, especially (2008); Troy Seeley (2009); and the essays in Riggio, Chaleff, and Lipman-Blumen, eds (2008).

6 The company's management quickly learned its lesson, re-hired a cadre of designers and engineers, and had a much more successful auto show circuit in 2010.

7 For excellent summaries of scientific management, see Taylor (1978) and Locke (1982). For a summary of Adam Smith's view of natural liberty, see Rosenberg (1968, 1990).

8 For a superb analysis of how "leadership" is treated in Western literature, see Northrop Frye (1976). Lawrence Prince (2005) provides an excellent analysis of the ways in which Western cultures foster either/or thinking, including about leadership and followership.

9 For broader historical and conceptual analyses of the process, see Jackall (1983, re-issued in 2009); Toffler (1986); McMillan (1988); Weaver, Trevino, and Cochran (1999); Clegg, Courpasson, and Phillips (2006); McMillan (2007).

10 There are literally hundreds of additional sources. One of the most important for the transformational leadership perspective was Conger (1991), which linked the movement to sociologist Max Weber's foundational work on charisma, and Tichy and Devanna (1986). Additional foundational works in the corporate culture paradigm were Ouchi (1981) and Schein (1985).

11 Howard Stein (1998) offers a very different analysis of leaders' use of these symbolic forms, especially during organizational downsizing, arguing that the forms are "really not much different from the euphemisms used by the Nazi German state to dehumanize and then systematically exterminate millions" (p. xx). See also Grint and Case (1998). Kenneth Burke (1966) offered a similar analysis of the role that framing plays in all symbolic action.

12 The popularity of the perspective is explained in Charles Conrad (1985).

13 For an early critique and summary of other early critiques, see Conrad (1985). The "excellence" series even spawned a parody: Chapman (2006).

14 The "witch doctor" metaphor was introduced by Clark and Salaman (1996). Guru studies draw heavily on the work of symbolic theorists Kenneth Burke (see, for example, 1962 and 1966) and Ernest Bormann (2001). It should be obvious that guru rhetoric is grounded in masculine imagery, which is not surprising, since the vast majority of US executives and gurus are male (see Alvesson and Sveningsson, 2003b; Buzzanell, Meisenbach, and Remke, 2008).

15 For parallels with the rhetoric of evangelical Protestantism, see Grint (1994) and Jackson (1996). Classic works on the American Jeremiad include Bercovitch (1978); Bormann (2001); Murphy (2008). For an excellent analysis of implementation as consummation, see Mangam and Overington (1983, 1987). In a provocative article, Nadesan (1999) has persuasively argued that this secular–religious form is essentially the same in two otherwise disparate versions of guru thought – "corporate spiritualism," based on New Age doctrine, and "evangelical capitalism" such as "servant leadership."

16 For the "classic" debate over this issue, see Marglin (1975) and Landes (1986).

17 The "romance of leadership" perspective is developed in detail in Salancik and Meindl (1984); Meindl (1995); Meindl, Ehrlich, and Dukerich (1985).

18 Excellent analyses of the revised social theory are available in Giddens (1984, 1991); Knights (1997); Reed (1997); Willmott (2005). For an analysis of the relationship between power and perceptions, see Conrad and Poole (2005); and for a summary of "dialectical" approaches to leader–follower relationships, see Fairhurst (2001); Sobo and Sadler (2002); Collinson (2005); Reicher, Haslam, and Hopkins (2005).

19 The most often cited model of resistance is Albert Hirschman's (1970, 1991) distinction between exit, voice, loyalty, and, in later versions, neglect. The first two are self-explanatory. The latter two involve continuing to cooperate with the organization, but loyalty is based on an optimistic hope that things will improve, while neglect is based on a pessimistic willingness to watch it fail.

20 For an analysis of the increasing use of electronic surveillance, see Collinson (2005) and Adler and Tompkins (1996). For work advocating increased electronic control as a means of reducing the *problem* of resistance, see Wicks (2002) and Sewell and Barker (2006).

21 The examples using flight attendants are from Hochschild (1985) and Murphy (1998). One of the best summaries of negotiation processes is Prasad and Prasad (1998). Additional "classic" studies of resistance and control include Rosen (1988); Hodson (1995); Tucker (1993). For analyses of humor as resistance, see Collinson (1988, 2002).

22 Banks (2008), Acroyd and Thompson (1999), and Jermier, Knights, and Nord (1994) all examine the ways in which dissenters improve organizational functioning. The experiences of, and contributions made by, whistleblowers are described at length in Farrell and Rusbult (1992) and in Graham (1986). For an analysis of whistleblowers, see McMillan (1990); Miceli and Near (1992); Conrad and Poole (2005). For an analysis of leadership and dissent at Enron, see Tourish and Vatcha (2005).

23 See Graham (1995), Fairhurst and Zoller (2007, 2008), and Zoller (2005). These analyses rely on Collinson's (2005) perspective on leadership as interaction.

24 For a related analysis of leadership as the suppression/channeling of dissent, see Reicher, Haslam, and Hopkins (2005); Sunstein (2007); Banks (2008).

25 For an analysis of how the "bad apple" metaphor was used to undercut meaningful systemic reforms during the last US financial crisis (Enron, WorldCom, Adelphia, etc.), see Conrad (2004); and for an analysis of how it was used to undercut reforms during the US Savings and Loan crisis and bailout, see Berg (1994).

26 Subsequent research has supported Kuhrana's analysis of the dynamics of peer-comparisons and their effects on executive compensation (see Sorkin, 2010). For an example of a board operating as they are supposed to, see Jeffrey Sonnenfeld's (2010) and Loren Steffy's (2010d) analyses of the dismissal of HP CEO Mark Hurd.

Chapter 4

1 Hodge and Coronado (2006) have coined the terms "corporoid" to refer to countries that are too small to resist pressure from multinational corporations (MNCs) and hence opt to become their allies, and "nationoid" to refer to MNCs that have become so powerful that they are able to act like nations.

2 Baumgartner et al.'s (2009) study of ninety-eight issues debated during multiple presidencies found that lobbying campaigns failed 60 percent of the time. The possibility of elites competing with one another was the foundation of what came to be called "pluralist theory." This perspective asserted that alliances among elites constantly coalesce, divide, and re-form as significant issues on the public agenda are debated. This ensures that no single group, or coalition of elite groups, dominates policymaking all of the time (see Clegg, 1989 and Stone, 2001). By the 1970s, pluralist theory was the dominant perspective in political science, but it was quickly attacked for not being empirically accurate. Research increasingly indicated that American pluralism systematically excludes many groups on the basis of class, race, and gender. This conclusion was also supported by Baumgartner and colleagues' study. Eventually even Robert Dahl, the founder of pluralist theory, accepted this critique and focused his research on examining how unequal power relationships were perpetuated in US politics (Dahl, 1998, 2002; see also Swanson, 2007).

3 This section is based on Stone's (2001) superb analysis.

4 For some reason, these arguments never seem to be applied to "corporate welfare." Stone (2001) points out that the preponderant part of evidence fails to support these assumptions when applied to individuals; but, as I have suggested throughout this book, cultural myths and empirical evidence are only loosely connected to each other.

5 The numbers of lobbyists and lobbying expenditures listed in this book underestimate the scope of the activity because many lobbyists do not register with

the federal government. The number of full-time paid lobbyists peaked in 2007 at 13,200 (Kirkpatrick, 2010a). After the Enron, WorldCom, and so on bankruptcies at the turn of the century, Vanguard Investments founder John Boggle estimated the potential payoff of campaign contributions and lobbying at 10:1; in the preface to *Still the Best Congress Money Can Buy*, former Senator William Proxmire estimated it at 1000:1. Although these figures seemed fanciful and neither source explained how they developed them, the 2008–2009 financial industry bailout makes them seem credible. The ratio of six months of lobbying and one year of campaign contributions to the size of the bailout (assuming that the *lowest* estimate – 2.1 trillion – is used) is 4000:1; the ratio of campaign contributions alone to the bailout is 1000:1, as Senator Proxmire predicted. Of course, these figures do not include subsidies and tax breaks granted to the financial services industry by the federal government through normal legislative procedures.

6 The Court did retain a 1907 ban on direct corporate (and labor union) contributions to politicians, so the precise effects of the decision will depend on how much corporations increase their political spending and on how Congress and state legislatures respond to it. For an extended debate over the likely effects of the decision, see http://roomfordebate.blogs.nytimes. com/2010/21/how-corproate-money-will-reshape-politics (New York Times Editorial Board, 2010). A couple of weeks after the decision an ABC News/ *Washington Post* poll found that the American public strongly opposed it: 80 percent overall (with 65 percent strongly opposing it, an unusually intense expression of opposition) – 76, 81, and 85 percent of self-identified Republicans, independents, and Democrats; and 73, 85, and 96 percent of self-identified conservatives, moderates, and liberals. Similar percentages favored Congressional action to reinstate the limits (Langer, 2010).

7 See Dionne (2010). David Broder (2010) explains how increasing ideological polarization of Congress exacerbates these structural changes. But filibusters are only part of the problem – a president's nomination of a candidate for a federal judgeship or as the head of an important federal agency can be blocked permanently by one senator, who does not even have to reveal his or her identity.

8 I discuss blame-shifting as a crisis management strategy in Chapter 5. For a brief summary of BP's repeated use of internal reports as blame-shifting, see Mouawad (2010) and Steffy (2010a).

9 An extended analysis, and copies of the Congresspersons' letters, are available in an episode of the PBS show "Frontline" entitled "Bigger than Enron," which is available on the pbs.org website.

10 Many political scientists argue persuasively that cases of regulatory capture rarely result from the actions of career regulators, although excessive caseloads in regulatory agencies make errors inevitable. Far more often, "regulatory failures" stem from actions taken by Congress and/or by the

executive branch, through the political appointees who are selected to head regulatory agencies. For example, Congress has required the Food and Drug Administration (FDA) to rely almost completely on industry research regarding drug efficacy and side-effects; Congress has dictated that the FDA not conduct research on the relative cost-effectiveness of various drugs and/or treatment options or publicize existing research relative to cost-effectiveness; Congress passed the Hatch-Waxman Act, which extended patent protection for the pharmaceutical industry far beyond that afforded any other industry (Angell, 2004), and so on. Of course, none of these actions would have been implemented had they not received support from a president.

11 For example, the primary responsibilities of the contemporary FDA were developed and legitimized in precisely this way – the Pure Food and Drug Act and the Meat Inspection Act of 1906 (which resulted in part from advocacy by Upton Sinclair); the Food, Drug, and Cosmetic Act of 1938; and the Kefauver drug probe of 1962. In these cases, public interest regulation is designed to achieve what economic self-interest cannot, and regulation is enacted because "the imperfections of government action are [viewed as] preferable to the imperfections of the market" (Wilson, 1974, 137).

12 The "classic" case studies in this debate involve the creation of the Interstate Commerce Commission and of the Federal Aviation Administration/Civil Aeronautics Board (Kuttner, 1996). Recent revelations concerning safety problems with virtually everything imported from China by US firms have even led industries to seek additional regulation, in order to protect themselves from themselves.

13 Wilson (1974) argues that moribund regulatory agencies can be stimulated into action through the appointment of leaders who are especially committed to social action and/or through the emergence of an especially zealous professional staff. This argument is often used to explain the FDA's 1966 shift from having a "solicitous and benign attitude toward the pharmaceutical manufacturers" (p. 159) to adopting a more activist position for a time, and then returning to passivity during the 1980s, to activity during the 1990s (Angell, 2004), and to passivity again during the W. Bush Administration.

14 This challenge is especially difficult when a regulatory agency is charged with inconsistent goals. For example, the Food and Drug Administration must get needed drugs to market as quickly as possible *and* ensure the safety of the drugs it approves (see Angell, 2004).

15 Mr. Bartlett was the first in a large number of former Reagan Administration officials to publish books during 2006 and 2007 attacking the Bush Administration and Republican Congress for abandoning the principle of fiscal conservatism. For an analysis of the bill from a broader health policy perspective, see Weissert and Weissert (2006). For an updated analysis of drug costs in the program, see Dicken (2009) and Cubanski et al. (2010).

16 For a comprehensive comparison of the costs of drugs charged by Medicare,

which is not allowed to negotiate with drug companies, and those charged by the Veteran's Administration, which is allowed to negotiate, although from a much weaker position than Medicare would be, see Familes USA (2007).

Chapter 5

1 For a superb, detailed analysis of the development of such programs, including resistance to them by upper management, see Marchand (1998).

2 For excellent examples of dialogic perspectives, see Boys (2009); Meisenbach and Feldner (2009). Robert Heath (1988) traces the growth and increased influence of advocacy groups, and so does Jarol Manheim (2001).

3 Somewhat surprisingly, university administrators often do not seem to understand the value of identification processes. During the 1990s it became commonplace for the PR departments in US universities to explicitly describe their students as consumers. The goal of this rhetoric was to make them feel empowered, and thus even more committed to their alma mater. But, in a tribute to the power of the interpretive processes of audiences, many alumni actually started to think and act like consumers who were empowered to make demands of their institutions. For example, Syracuse University, a pioneer in student-as-consumer rhetoric, found that contributions to its alumni fund declined sharply during the mid-1990s in spite of a booming economy. Perplexed, university fundraisers started asking their alumni to discuss their relationship with the organizations, fully expecting them to revel in their identification with it. Instead, many of them responded: "[I]f I buy a car from General Motors, they don't expect me to make voluntary contributions to the company for the rest of my life. Why does a university?" (Readings, 1996). The student-as-consumer rhetoric soon disappeared.

4 See the summary in Susan Strom (2006) and B. Ghose (2007).

5 Excellent analyses of the tension between identity/crisis management and litigation are available in Cohen (2002); Kellerman (2006); Hearit (2007); Llewellyn (2007); Seeger and Hipfel (2007). For brief analyses of tort reform, see Conrad and Abbott (2007). The Ford Pinto case appears in almost every textbook of organizational or engineering ethics, for example Harris, Pritchard, and Rabins (1995). The story was first told by Dowie (1977). Gary Schwartz' (1990–1991) review of related court cases concludes that the number of lives lost was exaggerated by the plaintiffs and the media, but accepts the standard summary of Ford's decision process.

6 For a superb analysis of a similar rhetoric, used by UK bank CEOs when they were forced to defend their actions to Parliament, see Hargie, Stapleton, and Tourish (2010).

7 This documentary was released in early November 2005 in selected movie theaters around the US. Greenwald's production company is Brave New

218

Films. The press release for the film is available at www.walmartmovie.com/wmsales.php.

8 See Kuttner (1996), for an analysis of the Moore film; see also Mandle (1999); Fetherston (2002); Peretti with Micheletti (2003).

9 And the story continues. In July, 2010 Nike accepted responsibility for the actions of two of its contractors, who closed plants in Honduras without giving workers the severance pay required by Honduran law. The decision resulted from pressure from universities and student anti-sweatshop groups (Greenhouse, 2010b).

10 In the case of environmental discourse this kind of rhetoric has even been given a name of its own: "greenwashing." For contrasting examples of legitimate change and of illusion, see Bendell and Bendell (2007); Cheney, Roper, and May (2007); McMillan (2007); Stohl, Stohl, and Townsley (2007); Waddock (2007).

11 For extended analyses of the Audi case, see the series of reports by J. V. Higgins and his associates in the *Detroit News*, and also Hearit and Courtright (2003). For an excellent summary of how Toyota's growth and management system contributed to its crisis, see Taylor (2010).

References

NOTE All websites were last checked on January 1, 2011, unless otherwise specified.

Abelson, Donald (2002). *Do think tanks matter?* Montreal: McGill-Queens University Press.

Abelson, Donald and Christine Carberry (1998). Following suit or falling behind? A comparative analysis of think tanks in Canada and the United States. *Canadian Journal of Political Science*, 31: 525–555.

Abelson, Robert (1959). Modes of resolution of belief dilemmas. *Journal of Conflict Resolution*, 3: 343–352.

Abercrombie, Nathan, Stephen Hill, and Bryan Turner (1980). *The dominant ideology thesis*, 2nd edn. London: George Allen and Unwin.

Abrahamson, Eric (1991). Managerial fads and fashions. *Academy of Management Review*, 16: 586–612.

Acosta, Carlos, V. Jorge Leon, Charles Conrad, and Cesar Malave (2009). *The global engineer*. New York: Taylor and Francis.

Acroyd, Steven and Paul Thompson (1999). *Organizational misbehavior*. London: Sage.

Adler, G. Stoney and Phil Tompkins (1996). Electronic performance monitoring. *Management Communication Quarterly*, 10: 259–288.

Agovino, Theresa (2006). Drug makers re-evaluate approaches to research. *Houston Chronicle*. December 10: 9D.

Alinsky, Saul (1989). *Rules for radicals*. New York: Vintage.

Allen, Myria Watkins and Rachel H. Caillouet (1994). Legitimation endeavors: Impression management strategies used by an organization in crisis. *Communication Monographs*, 61: 44–62.

Alsop, Ron (2008). *The trophy kids grow up*. San Francisco: Jossey-Bass.

Altheide, David and John Johnson (1980). *Bureaucratic propaganda*. Boston: Allyn and Bacon.

References

Alvesson, Mats (1990). On the popularity of organizational culture. *Acta Sociologica*, *33*: 31–49.

Alvesson, Mats (2002). *Understanding organizational culture*. Thousand Oaks, CA: Sage.

Alvesson, Mats and Stefan Sveningsson (2003a). Good visions, bad micro-management, and ugly ambiguity. *Organization Studies*, *24*: 961–988.

Alvesson, Mats and Stafan Sveningsson (2003b). The great disappearing act. *Leadership Quarterly*, *14*: 359–381.

Alvesson, Mats and Stefan Sveningsson (2003c). Leadership is the extra-ordinization of the mundane. *Human Relations*, *56* (12): 1435–1459.

Andrews, E. (2009). Bank aid programs are seen as open to fraud. *NYTimes on the web*, April 21. Available at: http://dealbook.nytimes.com/2009/04/21/bank-aid-programs-are-seen-as-open-to-fraud/?scp=1&sq=%22bank%20aid%20programs%22&st=cse.

Angell, Marcia (2004). *The truth about the drug companies*. New York: Random House.

Anthony, Paul (1977). *The ideology of work*. London: Tavistock Publications.

Aristotle (1962). *The politics of Aristotle*, ed. and trans. by Ernst Barker. New York: Oxford University Press.

Aristotle (1991). *Aristotle on rhetoric: A theory of civic discourse*, ed. and trans. G. Kennedy. New York: Oxford University Press.

Atkinson, Sherry (2002). *Red faces at the Red Cross*. CBS Evening News [Televison broadcast transcript], July 30. Available at: www.cbsnews.com/stories/2002/07/30/eveningnews/main516886.shtml.

Aune, James Arnt (2001). *Selling the free market*. New York: Guilford Press.

Aune, James Arnt (2007). How to read Milton Friedman. In Steve May, George Cheney, and Juliet Roper (eds), *The debate over corporate social responsibility* (pp. 207–218). New York: Oxford University Press.

Baber, L. and H. Khondker (2002). "Sites" of resistance: Alternative websites and state–society relations. *British Journal of Sociology*, *53*: 127–148.

Bailey, David (2006). America's capitalist covenant: Using the jeremiad to defend Wal-mart's corporate image. Paper presented at the National Communication Association Convention, Chicago (November).

Bajaj, Vikas (2010). Bangladesh, with low pay, moves in on China. *NYTimes on the web*, July 16. Available at: www.nytimes.com/2010/07/17/business/global/17textile.html.

Bakan, Joel (2004). *The corporation*. Boston: Free Press.

Baker, Jane Stuart, Charles Conrad, Chris Cudahy, and Jennifer Willyard (2009). The devil in disguise: Vioxx, drug safety, and the FDA. In Robert Heath, Elizabeth Toth, and Damion Waymer (eds), *Rhetorical and critical approaches to public relations*, vol. 2 (pp. 170–194). New York: Routledge.

Banks, Stephen (2008). The troubles with leadership. In Stephen Banks (ed.), *Dissent and the failure of leadership* (pp. 1–21). Cheltenham, UK: Edward Elgar.

References

Banting, Keith and Stan Corbett (2002). *Health policy and federalism: A comparative perspective on multi-level governance.* Montreal: McGill-Queens University Press.

Barker, James R. (1993). Tightening the iron cage: Concertive control in self-managing teams. *Administrative Science Quarterly, 38:* 408–437.

Barker, James R., C. W. Melville, and Michael Pacanowsky (1993). Self-directed teams at Xel: Changes in communication practices during a program of cultural transformation. *Journal of Applied Communication Research, 21:* 297–313.

Barker, Richard (1997). How can we train leaders if we do not know what leadership is? *Human Relations, 50:* 343–362.

Barker, Richard (2001). The nature of leadership. *Human Relations, 54:* 469–494.

Barley, Stephen and Gideon Kunda (1992). Design and devotion. *Administrative Science Quarterly, 37:* 363–399.

Barley, Stephen, G. W. Meyer, and Debra Gash (1988). Cultures of culture. *Administrative Science Quarterly, 33* (1988): 24–60.

Barrett, Kate (2009). Health care battle: Lobbyists outnumber lawmakers, August 14. Available at: http:abcnews.go.com.

Bartlett, Bruce (2006). *Imposter.* New York: Doubleday.

Barton, Lawrence (2001). *Crisis in organizations,* vol. 2. Cincinnati, OH: College Divisions South-Western.

Bass, Bernard (1985). *Leadership and performance beyond expectations.* New York: Free Press.

Bass, Bernard and Ruth Bass (2008). *The Bass handbook of leadership,* 4th edn. New York: Free Press.

Baumgartner, Frank and Bryan Jones (1993). *Agendas and instability in American politics.* Chicago: University of Chicago Press.

Baumgartner, Frank and Beth Leech (1998). *Basic interests: The importance of interest groups in politics and political science.* Princeton: Princeton University Press.

Baumgartner, Frank, Jeffrey Berry, Marie Jojracki, David Kimball and Beth Leech (2009). *Lobbying and policy change: Who wins, who loses, and why.* Chicago: University of Chicago Press.

Beard, Charles (1986). *An economic interpretation of the Constitution of the United States* [1913]. New York: The Free Press.

Bellah, Robert, Richard Madsen, William Sullivan, and Ann Swidler (1995). *Habits of the heart,* 2nd edn. Berkeley: University of California Press.

Bendell, Jem and Mark Bendell (2007). Facing corporate power. In Steve May, George Cheney, and Juliet Roper (eds), *The debate over corporate social responsibility* (pp. 59–73). New York: Oxford University Press.

Bennett, William (2003). Communicating global activism: Strengths and vulnerabilities of networked politics. *Information, Communication and Society, 6:* 143–168.

References

Bennis, Warren and Brian Naus (1985). *Leaders*. New York: Harper and Row.

Bennis, Warren, Jagdish Parikh and Ronnie Lessem (1994). *Beyond leadership: Balancing economics, ethics, and ecology*. Cambridge, MA: Basil Blackwell.

Benoit, William L. (1995). *Accounts, excuses, and apologies: A theory of image restoration strategies*. Albany, NY: SUNY Press.

Benoit, William and J. J. Lindsay (1987). Argument strategies: Antidote to Tylenol's poisoned image. *Journal of the American Forensics Association*, 23: 136–146.

Benson, J. A. (1988). Crisis revisited: An analysis of the strategies used by Tylenol in the second tampering episode. *Central States Speech Journal*, 39: 49–66.

Bercovitch, Sacvan (1978). *The American Jeremiad*. Madison, WI: University of Wisconsin Press.

Berg, John C. (1994). *Unequal struggle: Class, gender, race, and power in the US Congress*. Boulder, CO: Westview Press.

Berger, Eric (2010). Free markets in outer space. *Houston Chronicle*, May 1: D1.

Biersack, Robert, Paul Hernson and Clyde Wilcox (1999). *After the revolution*. Boston: Allyn and Bacon.

Black, Edwin (1970). The second persona. *Quarterly Journal of Speech*, 61: 235–249.

Blake, Rich (2010). Financial overhaul nothing for Wall Street to cry about. *ABC News on the web*, July 15. Available at: http://abcnews.go.com/Business/financial-bill-set-pass-wall-street-returns-form/story?id=11165278.

Blanton, Brett (2010). Blame game has no end in sight: Pointing finger at contractors. BP seeks to distance itself from spill. *Houston Chronicle*, May 10: A4.

Blow, Charles (2010). Give them something they can feel. *NYTimes on the web*, May 28. Available at: www.nytimes.com/2010/05/29/opinion/29blow.html.

Boje, David (1999). Is Nike Roadrunner or Wile E. Coyote? A postmodern organization analysis of double logic. *Journal of Business and Entrepreneurship*, 2: 77–109.

Boje, David (2000). Nike corporate writing of academic, business, and cultural practices. *Management Communication Quarterly*, 14: 507–516.

Boje, David, G. N. Rosile, R. Dennehy, and D. J. Summers (1997). Restorying re-engineering. *Journal of Applied Communication Research*, 6: 631–668.

Bormann, Ernest (2001). *The force of fantasy* [1985]. Carbondale, IL: Southern Illinois University Press.

Botan, Carl and M. Taylor (2004). Public relations: State of the field. *Journal of Communication*, 54: 645–661.

Boys, Suzanne (2009). Inter-organizational crisis communication: Exploring source and stakeholder communication in the Roman Catholic clergy sex abuse case. In Robert Heath, Elizabeth Toth, and Damion Waymer (eds), *Rhetorical and critical approaches to public relations*, vol. 2 (pp. 290–310). New York: Routledge.

References

Breen, Marcus (2007). Business, society, and impacts on indigenous peoples. In Steve May, George Cheney, and Juliet Roper (eds), *The debate over corporate social responsibility* (pp. 292–384). New York: Oxford University Press.

Brewster, Mike (2003). *Unaccountable: How the accounting profession forfeited a public trust.* New York: John Wiley.

Broder, David S. (2010). The Senate, stuck on partisan and parochial battles. *Houston Chronicle*, August 5: B9.

Broder, John and Helene Cooper (2010). Obama vows end to "cozy" oversight of oil industry. *NYTimes on the web*, May 14. Available at: www.nytimes. com/2010/05/15/us/politics/15obama.html.

Brooks, David (2010). The return of history. *NYTimes on the Web*, March 26. Available at:www.nytimes.com/2010/03/26/opinion/26brooks.html.

Brooks, John (1900). The morals of shopping. *Women's Journal*, December 22: 400–409.

Brummett, Barry (1995). Scandalous rhetorics. In W. N. Elwood (ed.), *Public relations inquiry as rhetorical criticism* (pp. 13–23). Westport, CT: Praeger.

Bucholz, Robert (1988). Adjusting corporations to the realities of public interests and policy. In Robert L. Heath (ed.), *Strategic issues management: How organizations influence and respond to public interests and policies* (pp. 50–72). San Francisco: Jossey-Bass.

Buder, Stanley (1967). *Pullman.* New York: Oxford University Press.

Burke, Kenneth (1941). *A philosophy of literary form.* Berkeley: University of California Press.

Burke, Kenneth (1962). *A grammar of motives* [1945]. Berkeley: University of California Press.

Burke, Kenneth (1966). *Language as symbolic action.* Berkeley: University of California Press.

Burke, Kenneth (1969). *A rhetoric of motives* [1950]. Berkeley: University of California Press.

Burke, Kenneth (1970). *A rhetoric of religion.* Berkeley: University of California Press.

Burns, James (1978). *Leadership.* New York: Harper and Row.

Bush, Darren (2008). Mergers: An idea that shouldn't fly. *Houston Chronicle*, May 4: E1.

Buzzanell, Patrice, Rebecca Meisenbach, and Robyn Remke (2008). Women, leadership, and dissent. In Steve Banks (ed.), *Dissent and the failure of leadership* (pp. 119–133). Cheltenham, UK: Edward Elgar.

Calder, Bobby (1977). An attribution theory of leadership. In Barry Staw and Gerald Salancik (eds), *New direction in organizational behavior* (pp. 179–204). Chicago: St. Clair.

Calder, Bobby (2002). *Leaders' personalities and the outcome of democratic elections.* Oxford: Oxford University Press.

Calmes, Jackie (2010). With populist stance, Obama takes on banks. *NYTimes on the web*, January 22. Available at: www.nytimes.com/2010/01/22/22policy. html.

Campbell, James (1977). The cutting edge of leadership: An overview. In J. Hunt and L. Larson (eds), *Leadership: The cutting edge* (pp. 106–147). Carbondale, IL: Southern Illinois University Press.

Campbell, Karlyn Kohrs (1970). The ontological foundations of rhetorical theory. *Philosophy and Rhetoric*, 3: 97–108.

Canadian Press (2007a). Demand for human organ transplants far exceeds supply, fuels "tourism": WHO, March 30. Available atwww.cbc.ca/cp/health.

Canadian Press (2007b). Mad cow ban leads to US shortage of "European" sperm, September 21. Available at: www.cbc.ca/news/health/story/2007/09/21/sperm-shortage.html.

Cappelli, Peter (1999). *The new deal at work: Managing the market-driven workforce*. Boston: Harvard Business School Press.

Carroll, Brigid and Lester Levy (2008). Defaulting to management: Leadership defined by what it is not. *Organization*, 15: 75–96.

Carroll, Glenn and Michael Hannan (2000). *The demography of corporations and industries*. Princeton, NJ: Princeton University Press.

Carroll, Susan (2009). Immigration crackdown goes after employers. *Houston Chronicle*, July 2: A1.

Casey, Whitney (2008). Treat dating like a business to help close the deal. *Houston Chronicle*, November 23: G4.

Cassidy, John (2002). The grand cycle: How the financial systems encouraged corporations to go crazy. *New Yorker*, 23 September: 64.

Cawelti, John (1974). *Apostles of the self-made man*. Cambridge, MA: Harvard University Press.

CBC News (2006). Sperm donor shortage hits Canadian infertility clinics, December 19. Available at: cbc.com.

CBC News (2007). Mapping genes opens Pandora's box of issues: researcher, September 21. Available at: www.cbc.ca/health/shorty/2007/09/21/genomic-study.html.

Chaleff, I. (2003). *The courageous follower*, 2nd edn. San Francisco, CA: Berrett-Koehler.

Chan, Sewell (2010). Reconciliation for 2 financial overhaul bills. *NYTimes on the web*, May 21. Available at: www.nytimes.com/2010/05/22/business/22regulate.html.

Chapman, Rick (2006). *In search of stupidity*, 2nd edn. Berkeley, CA: Apress.

Chen, Chao and James Meindl (1991). The construction of leadership images in the popular press: The case of Donald Burr of People Express. *Administrative Science Quarterly*, 36: 521–551.

Cheney, George (1992). The corporate person re-presents itself. In Elizabeth Toth and Robert Heath (eds), *Rhetorical and critical approaches to public relations* (pp. 165–184). Hillsdale, NJ: Lawrence Erlbaum.

References

Cheney, George and Craig Carroll (1997). The person as object in discourses in and around organizations. *Communication Research*, 24: 593–630.

Cheney, George and Lars Christensen (2001). Organizational identity: Linkages between internal and external communication. In Fredric Jablin and Linda Putnam (eds), *The new handbook of organizational communication* (pp. 231–269). Thousand Oaks, CA: Sage.

Cheney, George, Juliet Roper, and Steve May (2007). Overview. In Steve May, George Cheney, and Juliet Roper (eds), *The debate over corporate social responsibility* (pp. 3–14). New York: Oxford University Press.

Cheney, George, Lars Christiansen, Charles Conrad, and Dan Lair (2007). Corporate rhetoric as organizational discourse. In Linda Putnam, Cynthia Hardy, and Cliff Oswick (eds), *Handbook of organizational discourse* (pp. 79–103). London: Sage.

Cheney, George, Lars Christensen, Theodore Zorn, Jr., and Shiv Ganesh (2004). *Organizational communication in an age of globalization*. Prospect Heights, IL: Waveland Press.

Cheney, George, Dan Lair, Dean Ritz, and Brenden Kendall (2010). *Just a job?* New York: Oxford University Press.

Child, John (1972). Organizational structure, environment, and performance. *Sociology*, 6: 1–22.

Clair, Robin (1996). The political nature of the colloquialism, "A real job." *Communication Monographs*, 63: 249–267.

Clair, Robin, Stephanie Bell, Kyle Hackbarth, and Stephanie Mathes (2008). *Why work?* West Lafayette, IN: Purdue University Press.

Clark, Timothy and Graeme Salaman (1996). The management guru as organizational witch doctor. *Organization*, 3: 85–107.

Clark, Timothy and Graeme Salaman (1998). Telling tales: Management gurus' narratives and the construction of managerial identity. *Journal of Management Studies*, 35: 137–160.

Clegg, Stewart (1989). *Frameworks of power*. Thousand Oaks, CA: Sage.

Clegg, Stewart, David Courpasson, and Nelson Phillips (2006). *Power and organizations*. London: Sage.

Cleverly, Graham (1971). *Managers and magic*. London: Longman.

Cloud, Dana (1996). Hegemony or concordance? *Critical Studies in Mass Communication*, 13: 115–137.

Cloud, Dana (2005). Fighting words. *Management Communication Quarterly*, 18: 509–542.

Cobb, Roger and Marc Ross (1997). *Cultural strategies of agenda denial*. Lawrence, KS: Kansas University Press.

Cohan, William (2010). Will Wall Street go free? *NYTimes on the web*, May 27. Availabkle at: http://opinionator.blogs.nytimes.com/2010/05/27/will-wall-street-go-free.html.

References

Cohen, J. R. (2002). Legislating apology: The pros and cons. *University of Cincinnati Law Review, 70*: 101–122.

Collier, Roger (2009) Drug development cost estimates hard to swallow, *Canadian Medical Association Journal, 180*(3): 279–280.

Collinson, David (1988). Engineering humor. *Organization Studies, 9*: 181–199.

Collinson, David (1992). *Managing the shop floor*. New York: DeGruyter.

Collinson, David (2002). Managing humor. *Journal of Management Studies, 39*: 269–288.

Collinson, David (2005). Dialectics of leadership. *Human Relations, 58*: 1419–1442.

Comerer, Colin and George Lowenstein (2004). *Advances in behavioral economics*. Princeton, NJ: Princeton University Press.

Conger, Jay (1991). *The charismatic leader*. San Francisco: Jossey-Bass.

Connelly, Julie (2003). Youthful attitudes, sobering realities. *NYTimes on the web*, October 28. Available at: www.nytimes.com/2003/10/28/jobs/the-new-generation-youthful-attitudes-sobering-realities.html?scp=15&sq="julie connelly"&st=cse.

Conrad, Charles (1983). Organizational power: Faces and symbolic forms. In Linda Putnam and Michael Pacanowsky (eds), *Communication and organizations: An interpretive perspective* (pp. 173–194). Beverly Hills: Sage.

Conrad, Charles (1985). Review of *A passion for excellence*. *Administrative Science Quarterly, 30*: 426–429.

Conrad, Charles (2003). Stemming the tide. *Organization, 10*: 549–560.

Conrad, Charles (2004). The illusion of reform. *Rhetoric and Public Affairs, 7*: 311–338.

Conrad, Charles (2009). Smoke and mirrors. Paper presented at the International Communication Association Convention, Chicago, May.

Conrad, Charles and Je'Anna Abbott (2007). Corporate social responsibility and public policy making. In Steve May, George Cheney, and Juliet Roper (eds), *The debate over corporate social responsibility* (pp. 417–437). New York: Oxford University Press.

Conrad, Charles and Julie Haynes (2001). Key constructs: Views from varying perspectives. In Fredric Jablin and Linda Putnam (eds), *The new handbook of organizational communication* (pp. 47–77). Newbury Park, CA: Sage.

Conrad, Charles and Denise Jodlowski (2008). Dealing drugs on the border. In Heather Zoller and Mohan Dutta (eds), *Emerging perspectives in health* (pp. 365–389). Mahwah, NJ: Lawrence Erlbaum.

Conrad, Charles and Brad Millay (2001). Confronting free market romanticism: Health care reform in the least likely place. *Journal of Applied Communication Research, 29*: 153–170.

Conrad, Charles and M. Scott Poole (1997). Introduction. *Journal of Applied Communication Research, 6*: 580–596.

References

Conrad, Charles and M. Scott Poole (2005). *Strategic organizational communication*, 6th edn. Belmont, CA: Thomson Wadsworth.

Conrad Charles and Mary Ryan (1985). Power, praxis, and self in organizational communication theory. In Philip Tompkins and Robert McPhee (eds), *Organizational communication: Traditional themes and new directions* (pp. 345–364). Beverly Hills: Sage.

Conrad, Charles, Jane Stuart Baker, Chris Cudahy, and Jennifer Willyard (2010). The dialectics of organizational crisis management. In William Coombs and Sherry Holladay (eds), *The handbook of crisis communication* (pp. 607–634). New York: Wiley–Blackwell.

Coombs, W. Timothy (2004). Impact of past crises on current crisis communication. *Journal of Business Communication*, 41: 265–289.

Coombs, W. Timothy (2007). *Ongoing crisis communication: Planning, managing, and responding*. Los Angeles, CA: Sage.

Coombs, W. Timothy (2009). Crisis communication, reputation, and rhetoric. In Robert Heath, Elizabeth Toth, and Damion Waymer (eds), *Rhetorical and critical approaches to public relations*, vol. 2 (pp. 237–251). New York: Routledge.

Coombs, W. Timothy and Sherry Holladay, eds (2010). *The handbook of crisis communication*. New York: Wiley–Blackwell.

Cooper, Helene (2010). Obama says he doesn't begrudge bank executives' bonuses. *NYTimes on the web*, February 10. Available at: www.nytimes.com/2010/02/10/obama-says-he-doesn't-begrudge-bank-executives-bonuses.html.

Cooper, Michael (2006). New prescription pricing law faces repeal in Pataki budget. *NYTimes on the Web*, January 20. Available at: www.nytimes.com/2006/01/20/nyregion/20drugs.html?_r=1&ref=michaelcooper

Corak, M. (2006). *Do poor children become poor adults?* IZA Discussion Paper. Bonn, Germany: Institute for the Study of Labor.

Cox, J. Robert (2004). "Free trade" and the eclipse of civil society. In Steve Depoe, J. W. Delicath, and M. F. Aepli Elsenbeer (eds), *Communication and public participation in environmental decision-making* (pp. 201–219). Albany, NY: SUNY Press.

Crable, Richard and Steven Vibbert (1983). Mobil's epideictic advocacy: "Observations" of Prometheus-bound. *Communication Monographs*, 50: 380–394.

Crawford, Alan (1980). *Thunder on the right*. New York: Pantheon.

Creswell, Julie (2010). Will Goldman settlement be prize enough? *Houston Chronicle*, July 19: B1.

Cronin, Thomas (1987). Leadership and democracy. *Liberal Education*, 73(2) (March/April): 35–38.

Cronin, Thomas (1998). Leadership and democracy. In J. Thomas Wren (ed.), *The leader's companion: Insights on leadership thought through the ages* (pp. 303–309). New York: The Free Press.

228

References

Crook, Clive (2005). The good company. *Economist, 374* (January 22): 1–31.

Cropsey, John (2001). *Polity and economy.* South Bend, IN: St. Augustine's Press.

Cubanski, Juliette, Trician Neuman, Elizabeth Hargrave, Jack Hoadley, and Laura Summer (2010). Medicare Part D 2010 data spotlight: Prices for brand-name drugs in the coverage gap. Washington, DC: Kaiser Family Foundation. Available at: www.kff.org.

Cutlip, S. M. (1994). *The unseen power: Public relations.* Hillsdale, NJ: Lawrence Erlbaum.

Czarniawska, Barbara (1997). *Narrating the organization.* Chicago: University of Chicago Press.

D'Addio, Anna Cristina (2007). *Intergenerational transmission of disadvantage.* Available at: www.oecd.org/e1s.

Dahl, Robert (1998). *On democracy.* New Haven, CT: Yale University Press.

Dahl, Robert (2002). *How democratic is the American constitution?* New Haven, CT: Yale University Press.

Dash, Eric (2009). US may set debt test for banks. *NYTimes on the web,* May 6. Available at: query.nytimes.com/gst/fullpage.html?res=9C02E6D81538F935A 35756C0A96F9C8B63&scp=172&sq="Eric+Dash"&st=nyt.

Davies, G., R. Chun, R.V. da Silva, and S. Roper (2003). *Corporate reputation and competitiveness.* London: Routledge.

Deal, Terrance and William Jenkins (1994). *Managing the hidden organization.* New York: Warner.

Deal, Terrance and Allan Kennedy (1982). *Corporate cultures.* Reading, MA: Addison-Wesley.

Deetz, Stanley (1992a). *Democracy in an age of corporate colonization.* Albany, NY: SUNY Press.

Deetz, Stanley (1992b). Disciplinary power in the modern corporation. In Mats Alvesson and Hugh Willmott (eds), *Critical management studies* (pp. 21–45). London: Sage.

Deetz, Stanley (1995). *Transforming communication, transforming business.* Creskill, NJ: Hampton Press.

Dempsey, Paul (1989). *The social and economic consequences of deregulation.* New York: Quorum Books.

DeParle, Jason (2010). A world on the move. *New York Times,* June 27: A1, A4.

Dicken, John (2009). Brand-name prescription drug pricing: Lack of thera-peutically equivalent drugs and limited competition may contribute to extraordinary price increases. Washington, DC: Government Accountability Office, December. Available at: www.gao.gov/.

Dionisopoulos, George and Richard Crable (1988). Definitional hegemony as a public relations strategy: The rhetoric of the nuclear power industry after Three Mile Island. *Central States Speech Journal, 39*: 134–145.

Dionisopoulos, George and Steven Goldzwig (1992). The atomic power industry and the NEW woman. In Robert Heath and Elizabeth Toth (eds), *Rhetorical and critical approaches to public relations* (pp. 205–224). Hillside, NJ: Lawrence Erlbaum.

Dionne, E. J. (2009). America confronted with a silent crisis in education. *Houston Chronicle*, July 17: B9.

Dionne, E. J. (2010). Irrational ideas about fiscal policy undermining US. *Houston Chronicle*, July 30: B9.

DiTomaso, Nancy, Rochelle Parks-Yancy, and Corinne Post (2003). Structure, relationships, and community responsibility. *Management Communication Quarterly*, 17: 143–160.

Dlouhy, Jennifer (2010). Obama rips execs for blame game. *Houston Chronicle*, May 15: A1, A19.

Dougherty, Carter (2009). Debate in Germany: Research or manufacturing? *NYTimes on the web*, August 12. Available at: www.nytimes.com/2009/08/12/business/global/12silicon.html.

Dowd, Maureen (2010). *NYTimes on the web*, May 30. Available at: www.nytimes.com/2010/05/30/opinion/30dowd.html.

Dowie, Mark (1977). Pinto madness. *Mother Jones*, September/October. Available at: http://motherjones.com/politics/1977/09/pinto-madness.

Dowling, George (2001). *Creating corporate reputations: Identity, image, and performance*. Oxford: Oxford University Press.

Downs, Alan (1996). *Corporate executions*. New York: AMACOM.

Downs, Anthony (1972). Up and down with ecology. *Public Interest*, 28: 38–50.

Driskell, J. and Oscar Beckett (1989). Psychology and the military. *American Psychologist*, 44: 43–54.

Dunham, Richard and Stewart Powell (2010). Critics blame energy lobby for lax safety rules. *Houston Chronicle*, May 9: A21.

Eccles, R. G. and N. Nohria (1992). *Beyond the hype: Rediscovering the essence of management*. Cambridge, MA: Harvard University Press.

Egan, Timothy (2010). Groundhog day for oil. *NYTimes on the Web*, May 5. Available at: http:opiniionator.blogs.nytimes.com/2010/05/05/groundhog-day-for-oil.html.

Elliott, A. Larry and Richard Schroth (2002). *How companies lie*. New York: Crown Business Press.

Elsbach, Kimberly (1994). Managing organizational legitimacy in the California cattle industry: Construction and effectiveness of accounts. *Administrative Science Quarterly*, 39: 57–88.

Ewen, S. (1994). *All-consuming images*. New York: Basic Books.

Fairhurst, Gail (2001) Dualisms in leadership research. In Fredric Jablin and Linda Putnam (eds), *The new handbook of organizational communication* (pp. 379–439). Beverly Hills, CA: Sage.

Fairhurst, Gail (2005). Reframing *The art of framing*. *Leadership*, 1: 165–185.

References

Fairhurst, Gail and Robert Sarr (1996). *The art of framing.* San Francisco: Jossey-Bass.

Fairhurst, Gail and Heather Zoller (2007). Resistance leadership: The overlooked potential in critical organizational and leadership studies. *Human Relations*, 60: 1331–1360.

Fairhurst, Gail and Heather Zoller (2008). Resistance, dissent, and leadership in practice. In Steve Banks (ed.), *Dissent and the failure of leadership* (pp. 135–148). Cheltenham, UK: Edward Elgar.

Familes USA (2007). No bargain: Medicare drug plans deliver high prices, January. Available at: www.familiesusa.org.

Farrell, C. (2002). The other side of Adam Smith. *Business Week*, November 15. Available at: http://www.businessweek.com/bwdaily/dnflash/nov2002/nf20021115_2141.htm.

Farrell, D. and C. E. Rusbult (1992). Exploring the exit, voice, loyalty, and neglect typology. *Employee Responsibilities and Rights Journal*, 5: 201–218.

Farrell, Thomas and G. Thomas Goodnight (1981). Accidental rhetoric: The root metaphors of Three Mile Island. *Communication Monographs*, 48: 271–300.

Fetherston, Liza (2002). *Students against sweatshops: The making of a movement.* New York: Verso.

Fleming, Peter and Graham Sewell (2002). Looking for the good soldier, Svejk. *Sociology*, 36: 857–873.

Fleming, Peter and A. Spicer (2003). Working at a cynical distance. *Organization*, 10: 157–179.

Foderaro, Lisa (2010). From battlefield to Ivy League on the G. I. Bill. *NYTimes on the web*, January 9. Available at: www.nytimes.com/2010/01/09/nyregion/09gis.html.

Fombrun, Charles (1987). Creating an institutionally-informed ecology of organizations. In George Carroll (ed.), *Ecological models of organizations.* Cambridge, MA: Ballinger.

Fombrun, Charles and V. P. Rindova (2000). The road to transparency: Reputation management at Royal Dutch/Shell. In Majen Schultz, Mary Jo Hatch and M. H. Larsen (eds), *The expressive organization* (pp. 77–96). Oxford: Oxford University Press.

Fombrun, Charles and C. B. M. van Riel (2004). *Fame and fortune: How successful companies build winning reputations.* Upper Saddle River, NJ: Prentice Hall.

Foss, Sonja, Karen Foss, and Robert Trapp (1991). *Contemporary perspectives on rhetoric*, 2nd edn. Prospect Heights, IL: Waveland Press.

Fouhy, Beth (2009). Young Obama backers AWOL from reform fight. *Houston Chronicle*, August 25: A4.

Free, Joshua (2009). Southwest loses battle for Frontier. *Houston Chronicle*, August 14: D1.

231

References

Freeman, Richard (1994). *Working under different rules*. New York: Russell Sage.

Friedman, Milton (1970). The social responsibility of business is to increase its profits. *New York Times Magazine*, September 13: 30–36.

Friedman, Thomas (2010). Adults only, please. *NYTimes on the Web*, January 27. Available at: www.nytimes.com/2010/01/27/opinion/27friedman.html.

Fromm, Eric (1970). Psychoanalysis and Zen Buddhism. In D. Suzuki, Eric Fromm and R. DeMartino (eds), *Zen Buddhism and psychoanalysis* (pp. 3–37). New York: Harper and Row.

Frye, Northrop (1976). *The secular scripture*. Cambridge, MA: Harvard University Press.

Fuller, Colleen (1998). *Caring for profit*. Vancouver: New Star Books.

Galbraith, James K. (1998). *Created unequal*. New York: The Free Press.

Ganesh, Shiv (2007). Sustainable development discourse and the global economy: Promoting responsibility, containing change. In Steve May, George Cheney, and Juliet Roper (eds), *The debate over corporate social responsibility* (pp. 379–390). New York: Oxford University Press.

Ganesh, Shiv, Heather Zoller, and George Cheney (2005). Transforming resistance, broadening our boundaries. *Communication Monographs*, 72: 169–191.

Gardner, Amanda (2007). But out-of-pocket costs continue to rise, annual government report says, January 9. Available at: www.cbc.ca (accessed on 1/9/07).

Gemmill, Gary and Judith Oakley (1992). Leadership: An alienating social myth? *Human Relations*, 45: 101–131.

Geoghegan, Thomas (1992). *Which side are you on?* New York: Penguin.

Ghose, B. (2007). Ready or not? *Chronicle of Philanthropy*, 19, July 26: n.p.

Giddens, Anthony (1984). *The constitution of society*. Berkeley: University of California Press.

Giddens, Anthony (1991). *Modernity and self-identity*. Cambridge: Polity.

Gilman, Nicholas (1899). *A dividend to labor*. Boston: Houghton, Mifflin.

Ginsberg, Benjamin and John Green (1986). The best Congress money can buy. In B. Ginsberg and Alan Stone (eds), *Do elections matter?* (pp. 75–89). Armonk, NY: M. E. Sharpe.

Goffee, Richard and Gareth Jones (2001). Followership. *Harvard Business Review*, 79: 146–149.

Goldgar, Anne (2007). *Tulipmania: Money, honor and knowledge in the Dutch golden age*. Chicago: University of Chicago Press.

Goldstein, Kenneth (1999). *Interest groups, lobbying, and participation in America*. Cambridge: Cambridge University Press.

Goodman, Ellen (2008). Womb for rent: When does outsourcing cross the line? *Houston Chronicle*, April 13: E3.

Gordon, David (1996). *Fat and mean*. New York: Free Press.

References

Gordon, Nancy (2010). Citigroup settlement nears OK. *Houston Chronicle*, September 25: D3.

Gore, David (2005). The rhetoric of economic inquiry in Smith, Whately, and Mill. Doctoral dissertation, Texas A&M University, College Station, TX, May.

Gormley, Michael (2006). Bid to cut pollution reports criticized. *Houston Chronicle*, January 22: A6.

Gossett, Loril and Julian Kilker (2006). My job sucks. *Management Communication Quarterly*, 1: 1–32.

Gottfried, Hans (1994). Learning the score. In James M. Jermier, David Knights, and Walter Nord (eds), *Resistance and power in organizations* (pp. 102–127). London: Routledge.

Gowler, Dan and Karen Legge (1996). The meaning of management and the management of meaning. In Stephen Linstead, Robert Grafton-Small, and Paul Jeffcutt (eds), *Understanding management* (pp. 286–302). London: Sage.

Grady, Denise (2007) Girl or boy? As fertility technology advances, so does an ethical debate. *NYTimes on the web*, February 6. Available at: www.nytimes.com/2007/02/06/health/06seco.html?ref=denisegrady.

Graham, Julie W. (1986). Principled organizational dissent. *Research in Organizational Behavior*, 8: 1–52.

Graham, Laurie (1993). Inside a Japanese transplant. *Work and Occupations*, 20: 147–173.

Graham, Laurie (1995). *On the line at Subaru-Isuzu: The Japanese and the American worker*. Ithaca, NY: Cornell University Press.

Gramsci, Antonio (1992). *Prison notebooks*. New York: Columbia University Press.

Green, Heather (2007). The greening of America's campuses. *Business Week*, April 9: 62.

Greenhouse, Steven (2010a). Wal-Mart battles trampling case. *Houston Chronicle*, July 7: D1.

Greenhouse, Steven (2010b) Pressured, Nike to help workers in Honduras. *NYTimes on the web*, July 26. Available at: www.nytimes.com/2010/07/27/business/global/27nike.html?ref=honduras.

Greider, William (1992). *Who will tell the people?* New York: Simon and Schuster.

Greider, William (1997). *One world, ready or not*. New York: Simon and Schuster.

Grieshaber-Otto, Jim and Scott Sinclair (2004). *Bad medicine: Trade treaties, privatization and health care reform in Canada*. Montreal: Canadian Centre for Policy Alternatives.

Grint, Keith (1994). Reengineering history: Social resonances and business process reengineering. *Organization*, 1: 179–200.

References

Grint, Keith and Peter Case (1998). The violent rhetoric of re-engineering: Management consultancy on the offensive. *Journal of Management Studies*, 35: 222–238.

Gronn, P. C. (1983). Talk as the work. *Administrative Science Quarterly*, 28: 1–21.

Grossman, Gene and Elhanan Helpman (2001). *Special interest politics*. Cambridge, MA: MIT Press.

Grunig, James (2001). Two-way symmetrical public relations: Past, present, and future. In Robert Heath (ed.), *Handbook of public relations* (pp. 11–30). Thousand Oaks, CA: Sage.

Grunig, James and Laurie Grunig (2000). Public relations in strategic management and strategic management of public relations: Theory and evidence from the IABC excellence project. *Journalism Studies*, 1: 303–321.

Guest, Richard (1996). Right enough to be dangerously wrong. In Graeme Salaman (ed.), *Human resource strategies* (pp. 1–19). London: Sage.

Habermas, Jurgen (1984). *The theory of communicative action*, trans. T. McCarthy, vol. 1. Boston: Beacon Press.

Habermas, Jurgen (1987). *The theory of communicative action*, trans. T. McCarthy, vol. 2. Boston: Beacon Press.

Hacker, Joseph (1996). *The road to nowhere: The genesis of President Clinton's plan for health security*. Princeton, NJ: Princeton University Press.

Hambrick, Donald and Sidney Finkelstein (1987). Managerial discretion. *Research in Organizational Behavior*, 9: 369–406.

Hammer, Michael (1990). Reengineering work: don't automate, obliterate. *Harvard Business Review*, 67 (July/August): 104–112.

Hannan, Michael and John Freeman (1989). *Organizational ecology*. Cambridge, MA: Harvard University Press.

Hardin, Garrett (1968). The tragedy of the commons. *Science*, December 13: 1243–1248.

Hardy, Cynthia and Stewart Clegg (1999). Some dare call it power. In Stewart Clegg and Cynthia Hardy (eds), *Studying organizations* (pp. 622–641). London: Sage.

Hardy, Cynthia, Ian Palmer, and Nelson Phillips (2000). Discourse as a strategic resource. *Human Relations*, 53: 1227–1248.

Hargie, Owen, Karyn Stapleton, and Dennis Tourish (2010). Interpretations of CEO public apologies for the banking crisis: Attributions of blame and avoidance of responsibility. *Organization*, 17: 721–742.

Harris, Charles, Michael Pritchard, and Michael Rabins (1995). *Engineering ethics*. Belmont, CA: Wadsworth.

Harrop, Froma (2010). US could learn from Canada's immigration policy. *Houston Chronicle*, May 28: B9.

Hawken, Paul (1993). *The ecology of commerce: A declaration of sustainability*. New York: Harper Business.

References

Hawken, Paul, A. Lovins, and L. L. Lovins (1999). *Natural capitalism: Creating the next industrial revolution.* New York: Back Bay Books.

Hearit, Keith Michael (2007). Corporate deception and fraud: The case for an ethical apologia. In Steve May, George Cheney, and Juliet Roper (eds), *The debate over corporate social responsibility* (pp. 167–176). New York: Oxford University Press.

Hearit, Keith Michael and Jeffrey Courtright (2003). A social constructionist approach to crisis management: Allegations of sudden acceleration in the Audi 5000. *Communication Studies*, 54: 79–95.

Heath, Robert (1988). *Strategic issues management.* San Francisco: Jossey-Bass.

Heath, Robert (2009). The rhetorical tradition. In Robert Heath, Elizabeth Toth, and Damion Waymer (eds), *Rhetorical and critical approaches to public relations*, vol. 2 (pp. 17–47). New York: Routledge.

Heidelbaugh, Nola (2001). *Judgment, rhetoric and the problem of incommensurability.* Columbia, SC: University of South Carolina Press.

Heidelbaugh, Nola (2007). Invention and dialogue. *Communication Theory*, 18: 27–50.

Heilbroner, Robert (1982). The socialization of the individual in Adam Smith. *History of Political Economy*, 14: 427–439.

Hensel, Bill, Jr. (2009). Continental seeks path out of slump. *Houston Chronicle*, March 22: D1.

Herbert, Bob (2010). They still don't get it. *NYTimes on the web*, January 23. Available at: www.nytimes.com/2010/01/23/opinion/23herbert.html.

Higham, John (2002). *Strangers in the land.* New Brunswick, NJ: Rutgers University Press.

Hirschman, Albert (1970). *Exit, voice, and loyalty: Responses to declines in firms, organizations, and states.* Cambridge, MA: Harvard University Press.

Hirschman, Albert (1991). *The rhetoric of reaction: Perversity, futility, jeopardy.* Cambridge, MA: Belknap Press.

Hochschild, Arlie (1985). *The managed heart.* Berkeley: University of California Press.

Hodge, Bob and Gabriela Coronado (2006). Mexico Inc.? Discourse analysis and the triumph of managerialism. *Organization*, 13: 529–547.

Hodson, Robert (1995). Worker resistance. *Economic and Industrial Democracy*, 16: 79–110.

Hoffman, Renier (1997). Collectivism and individualism. In Daryl D'Art and Thomas Turner (eds), *Collectivism and individualism: Trends and prospects* (pp. 1–10). Dublin, Ireland: Oak Tree Press.

Hoffmeister, John (2010a). Stop outsourcing. *NYTimes on the web*, May 11. Available at: www.nytimes.com/2010/05/11/opinion/11oped2.html.

Hoffmeister, John (2010b). *Why we hate the oil companies: Straight talk from an energy insider.* New York: Palgrave Macmillan.

235

References

Hofstadter, Richard (1965). *The paranoid style in American politics and other essays*. New York: Alfred Knopf.

Hogarth, R. M. and M. W. Rader (1987). *Rational choice*. Chicago: University of Chicago Press.

Horwitz, Morton (1992). *The transformation of American law, 1836–1937*. Cambridge, MA: Harvard University Press.

Howe, Neil and William Strauss (2000). *Millennials rising*. New York: Vintage Books.

Howe, Neil and William Strauss (2003). *Millenials go to college*. Washington, DC: American Association of Collegiate Registrars and Admissions Officers.

Ibarra, P. R. and J. I. Kitsuse (1993). Vernacular constituents of moral discourse. In G. Miller and J. A. Hosteein (eds), *Constructionist controversies* (pp. 113–146). New York: Aldine de Gruyter.

Irwin, Neil (2010). Aughts were a lost decade for US economy, workers. *The Washington Post*, January 1. Available at: www.washingtonpost.com/wp-dyn/content/article/2010/01/01.

Iyengar, S. (1991). *Is anyone responsible?* Chicago: University of Chicago Press.

Jackall, Robert (1983). Bureaucracy and managerial work. *Harvard Business Review*, 61 (September/October): 99–123.

Jackall, Robert (2009). *Moral mazes*. New York: Oxford University Press.

Jackson, Brad (1996). Re-engineering the sense of self: The manager and the management guru. *Journal of Management Studies*, 33: 571–590.

Jackson, M. (1999). Business bends to include Generation X workforce. *Bryan/College Station Eagle*, January 31: E1.

Janeway, Elizabeth (1988). *Powers of the weak*. New York: Random House.

Jehenson, Roger (1984). Effectiveness, expertise, and excellence as ideological fictions. *Human Studies*, 7: 3–21.

Jermier, J. M., David Knights, and William Nord (eds) (1994). *Resistance and power in organizations*. London: Routledge.

Johnson, Carla and David Porter (2009). Brooklyn man's arrest on kidney-selling charges throws a spotlight on organ trafficking, July 24. Available at: www.cbc.ca/cp/health/090724.

Johnson, Simon (2009). TARP, the long goodbye. *NYTimes on the web*, April 3. Available at: www.nytimes.com/2009/04/03/business/economy/simonjohnson.ready/html.

Johnson, Simon (2010a). Breaking up the banks. *NYTimes Economix*, April 22. Available at: http://economix.blogs.nytimes.com/2010/04/22/breaking-up-the-banks.html.

Johnson, Simon (2010b). Under siege by the lobbyists. *NYTimes on the web*, May 27. Available at: http://economix.blogs.nytimes.com/2010/05/27/under-siege-by-the-lobbyists.html.

Johnson, Simon (2010c). The Fed, innovation, and the next recession. *NYTimes*

References

on the web, September 23. Available at: http://economix.blogs.nytimes. com/2010/09/23/the-fed-innovation-and-the-next-recession/?ref.=business.

Johnson, Simon and James Kwak (2010). *13 Bankers: The Wall Street takeover and the next financial meltdown*. New York: Pantheon.

Jones, Bryan and Frank Baumgartner (2005). *The politics of attention*. Chicago: University of Chicago Press.

Jonsson, Asgeir (2009). *Why Iceland?* New York: McGraw-Hill.

Kahneman, D. and A. Tversky (1982). *Judgment under uncertainty*. Cambridge: Cambridge University Press.

Kamenetz, Anya (2005). Call this passive? We're young and we do it our way. *The Washington Post*, August 28: B3.

Kaplan, Bernard and Walter Crockett (1968). Developmental analysis of modes of resolution. In Robert Abelson (ed.), *Theories of cognitive consistency* (pp. 661–669). Chicago: Rand McNally.

Kassing, Jeffrey (2001). From the looks of things: Assessing perceptions of organizational dissenters. *Management Communication Quarterly*, *14*: 443–471.

Kassing, Jeffrey and Theodore Avtgis (1999). Examining the relationship between organizational dissent and aggressive communication. *Management Communication Quarterly*, *13*: 76–91.

Kauffman, Jay (1997). NASA in crisis: The space agency's public relations efforts regarding the Hubble Space Telescope. *Public Relations Review*, *23*: 1–10.

Kellerman, Barbara (2008). *Followership*. Cambridge, MA: Harvard Business School Press.

Kellerman, Brad (2006). When should a leader apologize and when not? *Harvard Business Review* (April): 73–81.

Kelley, R. E. (1992). *The power of followership*. New York: Doubleday.

Kelley, R. E. (2004). Followership. In J. MacGregor Burns, G. R. Goethals, and G. I. Sorenson (eds), *Encyclopedia of leadership* (pp. 504–513). Thousand Oaks, CA: Sage.

Kendall, Brenden, Rebecca Gill, and George Cheney (2007). Consumer activism and corporate social responsibility: How strong a connection? In Steve May, George Cheney, and Juliet Roper (eds), *The debate over corporate social responsibility* (pp. 241–266). New York: Oxford University Press.

Kimberly, James (1981). Management innovation. In Paul Nystrom and William Starbuck (eds), *Handbook of organizational design*, vol. 1 (pp. 84–104). New York: Oxford University Press.

Kindleberger, Charles, Robert Aliber, and Robert Solow (2005). *Mania, panics, and crashes*, 5th edn. New York: Wiley.

Kingdon, John (1995). *Agendas, alternatives, and public policies*, 2nd edn. New York: HarperCollins.

Kirkpatrick, David (2010a). Law meant to curb lobbying sends it underground. *NYTimes on the web*, January 18. Available at: www.nytimes. com/2010/01/18/us/politics/18lobby.html.

References

Kirkpatrick, David (2010b). Lobbyists get potent weapon in campaign finance ruling. *NYTimes on the web*, January 22. Available at: www.nytimes. com/2010/01/22/US/politics/22donate.html.

Kleiner, Art (1996). *The age of heretics*. New York: Doubleday.

Knight, Graham and Josh Greenberg (2002). Promotionalism and subpolitics: Nike and its labor critics. *Management Communication Quarterly, 15*: 541–570.

Knights, David (1997). Organization theory in the age of deconstruction. *Organization Studies, 18*: 1–20.

Kocieniewski, David (2010). As oil industry fights a tax, it reaps billions from subsidies. *NYTimes on the Web*, July 3. Available at: www.nytimes. com/2010/07/04/business/04bptax.html?ref=business.

Kondo, D. K. (1990). *Crafting selves*. Chicago, IL: University of Chicago Press.

Korman, Gerd (1967). *Industrialization, immigrants, and Americanizers*. Milwaukee, WI: State Historical Society of Wisconsin.

Kotter, John (1988). *The leadership factor*. New York: The Free Press.

Kotter, John (1990). *A force for change*. New York: The Free Press.

Krischner-Goodman, Cindy (2010). Gen Y gets dose of job-market reality. *Houston Chronicle*, August 30: B6.

Krishner, Tom (2010). US automakers start to see improvement. *Houston Chronicle on the web*, January 11. Available at: www.chron.com/ fdcp?1263604173320.

Krugman, Paul (1994). The myth of competitiveness. *Harper*'s, 6 (June): 240–281.

Krugman, Paul (2003). The death of Horatio Alger. *The Nation on the web*, December 20. www.thenation.com/article/death-horatio-alger.

Krugman, Paul (2009). Missing Richard Nixon. *NYTimes on the web*, August 31. Available at: www.nytimes.com/2009/08/31/opinion/31krugman.html.

Krugman, Paul (2010a). Bankers without a clue. *NYTimes on the web*, January 15. Available at: www.nytimes.com/2010/01/15/opinion/15krugman.html.

Krugman, Paul (2010b). Close door on "zombie economics." *Houston Chronicle*, December 21: B11.

Kuhn, Tim (1997). The discourse of issues management: A *genre* of organizational communication. *Communication Quarterly, 45*: 188–210.

Kuhn, Tim and Karen Ashcraft (2003). Corporate scandal and the theory of the firm. *Management Communication Quarterly, 17*: 20–57.

Kuhnhenn, Jim (2010a). White House moves to clear up comments on bankers. *NYTimes on the web*, February 11. Available at: http://dealbook.blogs. nytimes.com/2010/02/11/white-house-moves-to-clear-up-comments-on-bankers.html.

Kuhnhenn, Jim (2010b). Obama takes it easier on high-earning bankers. *Houston Chronicle*, February 11: D2.

Kuhnhenn, Jim (2010c). Stores, banks clash over debit fees. *Bryan-College*

References

Station eagle, June 8. Available at: www.theeagle.com/Stores–banks-clash-over-debit-card-fees.html.

Kuhrana, Rakesh (2002). *Searching for a corporate saviour*. Princeton, NJ: Princeton University Press.

Kuhrana, Rakesh (2010). *From higher aims to hired hands*. Princeton, NJ: Princeton University Press.

Kuttner, Robert (1996). *Everything for sale?* New York: Random House.

Labaton, Steve and D. Dash (2009). Banks sway bills to aid consumers. *NYTimes on the web*, April 22. Available at: http://query.nytimes.com/gst/fullpage.html?res=9F0DEFDF1130F931A15757C0A96F9C8B63&ref=stephenlabaton.

Lancaster, K. L. and R. G. Lipsey (1956). The general theory of the second best. *Review of Economic Studies*, 24: 11–32.

Landes, D. S. (1986). What do bosses really do? *Journal of Economic History*, 46: 585–623.

Landes, L. and Richard Posner (1978). The economics of the baby shortage. *Journal of Legal Studies*, 7 (June): 323–348.

Langer, Gary (2010). In Supreme Court ruling on campaign finance, the public dissents, Feb. 17. Available at: http://blogs.abcnews/thenumbers/2010/02/in-supreme-court-ruling-on-campaign-finance-the-public-dissents.html.

LaNuez, D. and John Jermier (1994). Sabotage by managers and technocrats. In John Jermier, David Knights, and Walter Nord (eds), *Power and resistance at work* (pp. 219–251). London: Routledge.

Leeper, Robin (2001). In search of a metatheory for public relations: An argument for communitarianism. In Robert Heath (ed.), *Handbook of public relations* (pp. 93–104). Thousand Oaks, CA: Sage.

Levine, Marc and Agence France-Presse (2006). Canadian parents flock to US expert to end age-old gender question, May 24. Available at: www.Canada.com.

Levinson, Mark (1996). Not everyone is downsizing. *Newsweek*, March 18: 42–44.

Levitt, Arthur (2002). *Take on the street: What Wall Street and corporate America don't want you to know and what you can do to fight back*. New York: Pantheon.

Lichtblau, Eric and Robert Pear (2010). Washington rule makers out of the shadows. *NYTimes on the web*, December 8. Available at: www.nytimes.com/2010/12/09/us/politics/09rules.html.

Lindblom, Charles (1977). *Politics and markets*. New York: Basic Books.

Lindblom, Charles (2001). *The market system: How it works and what to make of it*. New Haven, CT: Yale University Press.

Livesay, Sharon and Julie Graham (2007). Greening of corporations? In Steve May, George Cheney, and Juliet Roper (eds), *The debate over corporate social responsibility* (pp. 336–364). New York: Oxford University Press.

Llewellyn, John (2007). Regulation: Government, business and the self in the

References

United States. In Steve May, George Cheney, and Juliet Roper (eds), *The debate over corporate social responsibility* (pp. 177–190). New York: Oxford University Press.

Locke, Edwin (1982). The ideas of Frederick Taylor. *The Academy of Management Review*, 7: 14–24.

Lohr, Steve (2009). Wall Street's math wizards forgot a few variables. *NYTimes on the web*, September 13. Available at: www.nytimes.com/2009/09/13/business/13unboxed.html.

Louis, Meryl Reis (1980). Surprise and sense-making in organizations. *Administrative Science Quarterly*, 25: 226–251.

Lowe, K. B. (2006). Shared leadership: Reframing the hows and whys of leadership. Book review. *The Leadership Quarterly*, 17: 105–108.

Maffesoli, M. (1996). *The time of the tribes: The decline of individualism in mass society*, trans. D. Smith. London: Sage.

Maignan, I. (2001). Consumers' perceptions of corporate social responsibilities. *Journal of Business Ethics*, 16: 943–962.

Manber, Jeffrey (2010). *Selling peace*. New York: Collector's Guide Publishing.

Mandle, Jay (1999). The student anti-sweatshop movement: Limits and potential. *The Annals of the American Academy of Political and Social Sciences*, 570: 92–103.

Manga, Pranlal (1987). A commercial market for organs? Why not? *Bioethics*, 1: 321–338.

Mangam, I. L. and Michael Overington (1983). Dramatism and the theatrical metaphor. In Gareth Morgan (ed.), *Beyond method* (pp. 219–233). Beverly Hills, CA: Sage.

Mangam, I. L. and Michael Overington (1987). *Organizations as theatre*. Chichester: John Wiley.

Manheim, Jarol (2001). *The death of a thousand cuts: Corporate campaigns and the attack on the corporation*. Mahwah, NJ: Lawrence Erlbaum.

Manheim, Jarol (2004). *Biz-war and the out-of-power elite: The progressive-left attack on the corporation*. Mahwah, NJ: Lawrence Erlbaum.

Mann, Michael (1973). *Workers on the move*. Cambridge: Cambridge University Press.

Mann, Michael (2003). *Incoherent empire*. London: Verso.

Mansbridge, Jane (1973). Time, emotion, and inequality. *Journal of Applied Behavioral Science*, 9: 351–368.

Marchand, Roland (1998). *Creating the corporate soul: The rise of public relations and corporate imagery in American big business*. Berkeley, CA: University of California Press.

Marchione, Marylynn (2009). Loopholes for the rich and sick. *Houston Chronicle*, June 28: A4.

Marcus, A. A. and R. S. Goodman (1991). Victims and shareholders. *Academy of Management Journal*, 34: 284–305.

240

References

Margasak, Larry (2008). Farm payments for millionaires raise questions in GAO report. *Houston Chronicle*, November 25: A4.

Marglin, Steven (1975). What do bosses do? In Andre Gorz (ed.), *The division of labour: The labour process and class-struggle in modern capitalism*. Brighton, UK: Harvester Press.

Marmor, Theodore (2000). *The politics of Medicare*, 2nd edn. New York: Aldine de Gruyter.

Martin, Andrew and Micheline Maynard (2010). For bankers, saying "sorry" has its perils. *NYTimes on the web*, January 13. Available at: www.nytimes.com/2010/01/13/business/13blame.html.

Maynard, Micheline (2010). In Washington, a renewed taste for auto safety. *NYTimes on the web*, May 6. Available at: www.nytimes.com/2010/0/07/business/07auto.html.

McCann, Jess (2008). *You lost him at hello*. Deerfield Beach, FL: Health Communications, Inc.

McCloskey, Deirdre (1994). *Knowledge and persuasion in economics*. Cambridge: Cambridge University Press.

McCloskey, Donald (1985). *The rhetoric of economics*, 2nd edn. Madison, WI: University of Wisconsin Press.

McGann, James and Kent Weaver, eds (2000). *Think tanks and civil societies*. New Brunswick, NJ: Transaction Publishers.

McMillan, Jill (1988). Institutional plausibility alignment as rhetorical exercise. *Journal for the Scientific Study of Religion*, 27: 326–344.

McMillan, Jill (1990). Legal protection of whistleblowers. In S. Prosser. R. Wear and J. Nethercote (eds), *Corruption and reform* (pp. 203–211). St. Lucia, Queensland: University of Queensland Press.

McMillan, Jill (2007). Why corporate social responsibility: Why now? How? In Steve May, George Cheney, and Juliet Roper (eds), *The debate over corporate social responsibility* (pp. 15–29). New York: Oxford University Press.

Mead, George Herbert (1967). *Mind, self, and society* [1934], vol. I. Chicago: University of Chicago Press.

Meindl, James (1995). The romance of leadership as a follower-centric theory. *Leadership Quarterly*, 6: 329–341.

Meindl, James, Sanford Ehrlich, and Janet Dukerich (1985). The romance of leadership. *Administrative Science Quarterly*, 30: 78–102.

Meisenbach, Rebecca J. (2006). Habermas's discourse ethics and the principle of universalization as a moral framework for organizational communication. *Management Communication Quarterly*, 20: 39–62.

Meisenbach, Rebecca and Sarah Bonewits Feldner (2009). Dialogue, discourse ethics, and Disney. In Robert Heath, Elizabeth Toth, and Damion Waymer (eds), *Rhetorical and critical approaches to public relations*, vol. 2 (pp. 253–271). New York: Routledge.

Miceli, Micahel and Janet Near (1992). *Blowing the whistle*. New York:

Lexington Books.

Mishel, Lawrence, Jared Bernstein, and Heather Bousley (2003). *The state of working America, 2002/2003*. Ithaca, NY: Cornell University Press.

Mitchell, Lawrence (2001). *Corporate irresponsibility*. New Haven, CT: Yale University Press.

Mitroff, Ian and Susan Mohrman (1987). The slack is gone. *Academy of Management Executive*, 1: 65–70.

Mohammadi, A. (1997). Communication and the globalization process in the developing world. In A. Mohammadi (ed.), *International communication and globalization* (pp. 67–89). Thousand Oaks, CA: Sage.

Moore, D. B. (1995). Development discourse as hegemony. In D. B. Moore and G. R. Schmitz (eds), *Debating development discourse* (pp. 1–53). New York: St. Martin's Press.

Morgenson, Gretchen (2006). Outside advice on boss's pay may not be so independent. *NYTimes on the web*, April 10. Available at: www.nytimes.com/2006/04/10/business/10pay.html.

Mouawad, Jad (2010). For BP, a history of spills and safety lapses. *NYTimes on the web*, May 8. Available at: www.nytimes.com/2010/05/09/business/09bp.html.

Mumby, Dennis (1988). *Communication and power in organizations*. Norwood, NJ: Ablex.

Mumby, Dennis (2001). Power and politics. In Fredric Jablin and Linda Putnam (eds), *The new handbook of organizational communication* (pp. 585–623). Thousand Oaks, CA: Sage.

Munshi, Debashish and Priya Kurian (2007). The case of the subaltern public. In Steve May, George Cheney, and Juliet Roper (eds), *The debate over corporate social responsibility* (pp. 438–447). New York: Oxford University Press.

Murphy, Alexandra (1998). Hidden transcripts of flight attendant resistance. *Management Communication Quarterly*, 11: 499–535.

Murphy, Andrew (2008). *Prodigal nation*. New York: Oxford University Press.

Murphy, Tom (2009). Fine unlikely to end bogus drug marketing. *Houston Chronicle*, September 5: A20.

Nadesan, Majia Holmer (1999). The discourses of corporate spiritualism and evangelical capitalism. *Management Communication Quarterly*, 13: 3–42.

Narkunas, J. P. (2005). Capital flows through language. *Theoria*, 108: 28–55.

National Commission on the Cost of Higher Education (1998). *Straight talk about college costs and prices*, January 21. Washington, DC: US Department of Education.

Norris, Floyd (2009a). The problem? Bankers point to the rules. *NYTimes on the web*, March 13. Available at: http://www.nytimes.com/2009/03/13/business/economy/13norris.html?ref=floydnorris.

Norris, Floyd (2009b). Did unemployment really rise? *NYTimes on the web*, August 9. Available at: http://norris.blogs.nytimes.com/2009/11/09/did-unemployment-really-rise/?ref=floydnorris.

Norris, Floyd (2010). A window opens on pay for bosses. *NYTimes on the web*, January 15. Available at: www.nytimes.com/2010/01/15/business/15norris.html.

New York Times Editorial Board (2010) "How corporate money will reshape politics." *NYTimes on the Web*, Jan. 1. Available at: http://roomfordebate.blogs.nytimes.com/2010/21/how-corproate-money-will-reshape-politics.

NYTimes on the web (2010). Financial reform, May 21. Available at: www.nytimes.com/2010/05/22/opinion/22sat1.html.

O'Neill, John (1999). Economy, equality, and recognition. In L. Ray and A. Sayers (eds), *Culture and economy: After the cultural turn* (pp. 76–91). London: Sage.

Orr, James (1996). *Talking about machines*. Ithaca, NY: Cornell University Press.

Orren, Karen (1995). Ideas and institutions. *Polity*, 27: 97–101.

Ostas, Daniel (2001). Deconstructing corporate social responsibility. *American Business Law Journal*, 38: 261–299.

Ouchi, William (1981). *Theory Z: How American business can meet the Japanese challenge*. Reading, MA: Addison-Wesley.

Ozen, Sukru and Hayriye Ozen (2009). Peasants against MNCs and the state. *Organization*, 16: 547–573.

Parker, Barbara (2005). *Introduction to globalization and business*. London: Sage.

Parker, Patricia (2001). African–American women executives' leadership communication within dominant culture organizations. *Management Communication Quarterly*, 15: 42–82.

Pauchant, T. C. and Ian Mitroff (1992). *Transforming the crisis-prone organization: Preventing of individual, organizational, and environmental tragedies*. San Francisco: Jossey-Bass.

Pearson, Christine M. and Ian Mitroff (1993). From crisis prone to crisis prepared: A framework for crisis management. *The Academy of Management Executive*, 7: 48–59.

Pederson, Wes (2006). PR's "implausible deniabilities." *Public Relations Quarterly*, 51: 3–5.

Peoples, Clayton (2009). Campaign finance in Canada and the US. *ACSUS Occasional Papers*, 3: 3–7.

Peoples, Clayton and Michael Gortari (2008). The impact of campaign contributions on policymaking in the US and Canada. *Research in Political Sociology*, 14: 43–64.

Perelman, Chaim (1963). *The idea of justice and the problem of argument*. London: Routledge and Kegan Paul.

Perelman, Chaim (1967). *Justice*. New York: Random House.

References

Perelman, Chaim and Lucie Olbrechts-Tyteca (1991). *The new rhetoric* [1969]. West Bend, IN: University of Notre Dame Press.

Perelman, Michael (2006). *Railroading economics: The creation of free market mythology.* New York: Monthly Review Press.

Peretti, Jonah, with M. Micheletti (2003). The Nike sweatshop email: Political consumerism, internet, and culture jamming. In M. Cheheletti, A. Follesdal, and David Stolle (eds), *Politics, products, and markets* (pp. 127–142). London: Tavistock.

Perrow, Charles (1984). *Normal accidents.* New York: Basic Books.

Perrow, Charles (1991). A society of organizations. *Theory and Society, 20*: 725–762.

Perrow, Charles (2002). *Organizing America.* Princeton, NJ: Princeton University Press.

Peters, John (1995). Publicity and pain: Self-abstraction in Adam Smith's *Theory of moral sentiments. Public Culture,* 7: 657–684.

Peters, Tom (2007). Tom Peters's true confessions. *FastCompany.Com,* December 19. Available at: www.fastcompany.com/note/44077.

Peters, Tom and Nancy Austin (1985). *A passion for excellence.* New York: Random House.

Peters, Thomas and Robert Waterman (1982). *In search of excellence.* New York: Harper and Row.

Peterson, Tarla Rai and Todd Norton (2007). Discourses of sustainability in today's public sphere. In Steve May, George Cheney, and Juliet Roper (eds), *The debate over corporate social responsibility* (pp. 351–364). New York: Oxford University Press.

Pfeffer, Jeffrey (1998). Six dangerous myths about pay. *Harvard Business Review,* 76 (May/June): 109–111.

Pfeffer, Jeffrey (2007). *What were they thinking?* Cambridge, MA: Harvard Business School.

Pfeffer, Jeffrey and John Salancik (1978). *The external control of organizations.* New York: Harper and Row.

Pfeffer, Jeffrey and Robert Sutton (2006) *Hard facts, dangerous half-truths, and total nonsense.* Cambridge, MA: Harvard Business School.

Phillips, Kevin (1990). *The politics of rich and poor.* New York: Broadway Books.

Phillips, Kevin (2002). *Wealth and democracy.* New York: Broadway Books.

Piderit, Sandy (2000). Rethinking resistance and recognizing ambivalence. *Academy of Management Review,* 25: 783–794.

Popper, Karl (1944). *The open society and its enemies: Plato.* Princeton, NJ: Princeton University Press.

Porter, W. Marc (1992). The environment and the oil company. In Robert Heath and Elizabeth Toth (eds), *Rhetorical and critical approaches to public relations,* vol. 1 (pp. 279–300). Hillside, NJ: Lawrence Erlbaum Associates.

References

Posner, Richard (1987). Forum: Adopton and market theory: The regulation of the market in adoptions. *Boston University Law Review*, 67: 1–4.

Posner, Richard (1992). *Economic analysis of law*, 4th edn. Boston: Little Brown.

Posner, Richard (2009). *A failure of capitalism: The crisis of '08 and the descent into depression*. Cambridge, MA: Harvard University Press.

Posner, Richard (2010). *The crisis of capitalist democracy*. Cambridge, MA: Harvard University Press.

Prasad, Anshuman and Pushkala Prasad (1998). Everyday struggles at the workplace. In P. A. Bamberger and W. J. Sonnenstuhl (eds), *Research on the Sociology of Organizations*, 15: 225–257.

Prasad, Pushkala and Anshuman Prasad (2000). Stretching the iron cage: The constitution and implications of routine workplace resistance. *Organization Science*, 11: 387–403.

Prechel, Harlan (2000). *Big business and the state*. Albany, NY: SUNY Press.

Preston, Julia (2008). Employers fight tough measures on immigration. *NYTimes on the web*, July 6. Available at: www.nytimes.com/2008/07/06/employers-fight-tough-measures-on-immigration. html.

Prince, Lesley (2005). Eating the menu rather than the dinner. *Leadership*, 1: 105–126.

Quadagno, Jill (2005). *One nation, uninsured: Why the US has no national health insurance*. New York: Oxford University Press.

Rabin, Roni (2007). As demand for donor eggs soars, high prices stir ethical concerns. *NYTimes on the web*, May 15. Available at: http://www.nytimes.com/2007/05/15/health/15cons.html.

Raelin, John (2003). *Creating leaderful organizations*. San Francisco, CA: Berrett-Koehler.

Readings, B. (1996). *The university in ruins*. Cambridge, MA: Harvard University Press.

Reed, Michael (1997). In praise of duality. *Organization Studies*, 18: 21–42.

Reicher, Stephen, Alexander Haslam, and Nick Hopkins (2005). Social identity and the dynamics of leadership: Leaders and followers as collaborative agents in the transformation of social "reality." *The Leadership Quarterly*, 16: 547–568.

Reinert, Patty (2002). Ex-SEC chief tried to change auditing rules. *Houston Chronicle*, January 24: A13.

Reinhardt, Uwe (2010). On health care, the devil's in the details. *NYTimes on the web*, September 3. Available at: http://economix.blogs.nytimes.com/2010/09/03/on-heath-care-the-devil's-in-the-details.html.

Reynolds, C. W. and R. V. Norman (eds) (1988). *Community in America: The challenge of* Habits of the heart. Berkeley: University of California Press.

Rich, Frank (2010). Still the best Congress money can buy. *NYTimes on the web*, November 27. Available at: www.nytimes.com/2010/11/28/opinion/28rich.html.

References

Riggio, Ronald, Ira Chaleff, and Jean Lipman-Blumen (eds) (2008). *Followership*. San Francisco: Jossey-Bass.

Ritti, Richard and John Silver (1986). Early processes of institutionalization. *Administrative Science Quarterly*, 31: 25–42.

Ritz, Dean (2001). *Defying corporation, defining democracy*. New York: Apex.

Ritz, Dean (2007). Can corporate personhood be socially responsible? In Steve May, George Cheney, and Juliet Roper (eds), *The debate over corporate social responsibility* (pp. 190–206). New York: Oxford University Press.

Rorty, Amelie Oksenberg (1996). Structuring rhetoric. In Amelie Oksenberg Rorty (ed.), *Essays on Aristotle's Rhetoric* (pp. 1–33). Berkeley, CA: University of California Press.

Rosen, Michael (1988). You asked for it: Christmas at the bosses' expense. *Journal of Management Studies*, 25: 463–480.

Rosenberg, Nathan (1968). Adam Smith: Consumer tastes and economic growth. *Journal of Political Economy*, 76: 361–374.

Rosenberg, Nathan (1990). Adam Smith and the stock of moral capital. *History of Political Economy*, 22: 1–17.

Rosenblum, Jonathan (1995). *Copper crucible: How the Arizona miners' strike of 1983 recast labor-management relations in America*. Ithaca, NY: ILR Press.

Rost, Joseph (1991). *Leadership for the twenty-first century*. New York: Praeger.

Rothschild, Emma (2001). *Economic sentiments: Adam Smith, Condorcet, and the Enlightenment*. Cambridge, MA: Harvard University Press.

Rowland, Robert and Angela Jerome (2004). On organizational apologia: A reconceptualization. *Communication Theory*, 14: 191–211.

Roy, William (1997). *Socializing capital*. Princeton, NJ: Princeton University Press.

Salancik, Gerald and James Meindl (1984). Corporate attributions as strategic illusions of management control. *Administrative Science Quarterly*, 29: 238–254.

Salter, John (1992). Adam Smith on feudalism, commerce, and slavery. *History of Political Thought*, 13: 219–241.

Schein, Edgar (1985). *Organizational culture and leadership*. San Francisco: Jossey-Bass.

Schenkler, Barry (1980). *Impression management*. Monterey, CA: Brooks/Cole.

Schwartz, Gary (1990–1991). Review of Ford Pinto litigation. *Rutger's Law Review*, vol. 43.

Scott, James (1990). *Domination and the arts of resistance: Hidden transcripts*. New Haven, CT: Yale University Press.

Scott, Megan (2009). A bitter pill for 20-somethings. *Houston Chronicle*, March 22: D3.

Scott, William (1985). Organizational revolution: An end to managerial orthodoxy. *Administrative Science Quarterly*, 17: 149–170.

References

Scott, William (1995). Organizational revolution: An end to managerial orthodoxy. *Administration and Society*, 17: 149–170.

Seeger, Matthew and Robert Ulmer (2002). A post-crisis discourse of renewal. *Journal of Applied Communication Research*, 30: 126–142.

Seeger, Matthew and Steven Hipfel (2007). Legal versus ethical arguments: Contexts for corporate social responsibility. In Steve May, George Cheney, and Juliet Roper (eds), *The debate over corporate social responsibility* (pp. 155–166). New York: Oxford University Press.

Seeley, Troy (2009) *Followership*. Saarbrucken: VDM Verlag.

Sennett, Richard (1998). *The corrosion of character*. New York: W. W. Norton.

Sewell, Graham and James R. Barker (2006). Coercion versus care: Using irony to make sense of organizational surveillance. *Academy of Management Review*, 31: 934–961.

Sewell, Graham and Peter Fleming (2002). Looking for the good soldier Sveik. *Sociology*, 36: 857–874.

Shostak, Arthur and David Skocik (1986). *The air traffic controllers' controversy: Lessons from the PATCO strike*. New York: Human Sciences Press.

Skerry, Peter (2009). The real immigration crisis. In Robert Faulkner and Susan Shell (eds), *America at risk* (pp. 174–192). Ann Arbor, MI: University of Michigan Press.

Skinner, B. F. (1976). *Walden Two*. New York: Macmillan.

Sklair, Leslie (1998). Debate transnational corporations: As political actors. *New Political Economy*, 3: 284–287.

Sklar, Martin (1988). *The corporate reconstruction of American capitalism, 1980–1916*. New York: Oxford University Press.

Skocpol, Theda (1997). *Boomerang: Health care reform and the turn against government*. New York: W. W. Norton.

Smircich, Linda and Marta Calas (1987). Organizational culture: A critical assessment. In Fred Jablin, Linda Putman, Karlene Roberts, and Lyman Porter (eds), *Handbook of organizational communication* (pp. 228–263). Beverly Hills, CA: Sage.

Smith, Adam (1976). *An inquiry into the nature and causes of the wealth of nations* [1776], ed. by R. J. Campbell and A. S. Skinner. Oxford: Oxford University Press.

Smith, James A. (1991). *The idea brokers*. New York: Free Press.

Smith, W. Stanton (2008). *Decoding generational differences: Fact, fiction, or should we all just get back to work?* New York: Deloitte LLP.

Sobo, E. J. and B. L. Sadler (2002). Improving organizational communication and cohesion in a health-care setting through employee–leadership exchange. *Human Organization*, 61: 277–287.

Sonnenfeld, Jeffrey (2010). Another view: At H.P., Governance Trumps Gossip, August 26. Available at: http://dealbook.blogs.nytimes.com/2010/08/26/

References

another-viw-at-h.p.-governance-trumps-gossip.html.

Sorkin, Andrew (2010). Study: Boards use peers to inflate executive pay, July 26. Available at: http://dealbook.blogs.nytimes.com/2010/07/26/studey-boards-use-peers-to-inflate-executive-pay.html.

Soros, George (1998). *The crisis in global capitalism*. New York: Public Affairs Press.

Soros, George (2000). *Open society: Reforming global capitalism*. New York: Public Affairs.

Stabile, Carol (2000). Nike, social responsibility, and the hidden abode of production. *Critical Studies in Media Communication*, 17: 186–204.

Staw, Barry (1975). Attribution of the "cause" of performance. *Organizational Behavior and Human Performance*, 13: 414–432.

Steffy, Brian and K. Grimes (1986). A critical theory of organizational science. *Academy of Management Review*, 11: 322–336.

Steffy, Brian and K. Grimes (1992). Personal/organizational psychology: A critique of the discipline. In Mats Alvesson and Hugh Willmott (eds), *Critical management studies* (pp. 181–201). London: Sage.

Steffy, Brian and S. Maurer (1987). The dollar-productivity value of the human resource function. *Academy of Management Review*, 12: 335–351.

Steffy, Loren (2009a). Kellner's case for regulation. *Houston Chronicle*, March 22: D1.

Steffy, Loren (2009b). Some logic flies only in airlineland. *Houston Chronicle*, April 29: D1.

Steffy, Loren (2009c). Once upstart Southwest settles into the status quo. *Houston Chronicle*, August 9: D1–2.

Steffy, Loren (2009d). Keeping patients in the dark. *Houston Chronicle*, August 12: D1.

Steffy, Loren (2010a). A changed BP? It was only an illusion. *Houston Chronicle*, May 30: D1.

Steffy, Loren (2010b). Wall Street wins in Goldman deal. *Houston Chronicle*, July 21: 1D.

Steffy, Loren (2010c). Failure not as lucrative outside US. *Houston Chronicle*, August 4: D1–2.

Steffy, Loren (2010d). Alien theory to some CEOs: Rules matter. *Houston Chronicle*, August 11: D1.

Stein, Howard (1998). *Euphemism, spin, and the crisis in organizational life*. Westport, CT: Quorum Books.

Stein, Howard (2008). Organizational totalitarianism and the voices of dissent. In Stephen Banks (ed.), *Dissent and the failure of leadership* (pp. 75–96). Cheltenham, UK: Edward Elgar.

Stiglitz, Joseph (2002). *Globalization and its discontents*. New York: W. W. Norton.

Stiglitz, Joseph (2010). *Freefall*. New York: W. W. Norton.

References

Stogsdill, Ralph (1974). *Handbook of leadership*. New York: Free Press.

Stohl, Michael, Cynthia Stohl, and Nikki Townsley (2007). A new generation of global corporate social responsibility. In Steve May, George Cheney, and Juliet Roper (eds), *The debate over corporate social responsibility* (pp. 30–44). New York: Oxford University Press.

Stokes, Ashli Quesinberry and Rachel Holloway (2009). Documentary as an activist medium: The Wal-Mart movie. In Robert Heath, Elizabeth Toth, and Damion Waymer (eds), *Rhetorical and critical approaches to public relations*, vol. 2 (pp. 344–359). New York: Routledge.

Stone, Deborah (2001). *Policy paradox*, 3rd edn. New York: W. W. Norton.

Strauss, William and Neil Howe (1991). *Generations*. New York: William Morrow & Co.

Strom, Susan (2006). Red Cross plans changes after hurricane problems. *NYTimes on the web*, April 12. Available at: www.nytimes.com/2006/04/12/us/nationaspecial/12red.html.

Sunstein, Cass (2003). *Why societies need dissent*. Cambridge, MA: Harvard University Press.

Sunstein, Cass (2007). *Republic.com*. Princeton, NJ: Princeton University Press.

Superville, Darlene and Tom Raum (2010). Obama scolds leading bankers. *Houston Chronicle*, April 23: D1.

Swanson, James (2007). The economy and its relation to politics: Robert Dahl, neoclassical economies, and democracy. *Polity*, 39: 208–233.

Symon, Gillian (2005). Exploring resistance from a rhetorical perspective. *Organizational Studies*, 26: 1641–1663.

Takala, T. (1998). Plato on leadership. *Journal of Business Ethics*, 17: 785–798.

Taylor, Frederick (1978). The principles of scientific management. In Jay Shafritz and Philip Whitbeck (eds), *Classics of organizational theory* (pp. 12–13). Oak Park, IL: Moore.

Taylor III, Alex (2010). How Toyota lost its way. *Fortune* (July 26): 108–118.

Tedeschi, John (1981). *Impression management theory and social psychological research*. New York: Academic Press.

Tedlow, Richard (2002). *Giants of enterprise*. New York: HarperBusiness.

Therborn, Goran (1980). *The ideology of power and the power of ideology*. London: Verso.

Thompson, Walter (1983). Hanging tongues. *Qualitative Sociology*, 6: 215–237.

Tichy, Neil and Mary Ann Devanna (1986). *The transformational leader*. New York: John Wiley.

Toffler, Barbara (1986). *Tough choices*. New York: John Wiley.

Toffler, Barbara (2003). *Final accounting: Ambition, greed, and the fall of Arthur Andersen*. New York: Broadway Books.

Toulmin, Stephen (1972). *Human understanding*. Princeton, NJ: Princeton University Press.

References

Toulmin, Stephen (2003). *The uses of argument* [1958]. Cambridge: Cambridge University Press.

Tourish, Dennis and Naheed Vatcha (2005). Charismatic leadership and corporate cultism at Enron. *Management Communication Quarterly*, 12: 455–480.

Tucker, John (1993). Everyday forms of employee resistance. *Sociological Forum*, 8: 25–45.

Tuller, David (2010). Payment offers to egg donors prompt scrutiny. *NYTimes on the web*, May 11. Available at: www.nytimes.com/2010/05/11/health/11eggs.html.

Tuohy, Carolyn (1992). *Policy and politics in Canada*. Philadelphia, PA: Temple University Press.

Tuohy, Carolyn (1999). *Accidental logics*. New York: Oxford University Press.

Turner, Frederick Jackson (2008). *The frontier thesis in American history*. New York: Bibliolife.

Tyler, Liv (2005). Towards a postmodern understanding of crisis communication. *Public Relations Review*, 31: 566–571.

Uchitelle, Louis (2005). College degree still pays, but it's leveling off. *NYTimes on the web*, January 13. Available at: http://www.nytimes.com/2005/01/13/business/13pay.html.

Uchitelle, Louis (2007). *The disposable American*. New York: Vintage.

Uchitelle, Louis (2009). Obama's strategy to reverse manufacturing's fall. *NYTimes on the web*, July 21. Available at: http://www.nytimes.com/2009/07/21/business/economy/21manufacture.html.

Uchitelle, Louis (2010). American dream is elusive for new generation. *NYTimes on the web*, July 6. Available at: www.nytimes.com/2010/07/07/busienss/economy/07.generation.html.

Ulmer, Robert (2001). Effective crisis management through established stakeholder relationships: Malden Mills as a case study. *Management Communication Quarterly*, 14: 590–615.

Urbina, Ian (2010). US said to allow drilling without needed permits. *NYTimes on the web*, May 13: Available at: www.nytimes.com/2010/04/14/us/14agency.htm.

van Maanen, John and Edgar Schein (1979). Toward a theory of socialization. In Barry Staw (ed.), *Research in organizational behavior*, vol. 1 (pp. 209–264). Greenwich. CT: JAI Press.

Vaughan, Diane (1983). *Controlling unlawful organizational behavior*. Chicago: University of Chicago Press.

Vibbert, Steve and Denise Bostdorff (1993). Issue management in the "lawsuit crisis." In Charles Conrad (ed.), *The ethical nexus* (pp. 103–122). Norwood, NJ: Ablex.

Vietor, Richard (1994). *Contrived competition*. Cambridge, MA: Harvard University Press.

References

Viner, Jacob (1960). The intellectual history of laissez faire. *Journal of Law and Economics*, 3: 45-60.

Vogel, David (1989). *Fluctuating fortunes*. New York: Basic Books.

Vogel, Thomas (2006). *Reassessing intergenerational mobility in Germany and the US*. Discussion paper 2006-055. School of Business and Economics: Humbolt University, Germany.

Waddock, Sandra (2007). Corporate ctizenship: The dark-side paradoxes of success. In Steve May, George Cheney and Juliet Roper (eds), *The debate over corporate social responsibility* (pp. 74–86). New York: Oxford University Press.

Walker, C. and E. Moses (1996). The age of self-navigation. *American Demographics*, 18: 36–42.

Weaver, Gary, Linda Klebe Trevino, and Philip Cochran (1999). Integrated and decoupled corporate social performance. *Academy of Management Journal*, 42: 539–552.

Weissert, Carol and William Weissert (2006). *Governing health: The politics of health policy*, 3rd edn. Baltimore, MD: Johns Hopkins University Press.

Wells, C. A. H. (2002). The cycles of corporate social responsibility. *Kansas Law Review*, 51: 77–140.

Werhane, Patricia (1991). *Adam Smith and his legacy for modern capitalism*. New York: Oxford University Press.

Wessel, David (2009). *In Fed we trust*. New York: Crown Business.

Whoeriskey, Peter (2010). Chrysler comes to Detroit auto show without a splashy new lineup. *The Washington Post*, January 13: A14.

Wicks, David (2002). Successfully increasing technological control through minimizing workplace resistance. *Management Decision*, 2: 672–681.

Williams, George (2001). Turmoil at the Red Cross. *Chronicle of Philanthropy on the web*, November 1.

Willmott, Hugh (2005). Theorizing contemporary control. *Organization*, 12: 747–780.

Wilson, Duff (2009). Waxman takes on drug makers over Medicare. *NYTimes on the web*, August 26. Available at: www.nytimes.com/2009/08/26/health/policy/26dual.html.

Wilson, James Q. (1973). *Political organization*. New York: Basic Books.

Wilson, James Q. (1974). The politics of regulation. In J. McKie (ed.), *Social responsibility and the business predicament* (pp. 135–168). Washington, DC: Brookings Institution.

Wilson, Nick (2008). *An introduction to behavioral economics*. New York: Palgrave Macmillan.

Winders, Bill and James Scott (2009). *The politics of food supply*. New Haven, CT: Yale University Press.

Windes-Munoz, Laura (2009). Pro-immigration PACS see shift in fundraising. *Houston Chronicle*, November 27: A29.

251

References

Wise, Lindsay (2009). New GI Bill answer to veteran's dreams. *Houston Chronicle*, July 30: A1.

Wyatt, Edward (2010). Judge accepts Citigroup's settlement with S.E.C. *NYTimes on the web*, September 24. Available at: www.nytimes.com/2010/09/25/business/25sec.html.

Zalzenik, Abraham (1977). Managers and leaders: Are they different? *Harvard Business Review*, 55 (May/June): 73–74.

Zbaracki, Mark (1998). The rhetoric and reality of Total Quality Management. *Administrative Science Quarterly*, 43: 602–636.

Zemke, R., C. Raines, and B. Filipczak (2000). *Generations at work*. New York: AMACOM.

Zhang, Yan Anthea (2010). It matters whether a CEO comes from inside or outside. *Houston Chronicle*, February 14: D10.

Zoller, Heather (2005). Health activism: Communication and action for social change. *Communication Theory*, 15: 341–364.

Zoller, Heather and Gail Fairhurst (2007). Resistance leadership. *Human Relations*, 60: 1331–1360.

Index

253

Index

Index

checks and balances 53
Chen, C. 125
Cheney, G. xii, 27, 52, 64, 90, 96, 101, 105, 130, 155, 176, 195, 209, 219
Chevrolet 173
Chief Justice Marshall 25
Child, J. 89
child care 47–8
Christensen, L. 130, 176
Citigroup 138
Citizens for Tax Justice 208
Citizens United v. *Federal Elections Commission* 152
Civil Aeronautics Board 217
Clark, T. 107, 108, 213
Clay, H. 209
Clegg, S. 111, 132, 213, 215
Cleverly, G. 108
Clinton Administration 160, 200
Cloud, D. 43, 114
Cobb, R. 155, 157, 159
Cochran, P. 213
codes of conduct 199
Cohan, W. 157
"collateral damage" 193
college
    administrators 218
    alumni and identification 172
    and upward mobility 41–3
    completion rates 42
    student-as-consumer rhetoric 218
Collier, R. 35
Collinson, D. 84, 90, 91, 111, 214
Columbia University 202
Comerer, C. 211
community 65
    as constraint to greed 63
    interest of 85
    structure for society 21, 52
comparative advantage, doctrine of 53–4
    movement of capital 54

movement of labor 54
movement of technology 54
competition
    avoidance of 68–9
    government and 68
    incentives to avoid 67–9
    limits to 62–71
    predatory pricing and 68
confessions 187–8
Conger, J. 213
Connecticut 27
Connelly, J. 50
Continental Airlines 211
Coronado, G. 215
corporate campaigns as a war of maneuver 198–201
Conrad, C. 95, 106, 132, 155, 157, 159, 160, 162, 189, 191, 214, 215, 218
consumer(s)
    and economic demand 65
    availability bias and 61
    communication networks and 61
    information overload and 60
    information withheld from 61
    (non)rationality of 59–62
    spending 56
    trust and decision-making 65
    utility-maximization and 59–62
contradictions within cultural assumptions 12
Coombs, S. 176, 194
Cooper, H. 123, 160
Cooper, M. 20
copycat drugs (also "me too drugs") 35
Corak, M. 41
Corax 6
Corbett, S. 18, 131
corporate colonization 38
Corporate Cultures 102–3
corporate disloyalty 49

256

Index

Index

and downsizing 96
and World Bank / IMF policies 31
comparative advantage and 53–5
competition and 62–71
creative destruction and 53
critics of 56, 59–73
extreme v. moderate versions 59
faith and 53–6
heroic assumptions of 72–3
ideology industry 73–4
purists 62
free-market rhetoric 56, 71, 73–7,
    190, 195
absolutism and 76
boundary conditions and 76
realist style of 75–6, 151
structural maneuvering and 75
French Revolution 21
Friedman, M. 64–5
Fromm, E. 208
frontier experience 46, 50
Frontline 163, 208, 210, 216
Frye, N. 213
Fuerstein, A. 177–8
Fuller, C. 210
full-time housewives 147

G. I. Bill 42
gag orders 187
Galbraith, J. K. 87, 210
Ganesh, S. 90
Gash, D. 104, 106
Geithner, T. 157
Gemmill, G. 84, 92, 99, 109
General Accounting Office (GAO) 18
General Electric (GE) Capital 178
General Motors 218
Generation X 49–51
Geoghegan, T. 113
Georgetown University 200
Germany 55
Ghose, B. 183, 218
Ginsberg, B. 209

globalization 54, 77, 84, 96, 208
Goffee, R. 92
golden age (of Greek thought) 6
Goldman Sachs 17, 123–4
Goldstein, K. 209
Goodman, R. S. 178
Goodnight, G. T. 179
Gordon, D. 17
Gorgias 10
Gortari, M. 209
Giddens, A. 106, 214
Gill, R. 195, 209
Gilman, N. 94
Goldgar, A. 207
Good Works International 199
Goodman, E. 80
Gore, D. 212
Gossett, L. 117
Gottfried, H. 114
government 77
    and reproductive technologies 80–1
    direct subsidies to corporations
        69–70
    futility thesis and 58
    indirect subsidies to corporations
        through tax breaks 589
    jeopardy thesis and 58
    perversity thesis and 58
    restrictions on flow of capital and
        labor 54
    role in free-market theory 56–8
Grady, D. 80
Graham, J. 214
Graham, L. 181, 114, 119–20, 200
Gramsci, A. 207
Great Recession 17, 41–2, 51, 211–12
greed
    and power of the state 63
    community restraint on 63
    excessive 63
    managerial 90
    need to constrain 63
Green, H. 50

Index

Index

263

Index

Index

Index

Index